01010010 LEGEND-TRIPPING ONLINE 10001011010 0

1101010110

LEGEND-TRIPPING
Online

SUPERNATURAL FOLKLORE
AND THE SEARCH FOR ONG'S HAT

Michael Kinsella

UNIVERSITY PRESS OF MISSISSIPPI • JACKSON

www.upress.state.ms.us

The University Press of Mississippi is a member of the
Association of American University Presses.

First printing 2011
∞
Library of Congress Cataloging-in-Publication Data

Kinsella, Michael, 1973–
Legend-tripping online : supernatural folklore and the search for Ong's hat /
Michael Kinsella.
p. cm.
Includes bibliographical references (p.   ) and index.
ISBN 978-1-60473-983-1 (cloth : alk. paper) — ISBN 978-1-60473-984-8 (ebook) 1.
Supernatural. 2. Legends. 3. Parapsychology. I. Title.
BF1040.5.K56 2011
130—dc22   2010038182

British Library Cataloging-in-Publication Data available

For my mother, Cheryl McDonald

CONTENTS

In 1882, the Society for Psychical Research was established to empirically test firsthand accounts of ostensibly supernatural phenomena such as "raps," levitation, and apparitions commonly reported by persons participating in séances. Although religiously significant to Spiritualists, séances were also an extremely popular form of entertainment, as people wished to see for themselves whether the many stories and legends they had heard about the medium's abilities to summon the otherworldly were true. Four years earlier, in 1878, the Folk-Lore Society had been founded to collect and classify stories and customs of the Old World, including those that involved supernatural tales, beliefs, and practices. Andrew Lang, the only person elected president of both these organizations, assumed, as did his fellow folklorists, that supernatural tales and beliefs were "survivals" of primitive folk psychologies and remnants of ancient modes of thought. Lang, however, also proposed, along with other psychical researchers, that many supernatural stories were in some way related to actual psychical occurrences. Lang aggressively attempted to merge folklore and psychical research into the study of "psycho-folklorism" in order to examine how concepts of the supernatural relate to both individual experience and cultural traditions, but neither the Folk-Lore Society nor the Society for Psychical Research pursued this union.[1]

Historically, the disciplines of folklore and psychical research have shared an interest in the supernatural, although to very different ends. While the folklorist is concerned with the ways that supernatural traditions—consisting of behaviors, beliefs, narratives, and material culture—are transmitted and how they creatively express and address the worldviews of individuals and groups, the psychical researcher (today more commonly known as a parapsychologist, though these roles somewhat differ) investigates whether the experiences described by supernatural narratives are based in scientific fact. As a folklorist, I have studied people's versatile relationships to the supernatural and while observing and participating in psychic circles, ghost-hunting expeditions, Peruvian shamanic ceremonies, and UFO investigations, I've come to appreciate that many supernatural traditions operate in such an ingenious fashion as to motivate people to generate the very supernatural worlds these traditions portray. By harnessing the interpretive frameworks that supernatural traditions provide, people can enter particular states of mind in which they become especially inclined to have supernatural experiences that may consist of anything from seeing visions or conversing with the dead to encountering otherworldly intelligences. Such experiences, once recounted as legends, then become assimilated into the very traditions that described them.

Though folklorists and psychical researchers have for over a century preserved the distinction between "experience" and "tradition," I suggest we look at how people draw upon supernatural traditions to generate supernatural experiences. As both a thematic category and as a perspective with parameters dictated by sociocultural conventions, discourse communities, and individual experiences, the supernatural offers us opportunities to step outside the confines of the everyday, which, in turn, can reframe our expectations and modify our beliefs. The supernatural permits us and sometimes even forces us to go beyond the dichotomies of fact and fiction, truth and falsehood, reality and illusion, tradition and experience. In doing so, we become able to effect changes upon ourselves, although this process sometimes proves traumatic rather than therapeutic, bewildering instead of sagacious. But just as the legend transforms, it also preserves, maintaining long-held assumptions and beliefs about the otherworldly.

That we opportune supernatural experiences by no means precludes the possibility that some anomalous experiences occur in the absence of familiarity with supernatural lore.[2] But by examining both the experiential and traditional aspects of legends as performances, this book acknowledges that supernatural legends demonstrate efforts to codify and manage anomalous perceptions and states of mind, making them, at least in part, theoretically and experientially accessible. Supernatural legends are complex narratives that encourage ostensive reenactment of their content and inspire investigations of their veracity. Ostensive reenactments specifically motivated by the desire to test a legend's truth are known to folklorists as legend-trips—ritual performances in which participants seek to presence the very experiences chronicled in the legend.

Legends do not exist within a vacuum nor are they told exclusively in face-to-case interactions. Many people today regularly tell legends by using various combinations of image, audio, video, and text in online environments.[3] Legend-telling online operates slightly differently than when performed in face-to-face situations, since computer-mediated communication permits tellers to instantly present various kinds of "evidence" and to hypertextually connect their accounts to other legends to form vast legend complexes. And when people become immersed in these legend complexes, they may participate in an online form of legend-tripping.

In this work, I provide an ethnography of online legend-tripping performances surrounding two enigmatic documents collectively called "The Incunabula Papers." Anonymously written, the Incunabula Papers present a series of past accounts, blurring together factual and fictional information with various elements of supernaturalism; they are transmitted through the virtual equivalent of word of mouth and prompt much debate, since there is no consensus as to what these documents really "are." Although they may seem different from other kinds of supernatural legends people normally come in contact with, the Incunabula Papers and the communicative performances surrounding them constitute a legend complex. *Incunabula* is a term that generally refers to artifacts of an early period, particularly books printed before 1501; its literal meaning is "cradle," and the word itself denotes the earliest stages or traces of anything. The Incunabula Papers are arguably the first immersive online legend complex that introduced readers to a host of content, including what religious historian Robert Ellwood has called the "alternative reality tradition," which are those customs and beliefs that involve seeking out metaphysical or occult knowledge and experiences.[4]

Chapters 1 through 4 describe the various forms and functions of legends and legend-trips and show how supernatural legends and legend-trips operate akin to occult texts and magic rituals that promote shifts in attitudes and worldviews. These chapters also illustrate how supernatural concepts shape and are shaped by technological and scientific innovations. My presentation of the ethnography follows the structure of a legend-trip as described by folklorist Bill Ellis because this permits the clearest illustration of means by which immersion within an online alternate reality unfolds as a legend-trip.[5] As such, chapter 5 explores the Incunabula Papers' accounts of past happenings and its challenge to audiences to investigate these accounts; chapter 6 describes participants' journey into uncanny territory; chapter 7 recounts various reports of encounters with the supernatural; and chapter 8 summarizes the intense discussion and processing of events that conclude legend-trips. It is important to understand that the ritual structure of legend-trips is progressive as well as recursive; experiences resulting from legend-trips become incorporated into the legend narrative.

Many of the transcripts I've gathered include a number of idiosyncratic phrases and misspelled words. Perhaps some of these apparent errors are nothing more than typos (such as writing the word "catlogue" instead of "catalogue," etc.), but some indicate a specialized form of communication that participants of the Incunabula Papers legend-trip use to shift the mindset of the writer and/or reader. Because of this, I have left all distinctive and erroneous spelling, punctuation, and spacing unchanged. I have, however, occasionally provided excerpts in lieu of lengthier texts, though I've tried to prevent compromising the integrity and ideas of these posts. I do not refer to people who post on message boards as either male or female, unless their gender has been confirmed elsewhere. The phrases "Incunabula Papers" and "Ong's Hat" are used several times to refer to various phenomena, so Appendix 1 provides a key.

Legends are assuming ever-greater influence in a world confronting new speeds of diversity, connection, and knowledge. As guardians of tradition as well as agents of change, legends—especially *supernatural* legends—contextualize persistent and emergent ideas, behaviors, and technologies that challenge our familiar realities. This book offers a theoretical perspective that analyzes supernatural legends accordingly.

ACKNOWLEDGMENTS

I developed many of the ideas in this book while working toward my MA at Western Kentucky University, and I am indebted to the Department of Folk Studies for their guidance. I'm also grateful to all who shared their photographs, stories, and adventures with me over the years.

0100101001010101010110101001010001011 0

010010100101010101011010100101000010110

1. LEGENDS AND LEGEND ECOLOGIES

Introduction

In 329 C.E., Alexander the Great and his army were attempting to cross the Jaxartes River in Central Asia when two massive silver shields flying through the sky assailed them with bursts of flames. Except for Alexander, all of the men, as well as their elephants and horses, fell into a panic and fled.[1] In 776 C.E., the Saxons, while laying siege on Sigiburg Castle in France, sighted "two large shields reddish in color" hovering high in the air. The Saxons, believing these objects to be aiding the French, retreated from the battlefield in terror.[2] On March 13, 1997, thousands of people in Arizona and Nevada witnessed a series of strange lights floating overhead in a "V" formation, and many also reported seeing a gigantic, solid, wedged-shaped object. Ten years later, former Arizona governor Fife Symington revealed that he, too, had seen something that night. When asked about his experience by a reporter, Symington said, "It was enormous and inexplicable. Who knows where it came from? A lot of people saw it, and I saw it, too. It was dramatic. And it couldn't have been flares because it was too symmetrical. It had a geometric outline, a constant shape."[3]

Over two thousand years ago, the Chinese poet Qu Yuan wrote of the "shangui," mountain ghosts or ogres believed to inhabit the mountain ranges of Shennongjia. Centuries later, the Ch'ing Dynasty poet Yuan Mei (1716–1798) recorded in his book, *New Rhythms*, that creatures "monkey-like yet not monkey-like" roamed the wild regions of Shanxi Province.[4] In 1957, William Roe of Edmonton, Canada, gave a sworn affidavit stating that while climbing up Mica Mountain in 1955, he stumbled upon a creature "about six feet tall, almost three feet wide, and probably weighing somewhere near three hundred pounds. It was covered from head to foot with dark brown silver-tipped hair." As he debated whether to shoot it, he thought to himself, "Maybe this is a Sasquatch."[5]

3

The thirteenth-century Scottish lord Thomas Learmonth, familiar to many Scots as Thomas the Rhymer, is reputed to have prophesied the death of his monarch, Alexander the Third. Toward the end of the seventeenth century, another Scot known as the Brahan Seer foretold the demise of the MacKenzie Clan of Seaforth by proclaiming that a cow would one day give birth in the remnants of their castle's uppermost tower. In 1851, a farmer discovered one of his cows in the crumbling remains of the MacKenzie tower, where it had there birthed a calf, fulfilling the Seer's prophecy. Scottish-born mystic and ardent Spiritualist Daniel Dunglas Home gained international fame in the nineteenth century for demonstrating an array of fantastic abilities including acts of levitation. According to psychical researcher Frank Podmore, he and others witnessed Home "rise from the ground slowly to a height of about six inches, remain there for about ten seconds, and then slowly descend."[6]

These stories of strange objects in the skies, goliath bipedal monsters, and the Scottish inheritance of psychical powers comprise just a fraction of the subjects associated with supernatural legendry. Such accounts depict strikingly similar uncanny and extraordinary incidents that have transpired across space and time. We use supernatural legendry to explain anomalous experiences, but so, too, do these tales seemingly exert their own influences. Chain letters promising either blessings or curses circulate even if we scoff and refuse to pass them on. Rumors about vast satanic conspiracies, even when debunked, repeatedly surface. Reports of alien beings and unidentified craft, even from the staunchest of skeptics, flourish. And testimonies to the healing power of sacred sites continually reinforce our faiths and challenge our disbelief.

Efforts to collect legends began in the nineteenth-century by Europeans who believed they were "survivals" or remnants of much older mythologies. Though best known for their anthologies of German fairy tales, the Grimm brothers also published the *Deutsche Sagen* (1816–1818), a collection of Germanic legends.[7] Little if any time was spent on scholarly analysis, however, until the mid-twentieth century when German folklorist Will-Erich Peuckert began to examine legends in relation to magic, folk belief, and folk customs.[8] Academic attempts to classify the legend as a specific type of folk narrative distinguishable from other folk tales developed after the first International Congress of Folk Narrative Research in 1959, and debate only intensified thereafter.[9] If a rumor begins to circulate among a small group of people, can that rumor be categorized as a legend? If an event described in science fiction accurately precedes real-world events, does it qualify as a legend? If someone picks up a hitchhiker late at night, only to witness the hitchhiker vanish into thin air just minutes later, can his account of what happened be called a legend?[10] Likewise, can we consider personal experience narratives as legends? Are the contents of modern legends really so similar to ancient ones? Developing any classificatory system remains challenging because the qualities distinguishing a legend from a personal experience narrative or a folk tale are contextual. The complexity of legends and legend-telling events only adds to this difficulty, since they can appear as both memorates (first-hand accounts) or fabulates (stories told in the third-person), and they can address a wide variety of topics and elicit a broad range of audience responses. The modes of legend transmission also vary greatly: they are recounted in face-to-face situations, on radio, on television, in print media, and on the Internet. Due to such incredible variation, scholars have proposed a range of classifications such as "belief" legends, "popular" legends, "historic" legends, "urban" legends, and "rumor" legends, that are often inconsistent and, in some cases, incompatible.[11]

Perhaps Robert Georges best intimated the complexity of defining the legend when he described it as "a story or narrative that may not be a story or narrative at all; it is set in a recent or historical past that may be conceived to be remote or antihistorical or not really past at all; it is believed to be true by some, false by others, or both or neither by most."[12] While Georges illustrates the definitional disparities within legend studies, current legend scholars generally do agree that the most significant feature marking a legend *as* legend is that it is both a form of and channel for social behavior; legends are communicative acts that serve specific purposes for the groups in which the legends circulate. Furthermore, they express relationships people have with allied stories, beliefs, perceptions, customs, and ideas concerning common anxieties and longings. As such, the legend's primary characteristics are always context-dependent and align more closely with those of a performance rather than a kind of text or literature and warrant studies evaluating them accordingly. Precisely because scholars seek to contextualize legends, they should concentrate on legend ecologies—the interactions between legends, legend-telling situations and communities, the material means and technologies of communication, and the environments throughout which legends circulate. A legend-telling performance about a ghostly encounter, for instance, doesn't occur in a vacuum. Rather, the legend invites others to offer stories and anecdotes from their own repertoire of legends, to collectively debate about these legends' factuality, to appraise their significance, and to introduce material artifacts such as spirit photographs or anomalous electronic voice recordings. Moreover, since so many legends are told through or otherwise occasion the use of multiple media forms, folklorists exploring the reciprocity among media and the legend ecologies of which they are a part move far beyond the initial efforts to merely collect legends. Not only does this allow us to progress beyond definitional debates, it also reveals how legends can affect people's understandings of technology, how media and technology influence folk theories of the supernatural, and even how folk traditions can thrive in computer-mediated environments which, as we shall see, are particularly conducive to propagating legends.

A variety of narrative content typically falls under the rubric of legendry: examples include more "down-to-earth" stories relating unusual, macabre, or distasteful events. Many of us have heard about the hook-handed madman who murdered teenage lovers in parked cars and about the couple who unknowingly chomped away on deep-fried rats while at a drive-in movie theater (these two specific narratives are known as "The Hook" and "The Kentucky Fried Rat," respectively). As folklorist Carl Lindahl points out, many legends told today focus on extraordinary events that aren't considered supernatural at all.[13] The reasons for this are partially temporal; modern legends are told in environments considerably more religiously pluralistic and ambiguous about the reality of the supernatural. No longer do legends transpire within communities adhering to one exclusive creed or belief system; no longer are they capable of fully mapping out the terrains of the everyday and the otherworldly for everyone equally. This fact changes our relations to supernatural legends. Earlier legend narratives pertaining to the supernatural—the likes of which can be found in the Grimms's collections—contained obvious codes or systems of consistent values, rewards, and punishments; their narrative contents reflected this in a constant way (e.g., you always knew the devil *as* the devil by his hooves, and you always knew his moral code, which was governed by evil). The messages of these legends were clear. But modern supernatural legends exhibit significant content variance and interpretive freedom. We find stories of ambiguous shadow-creatures, human-like aliens, and discarnate spirits whose ethics and intentions are shaped by the legend-teller's and audiences' own personal interpretations. Instead of producing moral certainty ("You should not play cards with the devil"), many of today's supernatural legends generate uncertainty ("Should I try to communicate with the spirit in my house?"). Lindahl says, for example, that legends about UFOs change "according to individual perceptions of the value of new scientific and social developments," which illustrates the multiple types of coding transpiring within legends today.[14]

Unlike those stories told centuries before, today's supernatural legends instigate interpretive dilemmas, challenging audiences to construct their meanings by acquiring evidence, judging the tale's veracity, and filling in the legend content in order to make sense of the narrative.

The subject of belief, one of most politicized topics within legendry, largely informs the social acceptance or rejection of supernatural legends, even by folklorists—especially by folklorists whose entire discipline acknowledges the distinction between the privileged academic and the construct of the "folk." And while legends themselves certainly incite debates about belief, they also reveal that belief itself is a construct. Even if you don't believe that an alien spaceship crashed in Roswell, you are still faced with the fact that there are more than a few people who do. Legends can reduce the time and amount of information required to propagate certain beliefs. And some people tell legends without necessarily believing in their factuality, although they do demonstrate belief in the effects of the legends told.

Legends typically have multiple symbolic meanings and functions, but supernatural legends additionally and exclusively serve as interpretive frameworks through which people may actually produce their own supernatural experiences by way of performing belief: a self-conscious, affective act in which the interpretive framework(s) provided by legend complexes are utilized to facilitate ostensibly supernatural experiences.[15] Perhaps Peuckert offered the most correct description of the supernatural legend when he declared that it expresses a formulated truth transpiring in a magical world governed by mythic thinking.[16] Supernatural legends contain interpretive dilemmas that invite audiences to think in magical terms—this in turn can promote alternative viewpoints and experiences perceived as supernatural. In a very real sense, supernatural legends give modern audiences venues to engage in liminal modes of being otherwise generally inaccessible, discouraged, or unfamiliar. As we shall see, magic isn't the sole province of shamans and occultists; rather, it exists all around us, embedded in our stories, our technologies, and even in our behaviors and pastimes.

Characteristics, Functions, and Behaviors Associated with Legends

Legends circulate among folk groups, or groups of people who share things in common, like neighbors, co-workers, or family members. Legends can also occasion the development of folk groups, as when communities form among those who share similar supernatural experiences or who are enthusiastic about particular supernatural subjects. Since legends are a kind of folklore transmitted among folk groups, a condensed definition of folklore would be useful to consider: folklore is a term that encompasses traditional and traditionalizing ways people engage with and think about the world. It may indicate anything from your family's particular way of celebrating birthdays to Kentucky bluegrass music. Legends as a folklore genre represent communal efforts to adapt old customs and beliefs to new situations. Simultaneously, legends frame emergent customs and beliefs by placing them in a historic continuum, thereby connecting the activities, behaviors, and beliefs of individuals and communities in the present to those in the past. For instance, belief in and stories about ghosts have existed for millennia; such convictions and tales serve many functions, including fostering communal cohesion, explaining what happens after we die, and, of course, entertaining us. But modern ghost stories and beliefs also incorporate theories about the nature of ghosts largely informed by the discourse of contemporary science and technology: terms such as "electromagnetic frequencies," "electronic voice phenomena," and "residual hauntings" are all relatively recent additions to ghost lore.

One function of legends is to identify and channel the anxieties of folk groups. There are several documented cases in which communities shared legends targeting and stereotyping unwelcome immigrants. One such case emerged in 1980 when large numbers of South Asians from Vietnam, Cambodia, and Laos were relocated to Stockton, California. Legends spread through the community that the immigrants ate cats and dogs—a practice met with horror and revulsion by many. Florence E. Baer summarized one of these legends as follows: "A woman in North Stockton discovered that her expensive dog was missing; a boy in the neighborhood saw a Vietnamese family down the street eating the dog and reported the gruesome fact to the owner; the dog's head and fur were subsequently found by the garbage collector."[17] A variant of this legend was eventually published in the local newspaper, the *Stockton Record*, even without any evidence substantiating the claims. This had a significant impact on perceptions of the legend's veracity, however, and demonstrates how the politics of legend-telling can compromise journalistic ethics and news credibility. Shortly after the publication, in light of growing public hostility directed toward the South Asian immigrants, or the "Vietnamese," as they were collectively called, a councilman demanded a city ordinance banning the eating of cats and dogs.[18] The legends told by the Stockton community expressed their fear that the influx of outsiders would irrevocably change their way of life. Legend-telling became a means to exercise control over the situation and to encourage political action against the immigrants. Unfortunately, examples such as this are not uncommon, even today. Legends have repercussions, and xenophobia is alive and well in America; rumors and legends about immigrant groups are repeatedly told and retold, identifying them as deviants—criminals, satanists, or even terrorists.

A series of reports that spread throughout rural America during the 1980s and 1990s illustrate the capacity of legends to reinforce particular worldviews. Stories of a vast satanic conspiracy, which included child kidnappings, bizarre animal mutilations, and sexual abuse, were broadcast and spread through various media outlets. The increasingly visible role of "experts" on satanic activity—police-appointed investigators, self-purported victims of satanists, and organizations formed to combat satanism—also promoted belief in the reality of these legends; what has been dubbed a "satanic panic" swept through the nation as well as other parts of the world. The fact there was no concrete evidence to confirm the actuality of the conspiracy did little to alleviate the fears of those who believed such stories.

My hometown of Sidney, Ohio, was one of many towns caught up in this terror. Born in 1973, I moved around the outskirts of Sidney with my family throughout my childhood, and I grew up amid stories about satanic cults said to be operating in the area. I often heard scores of local legends about nearby caves where animal mutilations took place and stories about robed figures conducting strange rituals out in the countryside. I remember one morning when my mother, after arriving home late from the night shift, told us the road had been blocked by a string of strategically placed large rocks. As she was describing the scenario, I envisioned a group of hooded satanists frenzied with bloodlust lurking around the outlying woods, lying in wait for passing motorists. Like many other Christian communities, some among Sidney's residents braced themselves against an imagined, impending doom.

Jeffrey Victor, who has written extensively on the transmission of satanic legends, tracing their origins to several impoverished rural towns, proposes they are the symptoms of widespread social stress, economic hardship, and the breakdown of the familial unit. Victor examined one legend that began to circulate in Jamestown, New York, around October 1987 and lasted until May of the following year.[19] According to this legend, a satanic cult planned to kidnap a blonde, blue-eyed virgin on Friday the 13th of 1988. As the date drew closer, a few locals, viewed for whatever reason as different or weird, were maligned as possible satanists, and rumors multiplied about a number of odd incidents, like animal mutilations, supposedly taking place. Soon thereafter, the city of Jamestown began holding public meetings to discuss the impending threat. While the kidnapping never occurred as predicted, the legend and rumors did much to solidify parts of the community through their preparation for this looming tragedy. Variants of this legend existed in other parts of the nation. Bill Ellis writes of a rumor appearing around the end of May 1987 in Lansford, Pennsylvania, about a satanic cult conspiring to murder prom-goers at the upcoming dance.[20] Some legends asserted the satanists were planning to gun down students during the dance of the prom king and queen; others proposed the victims would be the first several couples either entering or leaving school premises. State and local authorities took a series of extra precautions during the Lansford prom, but neither the cult nor its crimes ever materialized.

Accounts like these were told throughout many rural communities supportive of Christian fundamentalist ideologies. Their religious background provided these groups the raw materials to give face to the encroachment of an urban, contemporary mores they considered threatening. A series of court trials eventually debunked the pervasive notion of a widespread satanic conspiracy at large, as did the actions of socially conscious and responsible members of both occult and Christian communities who spoke out to counter the growing hysteria. Rumors and legends about satanic cults returned to their origin—those small populations characteristically suspicious of the activities of the larger world, which they often attribute to demonic forces at work. Since the satanic panic, legend studies have taken on new importance and immediacy. The fact that a legend can spread from rural, poorly educated communities to encompass the whole of the United States testifies to the power of legends, especially when combined with communication technologies.

The communal behavior associated with the above legends typifies actions exemplifying witch-hunting behavior. Many of these legends spring from cultural misunderstandings. Of course, not everyone believed these various tales, just as not everyone in Stockton believed the rumors spread about the South Asian immigrants. But in these cases, legend-telling led to discussions about communal values and about what—and who—belonged in the community. These discussions spilled into town meetings and other public forums and arose from people making judgments about contemporary events based more on "traditional" communal values than on any available evidence. The politics of legends alter social configurations by polarizing ideologies, obliging people to test or judge the narrative's truth status, and identifying individuals and groups as being somehow the cause of misfortune and hardship.

The politics of legends need not always be destructive, however. Legends routinely offer folk histories, or symbolic histories, that impart favorable characterizations of their subjects and draw upon, or even create, perceived credibility of an alleged historic record. For instance, one legend about President George Washington depicts him as a young boy who cut down his father's prized cherry tree with a hatchet. When his father asked young Washington what had happened, Washington, through expecting punishment, nonetheless replied, "I cannot tell a lie, father, you know I cannot tell a lie! I did cut it with my little hatchet." This legend, by portraying the honesty of Washington, connects a moral ideal with a "founding father" and simultaneously presents a role model for all future Americans, and ensures that the American past is viewed favorably.

Legends also regularly provide narrative histories for specific geographical sites. Supernatural legends are especially tied to distinct locations that, for whatever reason, are perceived as being out of the ordinary. Because these places—old graveyards, bridges, caves, or deserted houses—don't usually fit in with the surrounding, familiar environment, supernatural legends offer a rationale for their existence and exploit their presence as concrete points of reference to lend credibility to the stories told about them. Furthermore, sites such as these easily attract legends because they symbolize the boundaries between the known and unknown.[21] And while legends offer histories for specific activities and customs as well, from Thanksgiving dinners to May Day celebrations, those legends concerned with the supernatural most prolifically demonstrate this function, evident in stories about miraculous cures surrounding pilgrimages to sacred shrines, tales recounting the efficacy of certain practices to foretell the future, and accounts of malevolent spirits summoned during various occult parlor games. These folk rituals express belief in legends told about them; supernatural legends perpetuate these rituals that in turn reinforce the supernatural legends. Through legends—both supernatural and otherwise—the synergies between narrative and performance can sometimes result in the legend coming to life.

In short, we use legends as manifestations of a collective imaginary in order to create, substantiate, and contest what we believe to be reality. But turning back to the beginning of this chapter, did Alexander the Great "create" anything when his army left him high and dry at the Jaxartes?

Did William Roe "substantiate" whatever beast he confronted on Mica Mountain? This is where things get a bit complicated. According to the account of Alexander's face-off with airborne shields, the young conqueror was the only one who stood fast against his flying foes. This story is a testament to his courage, and modeled that courage for young Greeks to imitate. Roe's encounter was completely outside his field of expectations, but his familiarity with Native American legends of Sasquatch provided a means to make sense of it. Such examples illustrate legends' usefulness in naming the unknown (what Ellis characterizes as the "Rumpelstiltskin principle") and presenting a kind of formulated truth.[22] Perhaps above all else, legends are communicative technologies in the sense that they are both assemblages of cultural memories and knowledge, and processes that convey these memories and knowledge; we employ them to manage and transmit ideologies, behaviors, and experiences.

Evaluating the Categories of Ostension

The word "ostension" comes from the Latin *ostendere*, meaning "to show." It often refers to instances in which an action is used to indicate an example (i.e., pointing to the color red rather than attempting to define what red "is"). In their article, "Does the Word 'Dog' Bite? Ostensive Action as a Means of Legend-Telling," folklorists Linda Dégh and Andrew Vázsonyi used the term in reference to ways real-life actions are guided by legends. Entire legend plots sometimes correspond to real-world activities, and these activities—intentional or accidental, forthright or deceitful— are thought of as types of ostensive action. Folklorists generally classify ostensive acts into three categories, although this evaluative system is subject to their whims and prejudices; all too often scholars try to discern the level of objective reality portrayed by legends, which can be an antithetical endeavor not determined by the factuality of events, but by the judgment of researchers. Still, reflecting upon each of these categories offers a means with which legend scholars may consider their own roles in evaluating and shaping legends. I don't mean to completely dismiss the utility of discriminating between different forms of ostension; I simply wish to point out its limitations and drawbacks.

Proto-ostension, the first in the categories of ostensive acts, is when individuals draw from a legend to claim it as their own experience. If you, after hearing personal accounts and legends about extraterrestrial visitation and human abduction, make up a story that you have been abducted by alien beings, you are engaging in proto-ostension. The motives for devising such a story are surely countless, but, regardless, one of the effects of proto-ostension is an enhancement of a legend's plausibility. By claiming a legend narrative as one's own personal experience, the legend is transferred from a third-person account to a first-person account and its number of transmissional links is reduced, which generally increases its credibility for audiences, especially if the individual claiming to have experienced the events described by the legend is seen as trustworthy. Acts classified as proto-ostensive do not involve those experiences that do correspond to legendry. If someone encounters a gigantic, reptilian creature while boating on the waters of Loch Ness, the subsequent report of a "Nessie" sighting would not be considered a proto-ostensive act (at least not to those who believe the story). We should keep in mind that it remains possible that some legends describing supernatural experiences have their origins in accurate interpretations of events. In sum, proto-ostensive acts can be defined as intentional lies influenced and/or shaped by legends and, as such, can be considerably challenging to study. For what if someone genuinely believes something depicted by legendry has happened to her, and yet no one believes her account? Furthermore, there is good cause for concern that folklorists might ascribe the label of proto-ostension to anything they themselves have a hard time believing.

Sometimes people deliberately act out legend narratives; folklorists call this pseudo-ostension. For decades, stories have been told about Halloween "trick-or-treaters" finding candy apples with razor blades inside them or other treats laced with strychnine. Even though there has never been a single report of anyone finding razor blades in candy apples, hospitals throughout the United States continue to offer free candy X-raying during Halloween. But there has been one—and only one—account of poisoned Halloween candy, and it exemplifies an act of pseudo-ostension. On October 31, 1974, eight-year-old Timothy O'Bryan died after eating Pixie Stix containing strychnine. Police investigating the case discovered the boy's father, Ronald Clark O'Bryan, had laced the candy, hoping to cash in on an insurance policy. At his trial, Ronald unsuccessfully tried to draw upon common knowledge of this legend and use its elements as evidence of his innocence. The fact that he had intentionally based his criminal actions on a preexisting legend narrative did little to prove his innocence, but it did much to perpetuate the legend, its core narrative becoming reality.

Many criminal activities patterned after legend narratives fall into the category of pseudo-ostension. While some people like Ronald Clark

O'Bryan might reenact legends to mask their activities or to claim they themselves are victims of ostensive legend behavior, others may reenact legends subconsciously. Such might be the case of Juana Leija, who, on April 18, 1986, reenacted the Mexican legend of La Llorona, or "The Weeping Woman." This legend, known to many Hispanics, is about a woman who, after having several children with a married man, drowns her infants and then herself after her lover leaves. Her roaming spirit is said to weep for her dead children. Emulating the actions of La Llorona (consciously or not), Leija attempted to drown six of her seven children before she was stopped (two of her children drowned before the others were rescued). Leija and her family were the regular victims of physical abuse by her husband, and perhaps she saw no other way out for her children. The problem with classifying Leija's actions as pseudo-ostension lays in our uncertainty that she was influenced by the legend. However if a folklorist attributes Leija's actions to either a subconscious or conscious emulation of a local legend, she would classify them as pseudo-ostension.

The third type of ostensive act, quasi-ostension, takes place when naturally occurring events are mistaken to be those divine or supernatural manifestations depicted by legends. The refraction of sunlight by small ice crystals in clouds sometimes gives the illusion of two or more suns in the sky. If someone observed this phenomenon, known as a "sun dog," and claimed he had witnessed a miracle or some other event of legendry, he would be engaging in quasi-ostension. Of course we can never be sure whether the witness honestly believes this, for he might actually be participating in an act of proto-ostension. A common example of quasi-ostension occurs when people wake up to the effects of sleep paralysis and interpret the accompanying sensations and hallucinations as an attack by supernatural entities, often incubi, alien intruders, or witches. In fact, sleep paralysis is intimately linked with legends of "The Hag," a demonic spirit who suffocates her victims while they sleep.[23] But to instantly relegate all reports of supernatural nocturnal attacks as misinterpretations of this naturally occurring phenomenon would be premature.

Regardless of the category or categories they may be assigned, ostensive acts perpetuate the legends that inspire, influence, or correlate with them, meaning that the more these legends spread, the more people will be inclined to engage in further ostensive acts. This is one reason why hoaxing, or fabricating material and/or narrative evidence to enhance the credibility of a legend, is so pervasive and cannot be divorced from the legend process. Sometimes, ostension involves behavior that sets aside conventional distinctions between "reality" and "fiction" and engages in the manipulation of belief. Ostension paradoxically shows that a legend is only a legend (as in the O'Bryan case) while at the same time perpetuating it as something more, initiating a kind of mystification.

Legend-Telling Online

People commonly understand legends, like much of folklore, to circulate primarily through oral culture—by word of mouth in face-to-face interactions. But with the advent and exponential growth of communications technologies, people increasingly transmit legends through a variety of available media; as we shall see, legends are particularly virulent in computer-mediated environments that provide opportunities to utilize textual, visual, and aural evidence. Plenty of assessments, assertions, and arguments posit that communication within computer-mediated spaces has radically altered human awareness. Advancements in technology certainly offer new ways to engage with the world, but virtual realities, cyberspace, and other computer-mediated spaces also represent environments wherein the products and processes of folklore circulate unabated. The discipline of folklore concentrates on the traditional formulas used within everyday existence to promote both cultural continuity and change, so the adaptations of these traditional formulas within online environments deserve our attention.

I should mention there are some folklorists who have argued that no legitimate human interaction occurs online. Only a few years ago Larissa Fialkova and Maria Yelenevskaya investigated online legend-telling and concluded that "virtual communication, being the surrogate of the real, can only give an illusion of friendship, involvement, and belonging."[24] But this position is unfounded, for how can anyone determine another's experience of belonging? Either someone senses belonging or doesn't. Due to the immense variety of communicative activities, sweeping generalizations like this are unproductive. Statements criticizing the reality of online communities or even the authenticity of online human interaction reveal more about the inherent biases of those proposing them than they contribute to our understanding of the fundamental dynamics of human communication. But this statement is by no means the only shortsighted analysis of online legend-telling. The prominent legend scholar Linda Dégh, commenting on the proliferation of online legends, asks, "Is this strange and unnatural new virtual community capable of replacing real human communities and maintaining old legends or creating and varying new legends? Can we expect human nature to change so radically as to develop perfect electronic, science-fiction-style storytelling centers that can fill social and cultural needs in splendid autonomous isolation?"[25] Of course, the answer is no. Dégh presumes that online communities are "unnatural," therefore so are online legends. But legend-telling is a performance-based activity that *demands* involvement. Though the medium of the Internet certainly assists in circulating and propagating both old and new legends, if some automated storyteller were to sputter out such tales, these texts would be nothing more than legend summaries—legends removed from the context in which they were previously told.

Perhaps Dégh, by exaggerating the computer's role in contemporary legend-telling, is attempting to emphasize the importance of performance and context, but still, should online legend summaries be generated by some automaton, they could potentially be integrated within new legend-telling acts. A number of legend summaries exist on the Internet, but in this environment, these summaries can be situated within many diverse contexts by way of connecting them to other legends, a process which can initially involve little more than cursory use of a search engine. If someone posts a legend summary online, that text may be discovered and then incorporated into an ongoing legend-telling event at a later date. The Internet provides a particularly rich climate for the evolution and expansion of legend complexes, which are assemblages of thematically related legends (ghost stories, psychic experiences, and UFO sightings may all be considered as distinct legend complexes, although these groupings can and do interweave). Using the narrative elements of legends as building blocks, people construct entire realities and worldviews. Legend-telling is fluid, dynamic, and a fundamentally *human* endeavor.

Perhaps it is precisely because the Internet is a contested, liminal space that occasions debate over the nature of what is "reality" that legends are being told about cyberspace itself, thus affecting people's relationships with the very media environment in which these legends transpire. Some legends speak of the Internet as a medium for spirit communication, others characterize it as a sentient entity, and some even describe cyberspace as a hyper-reality wherein legend-telling becomes a magical act of casting spells. In each of these cases, legends infuse the metaphoric space of the computer-mediated environment with meaning and invite active participation within their narratives. It makes perfect sense that legends have arisen about the Internet, for this is a medium in which the imagination, intuition, and fuzzy logic reign; ideas surrounding instantaneous global communication exhibit many supernatural themes, and cyberspace allows people to externalize or evince their imaginings in an environment where fact and fiction become intermingled with beliefs and hoaxes. In a very real sense, the Internet is a province for mysteries and the supernatural, and as such, legends about it flourish.[26]

Legends of the Supernatural

Numerous legends do not touch upon any overtly supernatural themes, but so many do because of the very character of legendry, which emphasizes aspects of the unknown. Supernatural legends are stories that generate complex and dynamic social realities by correlating with various folk metaphysics, or spiritual lore that Jason Marc Harris describes as consisting of "rules, behaviors, powers, tendencies, and borders of the spiritual world implied by popular belief."[27] The supernatural—those extraordinary or seemingly impossible perceptions or events that cannot be otherwise conventionally explained by the culture in which they occur—qualifies the otherwise unfathomable, and as our own views of reality change, so does what we perceive to be supernatural. As Timothy Lloyd points out, the supernatural represents the widest vision of the natural world, and characterizes "the realm of the fundamental patterns and rhythms—of time, space, growth, and decline, for example—which, connecting, give purpose and governance to life."[28] Here Lloyd articulates the idea that the supernatural is, itself, an underlying structure of our reality—that which allows us to imaginatively situate our own existential conditions and concerns. Take, for instance, the popular concept of guardian angels. Millions of Americans believe they are constantly watched over by these supernatural beings. Especially in times of despair, guardian angels are imagined to be protectors who inspire men and women to persevere. Expressions of belief in guardian angels, as well as other supernatural entities and events, help describe what is ultimately indescribable and connect us with the mysteries and awe of being. Often, they represent wishes for personal contact or interaction with our deepest desires and aspects of existence outside our control; they can give us comfort and alleviate anxieties. It is the two-fold character of the supernatural as subject matter and perspective that fuels much of legendry.

Given the nearly universal longings that the supernatural addresses, it makes sense that in a consumer-driven society, the supernatural has increasingly become incorporated into commercial products such as films, books, television shows, and games of all kinds. The associations that legend texts provide offer entertainment and excitement and can even increase the value of goods and properties.[29] Ghost tours are a perfect example of this. Such tours, according to Diane Goldstein, routinely utilize a process she identifies as "fragmentation"—they commonly deconstruct and reconstruct several existent and newly created legends and apply them to specific places (i.e., only a few rooms or locations are deemed to be haunted within a larger tourist area). Fragmentation gives operators of ghost tours the chance to cater to a select group—those interested in ghost lore—while also leaving space to appeal to a wider market of tourists.[30] Identifying ghost tours as a form of postmodern tourism, Goldstein describes how the people she interviewed who embarked on these outings were "in search of an authentic experience, but weren't, but were . . ."[31] This comment touches upon a fundamental component in audience participation in and receptivity toward supernatural legends—the performance of belief. Legends are not in and of themselves agents of conviction: they do not force us to believe them. Rather, they are part of a larger dynamic process wherein worldviews and beliefs are teased and tested, and one's receptivity to the legend's believability depends less upon absolute conviction and more upon an admixture of doubt and certainty; investigating such legends in the hopes of experiencing the supernatural for oneself involves a confluence of suspending disbelief, pretend play, and make-believe, all which contribute to the affect of legendry, as I discuss later.

Another valuable point singled out by Goldstein is that the commodification of supernatural legends and beliefs has contributed to the trivialization of the supernatural, especially among scholars. This is no doubt true, but it must be noted that the supernatural has always been a marginalized topic in the modern Western world because it undermines positivistic ways of thinking. The supernatural crosses and blurs boundaries: between mind and body, mind and matter, the limitations of space and time, and even life and death. It mystifies us, challenging us to realign basic ideas as to what is probable, possible, and impossible.

Whether or not supernatural legends are truthful (let alone, factual) accounts is a question I will intentionally leave open. Current legend scholarship contends both legend-tellers and their audiences perceive legends as possibly true, but Lisa Gabbert argues that the "truth status" of legends is not fixed within the legend-telling audience, underscoring the fact that "everyday knowledge" is equally unstable. She writes that legends represent "the unknowable as knowable, and . . . this role ultimately has a metaphysical function, one based in the idea that human knowledge is imperfect."[32] Because supernatural legends portray extraordinary events, they characteristically encourage ongoing discussions and debates. More so, they demand discussion and debate; for the critical force behind legends—above all else—lies not in the factuality of events that legends recount, but in the significance and meaning that people eventually ascribe to the story. Legends represent a kind of artistry.

Myths and Legends

Storytelling might be the most vital of all human activities, for we construct our sense of reality in narrative form in order to make sense of things. Those oldest stories on record, myths, offer supernatural explanations for how the world or particular customs began. The events, people, and places they describe are symbolic rather than historic, and are governed by the sociocultural imagination. During sacred rites of passage, people reenact the roles and events described by myths to acquire experiential knowledge. One such ritual, performed between roughly 1500 B.C.E. and the fourth-century C.E., was known as the Eleusinian Mysteries. At the ritual's core, the myth of Demeter and her daughter, Persephone, were symbolically reenacted to initiate men and women into the Cult of Demeter. We know little about the specifics of this ritual, as strict laws forbade attempts to openly discuss the Mysteries, however fragments of history attest to their function. According to Aristotle, the initiates participated in order to experience certain impressions and psychic moods.[33] By reenacting the story of Demeter and Persephone, an allegory for the cyclical nature of life, death, and renewal, the initiates endured figurative death and transcendence.

While myths are those unifying stories offering metaphors for what a culture or society generally contends to be a reality (although some believe in more literal interpretations), legends offer alternatives to these stories, oftentimes illustrating those points of contestation and doubt that occur whenever any official cultural myth or narrative, whether found in the Torah, the Koran, or even the annals of science, is championed as an exclusive avenue for objective truth. Many religious institutions embrace an official doctrine to which a myth story is central, but among the practitioners of these religions, legends are told and retold that are at odds with or absent from official theology. For example, some Catholics incorporate vernacular beliefs and rituals involving the Black Madonna in their personal worship. Such customs have arisen in part from the numerous legends associated with the supernatural powers of this icon. One Polish legend recounts how the Black Madonna of Czestochowa began to bleed after being defaced by a thief, who, only moments after applying his knife to the painting, succumbed to an agonizing death. Many Poles believe the Black Madonna's supernatural protection saved the Jasna Góra monastery from the seventeenth-century Swedish invasion. Although official Catholic belief censures all worship of idols, the Black Madonna nonetheless remains an integral fixture in the religious practices of numerous Catholics around the world.

The French anthropologist Claude Lévi-Strauss contended that "mythical thought always works from the awareness of oppositions towards their progressive mediation" and that "the purpose of myth is to provide a logical model capable of overcoming a contradiction."[34] Participation in the Eleusinian Mysteries events likely offered initiates a communicative means to overcome the contradictions between life and death, contradictions that couldn't be surmounted by stories alone, but by additional, experiential knowledge afforded by highly ritualized action. Supernatural legends provide for similar operations through an audience's use of legend narratives as frameworks for ostensive acts. But unlike rites of passage reenacting myths, the ostensive play involved in reenacting legends centers on ambiguity, for legends undermine all-encompassing truths much more than advancing them, instead supplying a format for ideation. Both legends and myths, however, offer the chance to conciliate diametrically opposite ideas the likes of which come into focus when reflecting on the nature of the supernatural, as we shall see. The kind of ostensive action I'm referring to arises from legends that inspire quests to test their veracity; it is a ritual performance known as legend-tripping.

2. THE PERFORMANCE OF LEGEND-TRIPPING

Visiting the Waverly Hills Sanitarium

The Bluegrass State is allegedly home to untold legions of *haints*—lost, disembodied souls who wander the southern landscape—and their enduring popularity ensures that the region's folklore will forever be entwined with Kentucky's history. Shortly after relocating from Los Angeles to begin graduate studies at Western Kentucky University, I became enamored with local ghost stories and eventually conducted research on how contemporary spirit photography, as a type of folk art, articulates belief in spiritual manifestations. Part of this research entailed interviewing ghost hunters, many who were members of either the Adsagsona Paranormal Society of Tennessee or the Louisville Ghost Hunters Society (LGHS). During these interviews, people inevitably asked me if I had ever been to Waverly Hills (I hadn't) and then shared their own stories about the place. One of my undergraduate students, a burgeoning ghost hunter, confessed sneaking into Waverly with some friends one afternoon (they were too spooked to enter at night). While walking around the sanitarium's perimeter, he saw what appeared to be a young woman staring down at him from the fifth floor. She was pale, sickly looking, wearing a white smock, and after only a few seconds, she simply disappeared.

A more experienced ghost hunter and member of the Adsagsona Paranormal Society shared a collection of photos taken inside the building's interior. Some of these photographs contained odd, mist-like forms while others depicted semitransparent spheres of different sizes. She believed these spheres were "orbs," a classification for what some argue are spiritual energies caught on camera. As she showed me these images, she reported that strange voices had been heard in the room just moments before snapping the pictures. During interviews with several members of the Louisville Ghost Hunters Society, people often referred to one incident involving the LGHS founder and president, Keith Age, who had given a

21

brief tour of Waverly to a local news reporter a few years before. Wanting the reporter to experience an anomaly for himself, Age began verbally antagonizing the spirits in hopes of provoking their appearance when a brick flew across the room and struck him in the head. All of these stories and accounts were told with considerable excitement that only built as they progressed, and it seemed as if simply by invoking the aura of Waverly, these people gave their narratives a tangible power. At the time, the Louisville Ghost Hunters were preparing to host the 2005 Mid-South Paranormal Convention at Waverly Hills, which would culminate with an all-night ghost-hunting tour of the premises. Figuring the event would afford me plenty of opportunities to interview ghost hunters and spirit photographers, as well as the chance to see Waverly for myself, I purchased a ticket for the tour, advertised to begin at precisely midnight.

Unconfirmed rumors place the number of tuberculosis patients who died at the sanitarium at 63,000. Fueling these rumors is the ominously named "Death Tunnel," an underground structure through which corpses were allegedly carted away from hospital grounds in order to avoid demoralizing the residential patients. Since the hospital's closing, even more sinister reports of strange medical operations performed to satisfy morbid scientific curiosities have appeared. Only a few miles away stands the Pope Lick Trestle, home to the Pope Lick Monster, a crazed half-man, half-goat creature that, according to most stories, lures hapless individuals with its hypnotic gaze onto the tracks and into the path of oncoming trains. These and many other legends surrounding Waverly Hills have solidified its reputation as a mid-South epicenter for paranormal activity.

As the date of the convention approached, something more than academic curiosity was at work, because having immersed myself in these tales, I found myself imagining and even *expecting* a supernatural encounter, coming face to face with something that would force me to acknowledge some power haunting the sanitarium. When I finally drove up a winding trail, past a large metal gate, and onto the front parking lot of Waverly, I was instantly taken aback by its sheer size and by how its rows of windowless frames revealed only darkness inside. At the building's corner, closest to the parking lot, perched a solitary stone grotesque.

The sanitarium's grounds were crawling with paranormal enthusiasts, curiosity seekers, and dedicated spirit photographers. They had traveled not only from Louisville, but from all over Kentucky, bordering states, and even as far away as Florida. Under the looming shadow of the sanitarium, I wasted no time setting up my recording equipment at a nearby picnic table. After briefly talking to two or three people, word spread that I was a folklorist interested in hearing supernatural experience narratives and in seeing evidence of ghosts. Soon it was impossible *not* to talk about spirit photography. A few people presented me with scrapbooks filled with photographs they had taken at other sites, as well as photos taken on prior trips to Waverly Hills, and I talked with them at length. It soon became apparent that one of the main criteria for judging whether a photograph actually contains the image of a spirit is an accompanying paranormal experience. Because of this, my interviews frequently became spontaneous storytelling performances, and just as someone would finish, others would chime in to share their own experiences.

As people began gathering and listening in on the stories being told around me, one woman introduced a photograph she'd taken on a previous tour of Waverly that contained the image of a ghostly face peering in from outside a second-story window. Prompted by the image, a young man then recalled that during the previous year's tour, his group witnessed a glowing white apparition dressed as a nurse, whose uniform appeared to date from the early 1900s. Another woman near us immediately corroborated his story and, almost simultaneously, they all clamored to tell the story of Room 502. According to this legend, the spirits of two nurses who committed suicide—one who hanged herself and one who jumped from the fifth-story window—manifest to those wandering through the sanitarium late at night.

While I was jotting down as many notes as I could, someone introduced me to LGHS member Jonathan Jurgenson. The previous year, Jonathan and his wife had captured an image of the ghost-child Timothy, a frequent subject of many Waverly sightings and stories, along with what some argue is the image of another entity: the "Lab Coat Man." Jonathan eagerly shared his account of what happened that night and in a follow-up interview he described events occurring immediately before the photograph was taken:

Well, we went on the third floor and there's a group called MESA, which tries to either prove or debunk paranormal activity with scientific equipment. They had set up some motion sensor cameras at the end of the hall. Well, we got to the third floor at about three A.M. that night. All of a sudden we saw a flash at the end of the hallway. Then we saw another flash, but this one was a little bit closer, so something was triggering the motion-sensor cameras. Then came another flash even closer and another flash, so something was coming down the hallway towards us. Then it went to pitch black.

*As we're sitting there in the darkness, wondering if something's com-
ing towards us, we hear footsteps coming up the hallway—just slowly
walking towards us. Well, that gets quite unnerving when you're sitting
in the dark and you see a motion-sensor camera go off and you hear
something coming towards you. Then we heard the sound of concrete
hitting the wall around us, like something was throwing little bits of concrete. Well, somebody got unnerved and turned on their flashlight and
everybody started taking pictures.[1]*

Jonathan handed me an enlargement of the photo taken by his wife
during this incident and said the image contains "a little boy who is wearing old-type clothes. It looks like a white collared shirt with a little jacket
. . . very formal, very '20s or '30s style clothing."[2] The events contextu-
alizing this photograph continue to be told and retold in a number of
storytelling sessions about Waverly Hills. Even today, people who explore
the grounds of the sanitarium regularly claim to see Timothy and describe
him as wearing the same type of clothes.

Early in the evening, everyone attending the all-night tour listened
to local storyteller Roberta Brown tell a number of ghost tales during an
informal dinner. After a short walking tour of haunted locales around
downtown Louisville, we then headed back to Waverly, where we were
placed into groups. Two women I talked with during dinner joined me
in Jonathan's group, and I was glad for the familiar company, especially
since they had reported having a number of supernatural experiences
during the previous year's tour with Jonathan. While the members of our
group were introducing themselves to one another, the women advised
everyone to expect a high degree of paranormal activity, the appearance
of shadow entities, and perhaps even a visit from Timothy. At precisely
midnight, we lit our flashlights and entered the sanitarium.

The hospital had no interior lighting. Its many halls, rooms, and tunnels were in a state of ruin, and broken furniture and other debris littered
the dusty floors. Graffiti, much of it depicting occult symbols, marked
the walls. We made our way into the building and in no time, a few of
the more fervent tour members began to see flickering, unaccounted for
distant lights and shadow forms moving through the halls. Every time
someone pointed out an unusual shadow, a dozen cameras, flashing simultaneously, blinded me. Throughout the tour, Jonathan served as the
consummate tour guide, immersing us in a steady stream of legends as the
others shared their own beliefs about the paranormal. For the first hour or
two, the most passionate members of our group, including my two dinner

Man

Boy

The photograph taken by Rhonda Jurgenson moments after the motion-sensor cameras were triggered. Rhonda later discovered the images of Timothy and an "extra" spirit. Photograph courtesy of Rhonda Jurgenson.

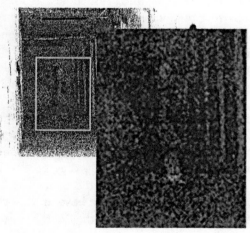

Close-up of Timothy and "extra" spirit. Photograph courtesy of Rhonda Jurgenson.

mates, a young couple, and an especially animated woman who carried practically an entire ghost-hunting laboratory on her back, repeatedly professed the reality of ghosts and staved off any prolonged period of silence with questions like, "Oh my God, what is that?" "Look, do you see that?" and, "What is that sound? Does anyone hear that?" Such queries invited others to participate in the ghost hunt, giving them permission, in a sense, to voice their own impressions. It definitely wouldn't have been as much fun without these enthusiasts who cheered on any and all potentially paranormal manifestations.

I must admit that I was somewhat distracted; I wanted to spend less effort recording the actions of the ghost hunters and more searching for ghosts. As I struggled to maintain at least a semblance of objectivity, we began walking down a long stretch of corridor on the third floor. I was checking my audio levels when I suddenly felt deathly ill. My stomach churned violently, my head swam in pain, and strong waves of chills wracked my entire body as an overwhelming sense of nausea forced me to the ground. Shocked by the abrupt onset and severity of the symptoms, I felt the urge to escape but I was paralyzed—completely helpless. Everyone else was in front of me, oblivious to my condition. I wondered if I might have gotten food poisoning and how I might be able to physically leave the building but then, after only a few moments, I felt completely normal, at least physically.

I had just rejoined the others in the hall when Jonathan exclaimed that he had heard the voice of a small boy; everyone immediately thought of Timothy. Huddling together in silence, the group peered into the darkness as someone shined a laser pointer down the corridor. Then, out of the corner of my right eye, I saw movement. Something rushed past as Jonathan cursed and my two friends from dinner screamed. A momentary whirl of confusion ensued as Jonathan exasperatedly told everyone Timothy had materialized in front of him and brushed against his flashlight. The women immediately corroborated this, and others claimed to have seen a shadow form or a blur. Again, I thought I saw something, although I'm still uncertain as to what it was.

While we trudged to the fourth-floor corridor, Jonathan related events purportedly occurring only a few years earlier. A group of teenagers who had broken into the sanitarium were exploring the fourth floor when they began to see shadow forms approaching. Panicking, they headed for a large metal door leading to the exit staircase, but the door, which had been rusted open, suddenly swung shut, locking the boys in. One of the teens grabbed a nearby axe and began chopping at the door. The sounds of the boys' screams and the axe strikes against the metal door alerted a night watchman, and when he arrived, he pulled the door open, revealing the boys covered with scratches and in hysterics. With a dramatic gesture, Jonathan pointed to notches on the door left by the axe blows, which our group then closely inspected. Shortly after entering the fourth-floor hallway, a member of our group began to experience chills and described feeling an icy, menacing presence behind him. Minutes later, a few claimed they saw the outline of a tall, shadowy figure following him. Jonathan instructed the man to walk down a corridor by himself and then return to the group. As he came back toward us, many (including myself) saw a large, black mass looming behind him that seemed to be well over seven feet tall. Whether it was an illusion created by the play of light and shadow, or a sinister energy seeking contact, I couldn't say, but as everyone stared, it lingered for a few seconds, then simply dissolved.

During our time in Waverly, it seemed as if we could never be sure of our senses or of what we had heard or seen, but by sunrise, virtually everyone believed they had encountered the supernatural (although some preferred the idea that they had experienced something natural, even if unrecognized by the scientific community as such). Some were convinced our experiences were due to ghosts and spirits, others attributed them to the combined psychic energies of everyone present, and others described them as the likely result of a kind of mass hysteria or hypnotic suggestion. Even those who had seen ghostly manifestations weren't in complete agreement as to their cause or source. Some thought the ghosts were sentient; others were convinced they had witnessed some kind of non-intelligent, residual energy in the area. Throughout the night, people saw eerie, glowing lights and shadow forms moving in peculiar ways, they smelled cigar smoke (which, according to some, indicated the presence of a doctor who had been fond of Cuban imports), and they heard loud thumps and crashes. I experienced a few oddities myself—orbs of light that danced about and what looked like the hazy outline of a person who walked across a hallway and passed through a wall. In Waverly, all of us felt we were in a separate reality, a bizarre place where the laws of the natural world seemed to work differently.

Well after this ordeal I was able to reflect on how many of these anomalous (as well as ordinary) events were experienced, described, and interpreted in a collaborative, open-ended process attempting to define what had transpired. After any anomalous experience occurred, each participant vocalized his or her opinions and beliefs, and then combined these with the others to generate possible explanations. Peoples' actions during these events were more chaotic, occasionally bordering on frenzy, with a few people screaming and pointing at shapes or movement in the distance, while others tried to rationalize or articulate logical explanations for what they were experiencing. The atmosphere was especially hectic with the ever-present flickering of camera flashes, laser beams, and other gadgetries. But, through the extensive, negotiative sharing of our experiences, these frenzied incidents and actions became narrative fragments, which then developed into fully detailed stories during the subsequent hours. When I returned the next day for a few follow-up interviews, the preceding night's events (most notably the encounter with Timothy) had already become part of the legend complex surrounding Waverly. Inadvertently, I too promoted Waverly as being haunted: during a casual conversation, I mentioned my sudden bout with illness. Several LGHS members identified the symptoms I described as "ghost-sickness," which they said had been experienced by a number of psychics while on the third floor.[3] These LGHS members said I, like the psychic investigators, must be sensitive to negative energies.

Legend-Tripping

My ordeal at Waverly Hills exemplifies what folklorists know as a legend-trip.[4] A legend-trip involves a journey to a specific location and/or the performance of certain prescribed actions that, according to local legend, have the potential to elicit a supernatural experience. Legend-tripping begins with the telling of one or more legends usually identifying a particular location as haunted or outlining a method with which to conjure supernatural powers—most typically, several legends and/or legend variations are told, the sum of which increase the believability of the overall narrative. Not all legend-trippers have strong convictions in regards to the truth status of narratives describing previous legend-trips or the legends associated with them. But one optimum precondition for a legend-trip is the belief that the legend could be more than just a fictional story. This is not to say that it must be believed to be true, but it must be believed to be possible, however improbable.[5]

The places these legends describe may be sites of past tragedies, such as murders; otherworldly events, like appearances of strange objects in the sky; or even locations reputed to have intrinsic magical abilities, such as graveyards where gravestones are said to return if moved or stolen. Often, legends also outline actions that must be performed in order to summon the supernatural elements associated with these places, although some legends focus more on describing activities that can summon the supernatural and less on where these activities are to take place. Many people have heard variants of the legend instructing how to summon the spirit of "Bloody Mary." In one version, the ritual involves standing in front of a mirror in any darkened room alight with a single candle. After chanting aloud "Bloody Mary" while spinning around in a circle three times, the spirit's face allegedly appears in the mirror. In some of these legends, Bloody Mary is merely a passive phantom; in others, she is violent and may physically assault people through the mirror. Besides mirror rituals like "Bloody Mary," other occult parlor games, such as the Ouija board, can also be the focus of legend-tripping performances.[6]

The German ethnographer Arnold van Gennep studied rites of passage, noting there were three stages of ritual: separation, transition, and reincorporation.[7] Building on van Gennep's work, the anthropologist Victor Turner redefined the transitional stage to include the concept of *liminality*. Through Turner's efforts, liminality has extended far beyond its original sense as a period of conversion and has taken on new meaning as an autonomous state described as "betwixt and between."[8] Now the term "liminal" designates persons, experiences, and activities (such as legend-tripping) that dissolve social norms or blur traditional categories. According to Turner, during the liminal phase of ritual, groups of individuals develop *communitas*, or a strong sense of community that promotes feelings of unity and equality. This is in contrast to traditional effects of social structures like the workplace and economic class in which differentiation and inequality dominate. While participants within rituals framed by myths must overcome some paradox or conflict by moving from one state to another (such as Christian baptisms, in which the baptized moves from a state of sin to a state of salvation), legend-tripping participants like those who claim to witness Bloody Mary may directly experience a paradoxical event in which there is no final resolution of the contradiction: should Bloody Mary actually appear, legend-trippers aren't provided with a description of how the experience should conclude.

In the absence of institutionalized rituals that offer supernatural experiences, people will invent their own, often by using themes available to them through the traditional expressive forms found in their folklore. At least partly because legend-tripping occurs outside of any institutionally sanctioned sphere, we are discussing a phenomenon that has for hundreds of years if not longer largely escaped social commentary and critique. Legends have been catapulted into the public spotlight by political controversy and popular culture, but the mechanisms by which they sustain and are sustained by legend-trips have been generally ignored, except by a few dedicated legend scholars.

All legend-trips open with the transmission of accounts of past happenings that usually appear as caveats against traveling to a site or against performing a ritual ("You better not summon Bloody Mary! She's real, and I heard she'll pluck your eyes out!"). However, underlying these warnings is an implicit challenge to test or explore the validity of the legend's claims. The telling of the legend creates a mood of excitement and anticipation that is nourished by its re-telling(s) during travel or other preparations, and, as Kenneth Thigpin points out, this encourages legend-trippers to interpret any near-future events or experiences as supernatural.[9] These experiences, in the end, become reabsorbed or added to the legend complex.

In sum, the basic structure of a legend-trip is as follows: (1) Accounts of past happenings are told in the form of legendry; (2) An uncanny journey is initiated wherein travel to a particular site or preparation for a specific ritual unfolds. At this time, the motivating legends are retold to evoke an anticipatory affect; (3) Encounters with the supernatural occur if the legend-trip is "successful"; and (4) Ongoing discussions and interpretations about what transpired occur among legend-trippers are then added to the legend complex.[10]

Because many legend-tripping themes include the search for monsters, extranormal powers, or spirits, most legend scholarship examines legend-tripping exclusively as an adolescent activity.[11] Many sites, such as the Pope Lick Trestle, for example, are seemingly visited much more frequently by teens than by adults. Legend-tripping induces a heightened degree of fear and excitement commonly associated with adolescent sexuality or delinquent activities like vandalism, and this performance allows teens to express courage and bravado in the face of the unknown. Another reason this performance is associated with adolescent behavior is due to the newfound freedom teenagers experience after getting their drivers' licenses, since access to transportation offers the opportunity to temporarily escape the watchful eyes of their families and neighborhoods. Most physical legend-tripping sites are out-of-the-way, secluded places, and just as a car allows teens to explore places that were previously inaccessible, so do legend-tripping locales provide for experiences generally inaccessible in everyday life.

The desire to test conventional, experiential, and metaphysical limits cannot merely be attributed to the adventurousness of rebellious youth, however, nor can simply visiting an alleged supernatural site be considered a legend- trip. *There must be some kind of openness or intent to summon the supernatural experience itself.* People of all ages legend-trip because it offers us a chance to play with conventional ways of perceiving reality. In the case of my legend-trip at Waverly Hills, everyone was over the age of eighteen and their motivation was colored by an adult attachment to rational explanation and scientific empiricism: they sought to record their experiences objectively through the various gadgets employed by modern-day ghost hunters. But while they wished to document evidence of a paranormal reality, they also wanted to have fun. To this end, many events in the legend-trip at Waverly were accompanied by squeals, screams, gasps, and laughter, and, at times, all of the participants seemed as if they were engaging in the types of make-believe and pretend play associated with children's games. Although bravado and merriment were certainly evident, so too were sincere efforts to test the experiential reality of spirit lore. Above all else, the experiences at Waverly resulted from a collective, sustained effort toward heightened awareness: straining to hear or see something out of the ordinary, reacting to numerous phenomena that just might be otherworldly, and maintaining the sense that the supernatural was *supposed* to be present. So while elements of play are crucial for legend-tripping, this doesn't necessarily rule out the fact that adults engage in this behavior. Rather, it might be stated that adults perform legend-trips, in part, because it allows them to participate in a type of group play.

Every ghost hunter in the Waverly Hills tour group claimed to have had both an ostensibly supernatural encounter and an emotionally rewarding or thrilling experience. For some who decided that their experiences originated from apparitions or spirits of the dead, the unknowable was represented as knowable and concerns about the nature of life after death were ameliorated. One ghost hunter confided in me that she no longer feared death since she now *knows* the soul endures. Additionally, the narratives arising from these performances contributed to the development of a sense of community and a shared sense of purpose by uniting spirit photographers to collectively deal with individual psychological and existential anxieties.

I was quite surprised to find out nearly every ghost hunter at Waverly was fascinated by the building's history even aside from its supernatural reputation. Only later did I realize that the legends about Waverly and the legend-trips they incite ensure that an abundance of regional folk stories endure and that local history will continue to be appreciated. The transmission of these narratives and the ostensive ordeals that perpetuate them converts the *space* Waverly occupies into a *place* offering Kentuckians a direct connection to their folkloric heritage.

Earlier I outlined the various ways legends may be reenacted as falling under three subcategories of ostension; legend-tripping, however, doesn't fit solely within any one of these. More than a simple legend reenactment, legend-tripping is a specific kind of ostensive play that can produce both wonder and fear. Folklorist Carl Lindahl was the first to suggest that ostension has the potential to inspire a sense of religious and spiritual awe. He studied the activities of a Hispanic San Antonio community whose members routinely visit "gravity hill"—a railroad crossing where the laws of gravity are seemingly defied. According to local legend, one rainy night a school bus stalled on the tracks and, despite the efforts of the driver to move it to safety, was smashed by an oncoming train, tragically killing all the children inside. If you stop your car at this precise spot, the spirits of the dead schoolchildren will push the car up the hill and off the tracks, out of harm's way. Like many legend-tripping sites, gravity hills (also known as ghost tracks) exist throughout the country. Lindahl observed that the ostensive reenactment of the accident solidified the Hispanic community by offering legend-trippers a sense of the miraculous. He noted that, to them, the legend-trip was "a religious experience through which they sought not to test their faith but to use it. Nevertheless, most experienced more immediately the thrill of a good scare, and only later a deeply spiritual sense of well-being."[12] We again see how legend-tripping involves play behavior that may also fortify cultural identity, group solidarity, a sense of place, and even occasion a spiritual or religious experience.

Early European Legend-Trips

There is no complete historic record of legend-tripping activities, as, like much of earlier folklore, supernatural legends and legend-tripping accounts were often transmitted through word of mouth. Bill Ellis identified one description of a legend-trip recorded in the thirteenth century, in Gervase of Tilbury's *Otia imperialia* ("Recreation for an Emperor"). This encyclopedic hodgepodge of the fantastic records a number of English folk beliefs and customs, including the following report, translated by Walter Scott:

Osbert, a bold and powerful baron, visited a noble family in the vicinity of Wandlebury, in the bishopric of Ely. Among other stories related in the social circle of his friends, who, according to custom, amused each other by repeating ancient tales and traditions, he was informed, that if any knight, unattended, entered an adjacent plain by moon-light, and challenged an adversary to appear, he would be immediately encountered by a spirit in the form of a knight. Osbert resolved to make the experiment, and set out, attended by a single squire, whom he ordered to remain without the limits of the plain, which was surrounded by an ancient entrenchment. On repeating the challenge, he was instantly assailed by an adversary, whom he quickly unhorsed, and seized the reins of his steed. During this operation, his ghostly opponent sprung up, and, darting his spear, like a javelin, at Osbert, wounded him in the thigh. Osbert returned in triumph with the horse, which he committed to the care of his servants. The horse was of a sable colour, as well as his whole accoutrements, and apparently of great beauty and vigour. He remained with his keeper till cock-crowing, when, with eyes flashing fire, he reared, spurned the ground, and vanished. On disarming himself, Osbert perceived that he was wounded, and that one of his steel boots was full of blood.[13]

Osbert's encounter is said to have taken place at Wandlebury Mound, the remains of a Neolithic garrison near Cambridge. Many European folk customs involve such monuments—ancient forts, henges, and stone circles—located throughout the British Isles. These formations, standing out in stark contrast to the ordinary landscape, have long been linked to the supernatural and are popular legend-tripping sites. According to legends, many of the large stones found at these Neolithic sites move of their own accord or have some other type of extraordinary powers associated with them. One legend about Stonehenge claims the large stones there cannot be counted without risk of death. Stonehenge, of course, may be the most popular Neolithic legend-tripping site in the British Isles, but it is by no means the only one. Many believe Doon Hill, located near Aberfoyle, Scotland, is actually a fairy mound. Atop the hill sits a single pine tree, called the "Minister's Pine," that supposedly imprisons the spirit of the seventeenth-century Episcopalian minister Robert Kirk.

Kirk followed his father's footsteps to become a man of the cloth, but held a lifelong fascination with all manner of folk beliefs in the supernatural. He was especially attracted to stories about fairies and was known to actively collect folk tales from his parish. In 1691, he completed an unusual essay on the social lives of legendary beings later entitled *The Secret Commonwealth of Elves, Fauns & Fairies*, but the manuscript wasn't discovered until after his lifeless body was found atop Doon Hill. After the document surfaced, many believed Kirk had revealed too many secrets of the fairy world, and so its denizens confined his soul to the tree. Even today, hundreds of years later, people adorn the trees surrounding the Minister's Pine with brightly colored votive messages as offerings to the fairies in hopes of receiving their blessings—or at least of avoiding their curses. For those who still believe in fairies, trips to Doon Hill strengthen their spiritual and cultural connections to these ancient elemental forces.

There do exist much older accounts of practices that may be identifiable as legend-trips, such as dream incubations, written about by Artemidoros of Ephesus around the second century B.C.E. Dream incubations were conducted by participating in certain rites followed by visiting particular temples or other places in the hopes of receiving prophetic dreams from supernatural sources. Though dream incubation was a popular form of oneiromancy, or dream prophecy, and was an institutionalized form of ritual practice, it also existed in many other regionalized forms, and its practice varied accordingly with accompanying local legends about different chthonic gods and heroes said to induce visionary sleep.

Today's legend-tripping activities aren't limited to exploring ancient sites where fairies are said to dwell or where the spirits of local figures remain after death, nor are they reliant on legends transmitted exclusively through word of mouth. Legend-trippers increasingly rely on computer-mediated communications to participate in rituals transpiring around the world in "real-time"; they also increasingly use an extensive array of technologies in attempts to prove or disprove paranormal phenomena. Because the otherworldly portrayed in supernatural legends and summoned by legend-trippers is encountered in that veiled place "betwixt and between" reality and the imagination, any attempts to obtain some irrefutable scientific "proof" of any supernatural experience that occurs are likely to fall short, for such evidence really constitutes but an additional claim made by legends. These claims do, however, fuel the transmission of legends.

Ouija Boards and Mediated Ostension

Many popular legends and legend-trips connected to the Ouija board frequently include warnings that malevolent spirits, after being summoned, will remain for an indefinite period of time to wreak havoc and generally pester their conjurors. Since these warnings invite people to test such stories by attempting to contact these forces themselves, the Ouija board is quite popular. However, if people actually come to believe they have brought forth supernatural entities, there are few outlets in which they can openly discuss and attempt to make sense of this experience, especially if the experience unnerves them. Erika Brady has written about the practice of "priesting," which she characterizes as "the calls and visits in which a priest is requested to interpret and sometimes intervene in paranormal matters."[14] She reports that priesting is "especially common in connection with the use of a Ouija board or other practices often undertaken to elicit a supernatural thrill."[15] Just as in the case of gravity hill, use of the Ouija board as a legend-trip has the potential to draw upon and elicit strong religious or spiritual convictions, positive or negative.

Legend-tripping at gravity hill underscores the supernatural aura of a particular place while using the Ouija board stresses the supernatural quality of interacting with a particular technology: the planchette. Other examples of ostension and legend-tripping, however, exhibit unique combinations of place-based and technology-based performances. Several years ago, Uri Geller, a self-proclaimed psychic, regularly appeared on television and radio broadcasts in Britain performing seemingly phenomenal feats, like bending kitchen utensils and stopping watches with the power of thought alone. Often, he would invite audience members to test their own spoon-bending skills during and after the show. One of the more remarkable outcomes of these performances is known as the "Geller Effect." After many of Geller's broadcasts, hundreds of people from all over the country claimed that forks, knives, and spoons in their homes had spontaneously bent and that clocks had stopped (or started) inexplicably. Even more baffling, some people claimed to have acquired Geller's abilities themselves; after watching or listening to one of his appearances, or after attending a live performance, they believed that they too were able to manipulate matter with their minds.

Allan Price, a medical doctor and parapsychologist, collected a series of case reports by persons claiming to have witnessed or experienced the Geller Effect and concluded, "it is not possible to be certain whether the Uri Geller Effect is due to the psychic ability of Mr. Uri Geller alone or to the arousal of latent psychic powers within the individual who experiences the Uri Geller Effect."[16] But might we also consider these as ostensive acts? We don't usually undertake careful examinations of common household utensils (unless we're expecting dinner guests), but many of us—should we choose to investigate—would likely find a few bent spoons, forks, and knives in our drawers. When members of the television audience scrutinized their forks and spoons, perhaps they noticed that one or more were twisted and imagined that either they or Geller were the cause. Thus, they experienced what they believed to be the results of genuine psychic phenomena. Of course, this is but one speculation (and one that doesn't preclude mass hypnosis).

Television programs associated with faith healing also invite ostensive acts. Among the most notable of these is *The 700 Club*, a talk show on the Christian Broadcasting Network whose personalities regularly participate in faith-based distance (mediated) healing. During these segments, the television personalities often utter phrases like "A woman living in Kansas has an abscessed tooth. She is healed!" or "Someone with arthritis in their knees no longer feels any pain." While such proclamations may be interpreted as statements informing the audience of events that have just occurred, they may also be interpreted as performative in that members of the audience believe in the statements to heal at the same time they are spoken. This illustrates a belief in the power of God in spite of—or perhaps because of—the great distances these healing operations immediately transcend. And like those reporting the Geller Effect, members of the viewing audience sometimes claim extraordinary experiences—in this case, miraculous healing. Both cases offer us examples of the ways that ostension can occur directly through communication media.

A Computer-Mediated Legend-Trip

Two years after my legend-trip at Waverly Hills, the sanitarium was the subject of the *Ghost Hunters Live 2007 Halloween Special* television show. *Ghost Hunters* is a reality TV series focusing on paranormal investigations by the members of The Atlantic Paranormal Society (TAPS). Weekly episodes follow a particular format: the show begins by offering a teaser trailer—a carefully edited montage of segments the episode will feature previewing the sites of featured hauntings. Voice-over narration simultaneously sets the supernatural context by recounting the events that have occurred at each location. After a standard opening credit sequence, the show begins with TAPS members discussing the place they are about to visit. Once TAPS arrives at the site, they meet with a local person who acts as the expert storyteller, sharing legends and personal experience narratives while giving TAPS a guided tour. Following this, the team calls for "lights out," and the ghost-hunting investigation, which includes gathering several types of audio and video footage, ensues. Some of the accumulated footage includes video of anomalous images and recordings of electronic voice phenomena (or EVP)—aural oddities often interpreted as disembodied voices and a form of spirit communication. While investigating the site during the night, members of TAPS themselves often experience anomalous events that aren't always captured on any recording devices, and these are used to contextualize the evidence collected. The next day they analyze the footage and TAPS members evaluate and debate the supernatural status of the recordings. Any evidence, including personal experiences deemed out of the ordinary, they present to the person providing the tour, who then reacts and incorporates this new information into the repertoire of previous stories. Essentially, *Ghost Hunters* is a televised legend-trip.

Folklorist Mikel J. Koven argues that "televisual text functions like a traditional legend-teller, creating a complex, matrixlike relationship among the supernatural belief traditions, the television show, and those watching that show."[17] In his analysis of the supernatural reality television show, *Most Haunted,* Koven reports that Richard Woolfe, the director of television programming at Living TV, noted: "We've since found out that loads of fans [of *Most Haunted*] have rituals attached to the way they watch the show; they turn off the lights, close the curtains, some burn candles and others set tape recorders running in case there's any EVP . . . We've also discovered that lots of people are getting together to watch the shows, even holding *Most Haunted* parties."[18] Although Koven is uncertain whether the truth-status of the recorded phenomena is discussed at these gatherings, he mentions that this show "elicits more comments on the show's veracity more than does the joint viewing of any other television program" he's watched.[19] But while episodes of *Most Haunted* offer audiences a televisual record of a legend-trip and instigate ritual viewing practices, they don't readily include audience members in the ritual, unlike the *Ghost Hunters Live 2007 Halloween Special,* which invited audiences to directly participate in the hunt online.

This episode of *Ghost Hunters,* filmed at Waverly, featured an online "interactive center," which posted photos and video streams of the investigation in real time. The center also employed a "Panic Button" feature with which online participants could, via special message boards, alert TAPS to any anomalous phenomena they witnessed. An unforeseen problem evident early within the six-hour interactive legend-trip was the addition of eerie mood music. One message board poster wrote during the show's airing, "it would be helpful if they took off the background music so the viewing audience could actually try to hear what they are hearing."[20] Another poster commented, "Funny how simple effects and music are hardly noticeable on other shows, yet when you are trying to be a part of the investigation, you want to hear whats [sic] going on."[21] Not only did the online audience members complain that the music disrupted their active involvement, affecting the anticipatory affect of the ritual, but many were also put off by the inclusion of an additional cast member, Elijah Burke, a wrestler featured on another Syfy Channel television series. His presence was interpreted as an obvious publicity stunt, and online participants routinely posted comments such as "Wrestler in the dredlocks [sic] . . . HAS GOT TO GO!!! 'Tell him to shut up and let them work'", and "I'm kinda feeling like the wrestler addition to the case is also needless, kinda takes away from the genuine ghost hunter feel."[22] Burke's involvement initially diminished the atmosphere the audience sought—an atmosphere that had been constructed in part by viewers' familiarity with previous episodes of *Ghost Hunters*. Since he was viewed as an uninformed skeptic, at least initially, his presence reduced the overall credibility of the investigation. However, unbeknown to viewers at the time, Burke had had strange experiences at Waverly hours before cameras began to roll, such as feeling "cold spots" and witnessing a child's ball (allegedly Timothy's) move on its own. In an interview with *Over the Ropes*, the online newswire for World Wrestling Entertainment, Burke talked about some of his experiences at Waverly during filming. He stated:

> *I was standing there and I motioned toward what appeared to be a window in the door. I was trying to get a reflection, and all of a sudden, I see some trees out there, but there's no reflection and I wanted to be sure my mind's not playing tricks on me . . . It was as if all of a sudden that shadow person said, "I'm going to show you this," and stuck his head straight in the window, covering the lights, covering the trees! All I saw was a silhouette of this shadow person, and then he moved back. I looked back at that door, and I saw absolutely nothing out there. There's no extra floor, or extra room—there's nothing out there![23]*

This interview reinforces the believability of legends portraying Waverly Hills as haunted, but more so, Burke eventually played a major role in what was to many online participants the most thrilling moment captured: at one point in the night, viewers witnessed Burke suddenly look to his side, scream in terror, and sprint away, only to come back and attempt to explain on camera his confusion and fright over something he heard and felt but couldn't explain. This act exponentially increased the believability that Waverly was haunted, since some audiences perceived Burke as a skeptic and/or as a nuisance, but whom they witnessed, in spite of this, have an intense experience. Burke's apparent transformation from a skeptic into a believer allowed the ghost hunters to accept him into their community. One poster commented, "I can't laugh at the ECW dude. The first time I saw a shadow person I was just going to retrieve a video camera . . . yeah . . . I was a State away by the time anyone realized what that woooshing sound was heading out the door."[24] Another participant added, "Heh, am I the only one that did see/hear something right before he ran off? Maybe I'm seeing things . . ."[25]

When several participants reported seeing the faint image of a face on the ceiling of the Death Tunnel, a TAPS member responded to their activation of the panic-button feature. After a cursory investigation of the ceiling, the TAPS member concluded it was either graffiti spray or a case of people misidentifying the pixel images on their computer screens. But this didn't end the audience's discussion of the matter. One poster wrote, "I saw a face that took over the whole ceiling it was pretty trippy."[26] Another said, "I saw this . . . scared the hell out of me."[27] Comments such as these testify to the experiential reality of the televised legend-trip for its online participants, whose actual presence was situated within virtual message boards.

Legend performances on message boards and other social networking and media sharing websites include discussions about video and audio "evidence," the telling of other, related legends, and becoming immediately connected to events transpiring in distant locations and periods. An obvious case in point is the video-sharing website *YouTube*, which contains thousands of video clips ostensibly revealing ghostly activities and other supernatural phenomena. Among these videos are also numerous parodies, hoaxes, and responses attempting to debunk allegedly "real" clips, thus illustrating that legendry perpetuated through media maintains an inherent ambiguity or lack of consensus opinion. Users regularly post comments and criticisms and engage in sometimes heated debates about these videos, making *YouTube* a fertile ground for examining the ongoing construction and transmission of supernatural legends online. Sites such as *YouTube* and the *Ghost Hunters* message boards bring multimedia presentations of the supernatural back into the corpus of oral or text-based storytelling and supply environments for entire legend complexes to spawn and thrive in the face of previous spatial and/or temporal confines.

The interactive format of *Ghost Hunters* is currently limited to their Halloween specials, but there are a growing number of websites devoted solely to interactive, online legend-tripping. The website *livescifi.tv* (which has no connection to the Syfy Channel) is one of many featuring live audio and video feed of paranormal investigations in which audience members may participate, and numerous websites feature "ghost-cams," providing live video and audio feed on sites reputed to be haunted. At the time of this writing, the Travel Channel's television show *Ghost Adventures is* preparing to air a live seven-hour ghost-hunting expedition of the Trans-Allegheny Lunatic Asylum in Weston, West Virginia. Their website promises, "Viewers at home will have complete access to the investigation on air and online as it occurs. They can monitor webcams throughout the building, chat with the guys during the lockdown, post messages on the bulletin board and send mobile text messages."[28] Without a doubt, multimedia sites flourish that host live feeds of ostensibly supernatural events and locations and that contain forums where online audiences can contribute to ongoing discussions.

Koven argues that the supernatural representations depicted in horror films and on television shows may result in audiences experiencing some effects similar to those that would occur should the subject matter actually be present in physical reality—he describes this process as "mass-mediated ostension."[29] Though the likes of Geller's performances and *The 700 Club* are examples of mass-mediated ostension, and though the special episode of *Ghost Hunters* and the upcoming episode of *Ghost Adventures* are examples of mass-mediated legend-trips, we shouldn't think them any less potent as rituals. The experiences these mediated performances bring about are real, present through the act of *presencing*.

Within the context of computer-mediated communication, media scholars Matthew Lombard and Theresa Ditton suggest that presence may be defined as the feeling of "being involved, engaged, and engrossed" by the environment created by the computer.[30] An important component of immersive presence is interactivity, realized "through the number of previous user inputs that are acknowledged in the current response of the technology."[31] On the Internet, legend-trippers use both archived and real-time audio and video feeds as well as message boards that provide a log of previous performances. These augment participants' efforts toward creating a shared ritual environment constructed from temporally or spatially distant real environments, or even from entirely mediated environments, which can provide for an overall sense of presence. But there is another kind of presence, one that involves what Rita Lauria characterizes as "being at the center of perspective of the observation while at the same time at the center of its construction."[32] In this sense, presence encapsulates the reflexive generation, reception, and evaluation of individual and group experiences within any environment. I use this sense of the word to indicate the manner in which supernatural experiences occur during legend-tripping performances. It is important to note that all Internet-based legend-trips necessitate that participants experience both the presence of their mediated environment as well as the presence of the supernatural.

We can say that legend-tripping presences the supernatural because this performance establishes the environment as supernatural, distinguishing the location and/or ritual—the center of upcoming events—as something other than ordinary. By utilizing legends and ostensive acts that conjure a portal to the world of the legend is opened. In this manner, legend-tripping operates as a *magical* ritual.

3. THE TECHNOLOGY OF MAGIC AND THE
MAGIC OF TECHNOLOGY

Magic, Legend-Tripping, and Interpretive Drift

In the nineteenth and early twentieth centuries, many Westerners thought belief in magic was a survival of primitive thinking, a remnant of an archaic pseudo-science. Regardless of this ethnocentric bias, some important observations were made about how magical beliefs function. In *The Golden Bough: A Study in Magic and Religion* (1890), the anthropologist James George Frazer classified magic as the belief that "things act on each other at a distance through a secret sympathy."[1] To this day, Frazer's description of "sympathetic magic" remains highly regarded as accurate. Another important "discovery" about magic belief came twenty-five years later, when the anthropologist Bronislaw Malinowski began studying the culture of the Trobriand Islanders. While observing local fishing customs, he noticed that the Trobrianders routinely performed elaborate magic rituals before their sea voyages. This was in stark contrast to their habits while fishing the lagoons. Malinowski concluded that the Trobrianders were using magic to psychologically prepare themselves for any situation beyond their control. Fishing the lagoons was simple, the water remained calm and fish were easily caught. But fishing at sea was perilous and a gamble—predators lurked beneath the waters, storms threatened to capsize boats, and the yield was never guaranteed. By noticing the Islanders' rituals gave them a sense of power, Malinowski helped lay the groundwork for the next century of Western scholars' conceptualization of magic.

Behaviors demonstrating belief in sympathetic correspondences are easily found in our own society. For example, in 2000, the anthropologist George Gmelch examined the superstitious rituals of professional baseball players and noted that players often wear the same (unwashed) clothing worn during the previous wins in hopes of attracting whatever force or luck that had affected the outcome.[2] Gmelch discovered that, like the Trobriand Islanders, these athletes use magic in preparation for activities that have a high degree of uncertainty, namely, pitching and hitting. Pitchers, for instance, may smooth the dirt on the mound before each batter or adjust their caps before each pitch. And hitters may smooth out the batter's box or tap their bat on the plate a specified nuumber of times. Besides superstitious rituals ("superstitious" usually being a title given to any other folk group's supernatural or magical beliefs), an abundance of explicitly magical practices exists within contemporary Western culture: witchcraft, ritual magick (spelled with a "k" by its practitioners to distinguish it from stage magic), and voodoo are but a few. Many of these operate as psychological self-help programs, inspire alternative types of religious thought, supply novel spiritual experiences, and act as alternative epistemological paradigms. Much to the chagrin of those intellectuals who see it as inimical to the advancement of reason, and those religious devotees who view it as demonic, magic thrives. Many people want to experience the otherworldly and the supernatural, and when institutionalized religions cannot or will not meet these experiential, people will turn to more dynamic systems of belief within their own traditions and folklore.[3]

In her book, *Persuasions of the Witch's Craft*, Tanya Luhrmann proposes that the practice of Western magic is a kind of play in which "belief and make-believe are intertwined" and the magician "plays at magic and understands the play as serious, and the truth of magical theory hovers in limbo between reality and fantasy."[4] This definition is quite compatible with that proposed by Margot Adler, who defines magic as "a convenient word for a whole collection of techniques, all of which involve the mind."[5] To this, she adds, "those who do magic are those who work with techniques that alter consciousness in order to facilitate psychic activity."[6] Together, Luhrmann and Adler's comments emphasize the imagination and intent—the most important elements of Western magic. Throughout this book, I will use the term *magic* to signify a complex process of imaginatively affecting perceptions of reality through distinctive and persistent rhetorical strategies and ritual performances. Adler claims most magicians don't concretely associate their practices with the supernatural, a statement I agree with, since the "supernatural" is a qualifier used largely by non-magicians (including legend-trippers) who generally remain unaware of advanced magical practices and lexicons (Adler acknowledges that most Americans consider magic to be "superstition or belief in the supernatural").[7] Legend-trippers are practicing the basics of magic—they are using techniques that artfully merge the rhetoric of supernatural legends with ritual behavior outlined by these same legends to effectively alter consciousness, facilitating psychic activity—that is, presencing—albeit usually without any personal attachments to or direct knowledge of magic as a system or systems proper. Legend-trippers generally approach, generate, and reflect upon supernatural encounters as untrained practitioners of the magical arts.

The experiences at Waverly Hills described in chapter 2 were the direct results of rhetoric and ritualized magical action. Magic rituals often begin at specific times, which are seen as windows of opportunity to effectively stop time; the magical ritual is meant to exist in between worlds where normal time and space cease to operate upon human consciousness as they ordinarily do. By setting out on our legend-trip at midnight, the peak of the "witching hour," we were correlating our activities with the implicit prescriptions for summoning the supernatural found in European folklore. The atmosphere of Waverly Hills was inherently uncanny—dilapidated, unlit, and fantastically eerie. The pervasive, natural darkness, punctuated by laser beams and flashes of electric gadgetry, distorted normal perceptions, and the many empty hallways and rooms dislocated the origins of any distant sounds. The overall effect was one of disorientation, which is critical in magical rituals designed to alter physical and psychological perceptions. Our familiarity with the variety of tales and belief statements about the sanitarium created certain expectations: to see the ghost of Timothy, to witness shadow forms, and to feel the presence of the dead. While the set and setting are vital to the outcome of a legend-trip, so is intent. Everyone wanted—and some fully expected—to have a supernatural encounter.

Performing either magic or a legend-trip traditionally necessitates the invocation or evocation of forces that constitute what most non-magicians refer to as the supernatural and what magicians call magic. The infamous magician Aleister Crowley clarified that "To 'invoke' is to 'call in,' just as to 'evoke' is to 'call forth'. . . In invocation, the macrocosm floods the consciousness. In evocation, the magician, having become the macrocosm, creates a microcosm."[8] According to Crowley, invocation is a magical act that can take the form of prayer, of possession, or of self-identification with certain literal or figurative supernatural spirits; invocation is the internal or mental presencing of these spirits. Evocation is the act of externally projecting these very forces in accord with the magician's will. To invoke power, magicians identify with or meditate upon spiritual forces or entities that are described by various legends, myths, and occult texts, concentrating upon their qualities in order to comprehend them. To evoke

pow
ma
pc
tr
e

cians engage in a process whereby these same spiritual forces
the evidence of the senses. Just as a successful evocation of
agical rituals first requires a successful invocation, in legend-
manifestation of the otherworldly in the form of a supernatural
es the invocation of the supernatural legend or legend com-
in best be thought of as preparation to interpret future events
ural. When the supernatural is considered to have appeared,
ers can then be said to have successfully brought the legend

similarity between the ritual performances of magicians and
end-trippers is that both employ the imagination to conjure
ibed by legends or occult texts for particular effects. By es-
ritual or ritual-like play frame in which the supernatural
ay operate, legend-trippers and magicians reframe their di-
experience. Tanya Luhrmann calls this process "interpretive
tendency for magicians to increasingly interpret events and
as magical the more they become involved with practicing
dentifies three loosely interlocking stages or conversions that
ft: interpretation, experience, and rationalization.[9]
ers to magic often face complicated concepts expressed in
oteric symbolism and discourse. But, as neophytes progress
ning, they begin to develop a hermeneutic system with which
nslating and applying this knowledge. When magicians insti-
dergo novel phenomenological experiences which are "salient
context of magical ideas but hard to account for outside,"
verful dreams, synchronicities, and ritual performances that
ousness, these experiences legitimate the magical framework
y transpire.[10] In effect, magicians begin to apply various sym-
respondences in which "ideas and beliefs drift, in a complex
ency of concept and experience"; these frames then permit
textualize the world within a magical paradigm.[11]
n notes that present-day Western practitioners of magic ex-
alence or otherwise remain equivocal as to whether they fully
agic. Because they acknowledge belief is a relative term, ma-
enerally inclined to profess that magic is *believable*. Similarly,
ing has less to do with belief in the objective truth status of
nd more to do with construction of meaning during and after
. We cannot say that all legend-trippers believe their actions
n the supernatural, but we can say that many legend-trippers
ief to this effect. Belief performances are the invocations of

legends enacted through legend-telling events and participatory behaviors that demonstrate an openness to the potential factuality of legend content. During the legend-trip at Waverly Hills, all of the stories told throughout the night, as well as the dozens of screams, gasps, exclamations, and camera flashes, encouraged us to begin interpreting the evidence of our senses through a supernatural frame. These belief performances catalyzed the process of interpretive drift.

A condensation of the stages involved in applying magical interpretive frameworks, the concept of interpretive drift is useful for explaining the process through which legend-trippers initiate and undergo ostensive ordeals. Legends provoke audiences to explore the supernatural realities they describe while providing a framework that may be used to instigate and subsequently interpret ostensive supernatural experiences aligned with these realities (those events salient within the ritual space of the legend-trip). Legend-trippers accept their experiences as out of the ordinary because they have shared and learned to interpret the experience with others (both in the immediate present and in the legend's past) within the frames provided by the ritual.

Daniel Lawrence O'Keefe stresses that "magic is real action . . . magic is more often than not *collective* social action."[12] What really separates us from preliterate societies like the Trobrianders is that they fully accept this whereas many of us do not.[13] Legend-tripping offers an opportunity to communally perform magic—albeit usually unknowingly—under the guise of traditional, playful behavior. Legend-trippers who encounter the supernatural and share their accounts with others are active performers—they are actors, directors, and stagehands in an unfolding and ongoing lively magico-performance, and not merely "spectators," as Bill Ellis insists.[14] By calling all legend-trippers spectators, Ellis mistakes legend-trippers' unawareness or disavowal that they are performing belief for inaction, for passivity. In fact, the frames supplied and reinforced during the legend-trip require participants to accept (or to believe/perform belief in) the idea that it is a supernatural force that causes their experiences. The difference between participants in magical rites and legend-trippers then is that the former are often keenly aware of the importance of performance in generating desired experiences, while the latter generally are not.

Magic and Technology

The wonders surrounding novel technologies have long worked to realign the boundaries between the possible and impossible, the known and

..., the natural and supernatural. Skeptics and debunkers often ask, "...hy do beliefs in the supernatural persist in the current technological, rational age we live in?" What they fail to acknowledge is that many of these beliefs thrive precisely because we live in an age full of technological wonder, and as long as new technologies continue to develop and transform the ways we interact with our environment and each other, so will supernatural beliefs. Both technology and magic exhibit humanity's desire and ability to affect or even design the future, and as essayist Erik Davis states, "Powerful new technologies are magical because they function as magic, opening up novel and protean spaces of possibility within social reality."[15] One of the most interesting illustrations of this can be found in the Modern Spiritualist Movement.

In the mid- to late 1800s, Spiritualism drew upon enthusiasm for empirical knowledge and novel technologies of communication in an effort to synthesize religious beliefs in an afterlife with contemporary scientific objectivism.[16] To Spiritualists both past and present, the term "supernatural" merely indicates those critical absences in society's understandings of the natural world. The main tenet of Spiritualism, namely, the belief that the living may commune with the spirit world, can be found in religious traditions throughout the world. Spiritualism is a movement intended to readily supply evidence of the afterlife, and as such, great importance is placed on demonstrations of paranormal activity. At the religion's core is the medium, a person able to communicate with spirit entities who usually directs séances or psychic circles. Participation in the séance may be considered a legend-trip since it is a group performance influenced by legends portraying séances as gateways to spiritual realms. Ardent Spiritualists, curiosity seekers, and scientists interested in paranormal manifestations all participated in séances during Spiritualism's peak of popularity during the latter half of the nineteenth century to the early twentieth century, although some participants in later years (such as Harry Houdini) were hell-bent on exposing all phenomena generated at séances as outright hoaxes. Like other legends describing the actions necessary for a successful legend-trip, narratives emerging from these rituals expounded upon the way séances should be conducted and included fantastic accounts of ghostly apparitions manifesting, ectoplasm materializing out of thin air, and even objects from afar teleporting or apporting into the room. Spiritualists and séance-goers eventually documented a wealth of anecdotes, theories, and legends. The sum of these writings provide key insights into how playframes and affective arousal shape the experiences of all who participated, and often read like textbooks on how to engage in legend-tripping.

Technological Mediums

Spiritualists' endeavors to unveil and communicate with invisible worlds corresponded with similar efforts by nineteenth-century scientists, and scientific discoveries and instrumentations were often incorporated into Spiritualist discourse as analogies for spirit contact. In 1844, the invention of telegraphy made wireless communication possible, and by 1882, it had become a source of popular metaphors for telepathy. In 1877, the phonograph began projecting disembodied voices much like spirit trumpets. The advent of radiographs after 1894 afforded people the ability to see inside the physical body, and these images were remarkably similar to the gauze-like apparitions caught by many Spiritualists with cameras.[17] But no device contributed to the expressive behaviors and physical artifacts of Spiritualism more than the daguerreotype and, later, the camera.

The earliest photographers were well aware that the photographic process could create transparent images if the plates were double exposed or if the figure to be photographed moved before a full exposure was made, and many novelty ghost photographs were created by these methods. But in 1861, a photographer named William Mumler composed a self-portrait that he claimed revealed the additional, anomalous image of a spirit after the photograph had been developed. Shortly thereafter, spirit photography became immensely popular and entire studios (including one run by Mumler) were devoted to its production, often in collaboration with Spiritualists. For Spiritualists, these photographs demonstrated the reality of the spirit world and authenticated their practices since the photograph—as an instrument of science—was commonly thought to be an accurate, true representation of the world.[18]

"Extras"—those inexplicable photographic images believed to be messages from spirits—included faces, bodies, and sometimes even writings. Many Spiritualists thought that the representations of spirits captured on film were partially the results of the paranormal abilities of either the photographer or a nearby sitter. But it was the medium of the camera itself that informed contemporary representations of ghosts and spirits. Before photography, pictorial representations of ghosts came from artistic illustrations, usually drawings and woodcuts that could only portray ghosts' appearances as solid. Interestingly, during this time, legends and personal experience narratives of hauntings mostly featured solid or embodied spirits. Only after the advent of the daguerreotype and other photographic processes could a disembodied, ethereal form be depicted.[19] And after such photographs were circulated legends and personal experience reports describing ghosts and spirits as insubstantial or semitransparent began to flourish.

In time, spirit photographers faced a surge of accusations of fraud as opportunistic hucksters began to take advantage of interest in the Spiritualist Movement for financial gain. Communities of spirit photographers rallied to defend and authenticate their photos and they developed a series of elaborate theories to counter their critics. They argued that spirit photos were feats of visual telepathy performed by Spiritualists; that those images containing apparent reproductions of photos taken before death were, in fact, evidence of the spirit's thoughtfulness, since it manifested in a form recognizable to loved ones; and that the crude images often found in the spirit photographs were evidence enough that they were real, since current technology would be able to construct more aesthetically pleasing images. Despite these efforts, by the second decade of the twentieth century, the spirit photography fad had subsided, as had the popularity of the Spiritualist Movement.

No doubt the incursion and exposure of charlatans contributed significantly to the eventual fragmentation of Spiritualism, because as a ritual performance, the séance's success depended on the communitas generated through shared experiences and interpretations. The function of the séance was dependent upon its structure as a legend-trip (or as a magic ritual) and once scientists, religious leaders, and others began publishing hoax reports and confessions, séances became occasions to discover fraudulent activities rather than performances to presence and experience the paranormal.

Contemporary Spirit Photography

With the introduction of new technologies, such as the Internet and digital cameras, spirit photography (a modern descendant of earlier Spiritualist practices) is once again immensely popular, especially within the context of legend-tripping. Entire online communities share photographic and video evidence of the paranormal, including UFOs, ghosts, and cryptids (creatures like Bigfoot and the Chupacabra). I've already mentioned that several television shows feature legend-trips—these have contributed thousands of hours of legend-tripping footage. Currently, most of these programs (such as the aforementioned *Ghost Hunters* and *Most Haunted*) center on contemporary ghost lore. Many ghost hunters are widely familiar with the tradition and history of spirit photography, but few profess to be Spiritualists. Rather than believing their photos, video, and audio equipment testify to the reality of the *supernatural*, these people, like their earlier-day Spiritualist counterparts, are inclined to posit that terms such as "supernatural" and "paranormal" exist due to our current inabilities to fully explain a range of naturally occuring phenomena. Like earlier Spiritualists, many of today's legend-trippers seek to verify the objective reality of ghosts and other so-called paranormal phenomena by technological means. Consciously or not, these individuals avoid the pitfalls of the earlier Spiritualist Movement's inability to successfully incorporate pluralistic interpretations of anomalous experiences. No single interpretation of photos is privileged, no one voice holds absolute authority when authenticating a photograph, and there are no canons of religious belief to observe or debunk, since there are usually no religious doctrines associated with this activity.

Some technological devices are certainly quite capable of recording phenomena that the human senses cannot perceive. Through our technology, we have the ability to see the wings of a hummingbird suspended in time, view the entire nightly procession of stars in a few seconds, and even scrutinize individual atoms on the head of a needle. Never before has humanity been able to extend the five senses to such a degree. But some still wonder if our technology is capable of revealing other hidden worlds. Addressing ghost hunters' claims that the camera is able to capture images of ghosts, the author and ghost hunter Troy Taylor writes, "Unfortunately no one really knows just how ghosts end up on film. Some believe that it has something to do with the camera's ability to freeze a moment of time and space in a way that the human eye cannot do. This may also combine with the intense energy pattern of the ghost, which somehow imprints itself through emulsion onto the film itself."[20] When I attended a meeting of the Adsagsona Paranormal Society in Nashville, one ghost hunter explained, "These spirits exist in a different spectrum of light that we're unable to see with our eyes but the camera can capture." Joshua Warren (nephew to the famous parapsychologists Ed and Lorraine Warren) claims that "Cameras allow us to see things we cannot see— things that move too fast or occupy a section of reality outside the scope of our natural observation . . . they can literally serve as our eyes into the spirit world."[21] The marvels of technology remind us of our limitations even as they offer us new ways to relate to the unknown and new media with which to propagate legendry.

The spirits that haunt the many photographs that communities of spirit photographers have taken over the years are, for some, evidence of a reality normally inaccessible to sensory operations. The photographer Mark Durant asserts, "The camera may sometimes act as a visual doorway to other worlds, but it is as if the lens were made of cheap plastic, offering only refraction, foggy figures, and ambiguity."[22] Spirit photography is a way to accumulate material that, when approached through particular interpretive frames, validates beliefs and ideas about spiritual and supernatural worlds for a number of people. While it may seem like the inward search for personal illumination is being replaced by the outward search for objective truth, the technology used in legend-tripping performances supplies ambiguous evidence that shapes and is shaped by people's wants, desires, and beliefs. The instruments and media ghost hunters emloy serve as their eyes and ears into the spiritual realms, and in this way function as extensions of the ritual.

Occult Software and Haunted Cyberspace

Some of the more inventive associations between magic and technology are evident in the development of occult software—computer programs used alongside or instead of more traditional magical practices. One website offers a number of occult programs "to help you with Sympathetic Magick."[23] Some of these claim to grant magicians the ability to "cast thousands of spells a minute," and even to "utilize the moon energy within the program." The website advertises:

> Is Image Magick your preferred style of Sympathetic Magick? Perfect then this is the perfect Magick Tool for you! The Source Software uses Image Magick perfectly enhanced and mingled with Biometrics. Biometrics has the ability to take the power of intent and your thought form to a whole new level of reality! Many have commented to the effect that it gives your intent a life form all of its own quickly and quite effectively. Imagine the way you craft spells, hexes, curses, etc., today and thousand fold it each and every minute you choose to run the program... This is what The Source software can do.[24]

Just as contemporary ghost hunters embrace the idea that digital technologies can assist them in finding ghosts, so too do some magicians entertain the idea that their spell casting may be enhanced by computer technology.

Magicians and psychics may also employ random number and/or text generators to test whether they can affect a random sequence of data through mind alone, to divine the future, and even as to communicate with discarnate beings. These last two applications are simply contemporary expressions of the ancient and universal belief that spiritual or otherworldly forces can deliver messages and make their presence known by manipulating human technology. Of course, there are more recent precedents as well. In the 1950s, UFO enthusiasts and amateur ham radio operators began receiving what they speculated might be communications from advanced, alien races. In 1985, a West German named Klaus Schreiber, a pioneer in electronic spirit photography, believed deceased loved ones were contacting him through his television set.[25] The folklorist Elizabeth Tucker writes of a ghost in a college residence hall that allegedly communicates by typing the words "!EM PLEH" ("Help me!") on the screen of a student's computer.[26] And several ghost hunters now use a device called the "Ovilus," an electronic gadget that translates different electromagnetic frequencies into words, purportedly allowing spirits to "talk" by manipulating local energies.[27]

Occult software has also been created to utilize the Internet as a magical tool to focus magicians' wills and manifest their intentions. Mark Pesche, co-creator of VRML (Virtual Reality Modeling Language, a text-based file format used to represent three-dimensional, interactive vector graphics) and a self-avowed witch, publicly launched VRML with a magical ceremony named CyberSamhain. On Friday, October 14, 1994, Pesche sent out an e-mail invitation to participate in this ritual:

On 27 October 1994, at Life On The Water in San Francisco, California, we will perform a ritual of CyberSamhain, a ritual which acknowledges and welcomes the God into his realm on the other side, within Cyberspace. He must pass through the Goddess, who is everywhere present and need be welcomed nowhere; before cyberspace took form, she was its firmament.

The great advantage of a ritual within cyberspace is very clear; everyone who wishes can join with us, *wherever they may be in the world*, and participate in the ritual. We will be using two wonderful channels into cyberspace; Mosaic, which allows you to view hypermedia documents which span the Internet, and Labyrinth, a brand-new

Internet visualization tool which creates a three-dimensional 'view'
of a space on the Internet. Real cyberspace.

   Using these tools, we will be casting a magick circle whose center
will be everywhere and perimeter nowhere. The ritual will be available through Mosaic and the World Wide Web, as well as a Labyrinth-
based view of the magick circle. Further, if anyone reading this
feels compelled to participate, they may contribute text, graphics,
or other media which will also be added to the site. Also, anyone who
wants to contribute a totem (a three-dimensional representation) to
be placed *within* circle during ritual will likewise be able to do
that.[28]

Pesche implies that cyberspace is particularly conducive to magical practice because it operates *as* magic, overcoming the limitations of space,
acting much like an astral plane. Moreso, cyberspace *is* magic, a manifestation of the divine. Pesche's magick circle permits any number of magicians to collectively presence the sacred, their numbers strengthening the
efficacy of this act.

   Folk belief in the supernatural or magical powers of the Internet arises partially because online communication connects people, places, and
events in ways that overcome conventional restrictions of time and space.
But the Internet also supplies two conditions that the political science
scholar Michael Barkun identifies as necessary for the construction of any
alternative belief system incorporating mystical awareness of immanent
and/or transcendent reality: access to a wide variety of thematic materials
or motifs—a database from which one may weave together many metaphysical ideas, and an environment that significantly lessens the influence
of existent authorities "so that novel combinations of ideas can be proposed and taken seriously."[29] One consequence of this is that people seek
to develop direct, personal relationships with the Internet, ascribing to it
a magical or supernatural character.

Cyberspace and the Noosphere

Over forty-five years ago, the media theorist Marshall McLuhan, argued
that computer technologies were collapsing space and time restraints, essentially turning the world into a "global village" where everyone could
actively participate in a worldwide conversation.[30] This belief echoed an

idea developed twenty years earlier by Pierre Teilhard de Chardin—the concept of the noosphere.[31] According to Teilhard, all human activity is oriented toward achieving a single point of convergence—a hypothetical, emergent, transhuman consciousness called the noosphere, which may be understood as a virtual space containing and emanating all human thought. In his posthumously published book, *The Phenomenon of Man*, Teilhard writes, "the noosphere tends to constitute a single closed system in which each element sees, feels, desires and suffers for itself the same things as all the others at the same time."[32] He continues: "All our difficulties and repulsions as regards the opposition between the All and the Person would be dissipated if only we understood that, by structure, the noosphere (and more generally the world) represent a whole that is not only closed but also centred. Because it contains and engenders consciousness, space-time is necessarily of a convergent nature. Accordingly its enormous layers, followed in the right direction, must somewhere ahead become involuted to a point . . . which fuses and consumes them integrally in itself."[33] The concept of the noosphere attempts to reconcile the metaphysical teleologies of singularity and radical plurality by codifying reality as a hermeneutic circle generating alternate worlds, which eventually, when interpreted, lead to understanding, which then recursively generates even more alternate worlds, *ad infinitum*—all of which eventually converge. Julian Huxley, in his introduction to the first English translation of *The Phenomenon of Man*, writes: "the increase of human numbers combined with the improvement of human communications has fused all the parts of the noosphere together . . . But when it is confined to spreading out over the surface of a sphere, idea will encounter idea, and the result will be an organized web of thought, a noetic system operating high tension, a piece of evolutionary machinery capable of generating high psychosocial energy."[34] The noosphere aligns temporal reality or history as a progressive series of stages, each growing in self-awareness and complexity toward a teleological singularity of space-time and matter. We may approach the noosphere as a kind of meta-reality incorporating a magical principle: everything is in some way connected to everything else regardless of temporal or spatial constraints. By identifying the noosphere as "a noetic system . . . generating high psychosocial energy," Huxley aligns this theory of grand unification with those magical practices that facilitate the development and application of psychic energy in efforts to presence into being infinite possible worlds that may be collectively experienced.

Many magicians, science fiction writers, and cyberculture enthusiasts have incorporated variations of the noosphere in their techno-evolutionary philosophies; among the more notable of these is the futurist Raymond Kurzweil, who argues in his transhumanist book, *The Singularity Is Near* (2005), that there will eventually be a hybridization of artificial intelligence and humanity, leading to immortality and the ability to re-fashion the entire physical universe. Kurzweil predicts the first artificially intelligent computer will emerge sometime around 2029. But others advocate that the Internet *is* the noosphere and is *already* sentient, and that our interactions with this consciousness have already begun the artificial intelligence/human hybridization that will manifest transhuman consciousness. These folk beliefs, in effect, reframe the concept of "natural" to allow experiences had through—and with—communication technologies to be interpreted as "supernatural." The legends that emerge from these experiences and lead others to seek them out contribute to vast, collective world-making enterprises that folklorists call legend complexes.

Legend Complexes and Occult Texts

Within a legend complex, narratives, practices, and experiences build upon and reinforce one another to encourage legend-tripping performances in a way one isolated tale never could. During my time at Waverly Hills I didn't meet a single person who had heard but one account of Waverly. Rather, everyone was familiar with many stories and legends about the sanitarium. They had contextualized these narratives within a larger sphere of folk metaphysics comprised of legends, rumors, opinions, ostensive acts, and beliefs related to New Age mysticism, psychic phenomena, institutional religious views, past personal experiences, information gleaned from the Internet, books, television, radio, and paranormal clubs and conventions. Legend-trippers draw upon these materials when interpreting any number of events. Shadow play on the walls of Waverly can become evidence for "shadow entities," a popular motif in contemporary supernatural folk discourse; the effects of sleep paralysis can be interpreted as demonic assaults or as an alien abduction. We can gain a better understanding of how legend complexes function as persuasive narrative worlds by investigating the operations of occult texts.

The term "occult," from the Latin *occulere*, meaning "to conceal," is often associated with, and sometimes used interchangeably with, the word "magic." Traditionally, the occult refers to a body of esoteric lore that profiles supernatural or magical provinces and powers for the benefit of an enlightened few. The historical threads of occultism run alongside yet separate from more conventional, everyday practices of folk magic.[1] Unlike folk magic, which usually relies on oral transmission for its circulation, practices in occult traditions are primarily transmitted through print, creating an intimate relationship between magicians and text. A few occult traditions continue to maintain elements of secrecy, but as a

56

truly secret tradition, it is no more. Anyone vaguely familiar with Western magic can readily gather occult texts online, and the secrets that occultism once strived to furtively preserve—magical records claimed to date from antiquity—are immediately accessible.

Occult texts were and are intentionally designed to introduce readers into new worlds of meaning; essentially, they serve as initiatory devices, acting as surrogate experts on the tradition. Western occultism employs its own discursive conventions, and its use of idiosyncratic symbolic, metaphorical, and allegorical language often requires strenuous interpretive efforts from readers. Similar to legends that promote legend-tripping activities, occult texts portray magical practices as effective for inciting extraordinary experiences. And like legends, they guide or even goad readers to use supernatural or magical frameworks to make sense of their contents. One example is found in the grimoire, *The Book of the Sacred Magic of Abramelin the Mage*.[2] This work, allegedly an autobiography, describes an elaborate ritual for summoning one's Holy Guardian Angel. It also outlines the procedures necessary to subjugate the Princes of Hell to one's bidding, though this book warns of the dangers inherent in cavorting with the demonic. Besides instructing how to conduct these rituals, *The Book of the Sacred Magic of Abramelin the Mage* also gives readers a series of past accounts concerning the author and how he came to acquire this potent magical knowledge. The esoteric nature of the text prevents any casual reader from fully understanding its contents, since many of its messages and instructions are encoded in various magical keys or word squares decipherable only through familiarity with other occult works, readers' previous experience with magical rituals, and faith in the efficacy of the grimoire.

Occult texts, philosophies, and practitioners commonly offer explicit warnings of the dangers inherent in occultism. Aleister Crowley's one-time secretary and fellow occultist, Israel Regardie, often commented that anyone wishing to seriously study magic (i.e., Western occult traditions) should first undergo extensive psychoanalysis, since pursuing magical knowledge may lead those who are fantasy-prone or who have any dissociative illnesses into a world where nonexistent signs and portents are habitually and erroneously uncovered. Occult researchers and those who investigate the paranormal commonly report being victimized by high strangeness.[3] In UFO lore, one readily finds anecdotes from UFO researchers who claim they are themselves alien abductees or that they are being persecuted by sinister government agents. And within occult circles, legends tell of magicians who have succumbed to insanity while pursuing forces far greater than themselves.[4] Such warnings may actually lead people to perform belief or even believe in the realities presented in occult texts. The magician, answering these as invitations to a challenge, and reading an occult text as a kind of instruction manual, simultaneously immerses herself into the world depicted by the text and presences this world through ostensive performances.

Unlike legends, which have traditionally been transmitted through oral culture, occult works must strategically develop believability in the absence of face-to-face interactions, often by alleging privileged knowledge based in claims of power, whether the ability to summon devils or to confer miraculous visions.[5] Occult texts necessitate specialized reading strategies in order to decode information culled from many related texts, each referring to one another in order to establish believability. Legend complexes operate upon the same principle: a single story about an extraterrestrial visitation might be considered preposterous but thousands of such tales told with sincerity makes what was once deemed impossible seem much less so.

Readers of occult texts receive various spells, rituals, and exercises prescribed for inducing altered states of consciousness. The same holds true for legend-trippers—supernatural stories and accounts, when reenacted, can alter consciousness (most supernatural legends don't expressly characterize the events contained therein as stemming from altered states of consciousness, however). In both cases, experiences within these altered states of consciousness, once narrativized, become part of the traditions that instigate them. The performance of the Bloody Mary ritual, for instance, transpires in accordance with the legend, which typically prescribes sitting in a darkened room, staring into a mirror, and repeating a series of verbal chants (sometimes repetitive tasks, such as spinning around in a circle, are requisite). The effects of sensory deprivation, concentrated awareness of the task at hand, and repetitive activity may trigger a degree of suggestibility—the narrative significantly influences the performer, who may interpret any unfolding experiences accordingly. Reports of these experiences may then become part of the overall legend and legend-trip, similarly to those reports magicians share with one another regarding their own experiences with rites and rituals laid out in various occult texts. One such rite, the summoning of one's Holy Guardian Angel, takes place over a time period of six months. *The Book of the Sacred Magic of Abramelin the Mage* prescribes a prolonged series of increasingly difficult tasks, including fasting, constructing a specific set of magical tools, and living in isolation, all of which incite a transformation in the magicians's consciousness.

Designed Tradition

The horror writer H. P. Lovecraft (1890–1937) is perhaps best known for his initial creation of the Cthulhu Mythos, a complex fictional world where ancient, all-powerful beings like the extraterrestrial "Outer Gods" and the ocean dwelling "Great Old Ones" lie just beyond the waking world of humanity—a world blissfully unaware of the truly incomprehensible, monstrous nature of reality. Many of Lovecraft's short stories uniquely blend folklore with science fiction and focus on characters that acquire glimpses of this truth while conducting various paranormal investigations. The author encouraged many of his peers to add to the Cthulhu Mythos, which has since evolved into a complete fictional universe transmitted through a variety of media, including role-playing games, television, film, and the Internet.

One artifact appearing throughout the Mythos is the *Necronomicon*, a grimoire said to contain spells for summoning the Old Ones. Originally constructed by Lovecraft's imagination, the *Necronomicon* has nonetheless developed a life all its own. Conjured by real-world magicians interested in tapping into the collective authority (as well as the economic potential) amassed by public interest in Lovecraft's work, several versions of the *Necronomicon* have actually been published, and each of these, like other occult grimoires, promises esoteric knowledge. If readers are seriously interested in exploring the Cthulhu Mythos, they will inevitably seek out occult materials that draw heavily upon Lovecraft's writings, such as the various versions of the *Necronomicon*. Several magicians claim Lovecraft had tapped into an occult reality that he had mistakenly assumed to be the product of his own imagination, and when their assorted works are explored, readers encounter numerous personal experience narratives describing ritual activities that have evoked visions of the Outer God Yog-Sothoth or the Deep One named Dagon. No longer is the Cthulhu Mythos framed as fiction, but, rather, as fact. This is hardly the first instance in which a legend complex has reframed fictional texts as "real," for the history of occultism is littered with such examples. The Rosicrucian Manifestos, two anonymously written documents initially appearing in the early 1600s, announced the existence of the Brotherhood of the Rose Cross, an ancient and secret fraternal order that believed the time was right for humanity to receive illuminated wisdom. Despite the fact these pamphlets were most likely carefully crafted works of fiction, their existence inspired people to seek out the Brotherhood, to develop occult groups declaring direct ties to the Brotherhood, and even to insist they themselves were members of this occult fraternal order.[6] Anyone familiar with occultism knows that these documents have decidedly shaped contemporary Western esotericism.

Occult texts strive to develop authenticity and authority by claiming, if not outright boasting, direct lineages from ancient cultures. Such creative means of authentication exist throughout many religious and secular customary practices. For instance, Wicca has quite successfully written its own history. As the folklorist Regina Bendix discusses in her work, *In Search of Authenticity*, the politics of cultural representations lie not in tradition, but in experiences. Through sustained world-making efforts, folk groups create more often than uncover their own heritage.[7] Supernatural legends and occult texts both illustrate attempts to become believable, or better yet, "real," by tying themselves to history through blending fiction with fact, infusing everyday reality with elements of the otherworldly and the fantastic. The interplay between ideas and experiences evident in supernatural legends and occult texts provides platforms for debate about the nature of reality and encourages particular interpretations of experiences, as well as retrospective interpretations of memories. By applying the frames of supernatural legends and occult texts, individuals and groups may discover and create, both individually and collectively, new ways of thinking about themselves and of interacting with the world.

Alternate Reality Games

At the end of the last chapter, I mentioned that experiences had through and with communication technologies can be interpreted as supernatural. Before exploring how these experiences can occur through legend-tripping performances, I'd like to first present a series of memorates gathered from players of *The Beast,* an alternate reality game (ARG). ARGs are open-ended gaming narratives that utilize transmedia storytelling and interweave the ideas and actions of both players and game designers (often called puppet masters) into an unfolding production. Jane McGonigal, a pioneer in the field of online performance gaming, defines an ARG as: "an interactive drama played out online and in real-world spaces, taking place over several weeks or months, in which dozens, hundred, thousands of players come together online, form collaborative social networks, and work together to solve a mystery or problem that would be absolutely impossible to solve alone."[8] According to the *2006 Alternate Reality Games SIG*

Whitepaper, what is now known as alternate reality gaming began with *The Beast*, the unofficial title for the game created by a team at Microsoft to promote Steven Spielberg's film, *A.I.*[9] Game play began in the summer of 2001 with three separate, yet related points of entry into the game—clues called "rabbit holes" by alternate reality gamers.[10]

The Beast's original rabbit holes took the form of advertisements for the film and included a credit listing for someone named Jeanine Salla—a "Sentient Machine Therapist," film trailers with an encoded telephone number in the promotional text, and a poster containing a message stating, "Evan Chan was murdered. Jeanine is the key." The film credit for a "Sentient Machine Therapist" struck some people as odd, so they conducted online searches for the name Jeanine Salla, which led them to several webpages intentionally created for gameplay containing fictitious contents camouflaged as "real." These, in tandem with additional clues provided, eventually led players into a complex mystery. When people called the phone number listed in the trailers, they received a series of instructions, which, if followed, would send them an e-mail stating, "Jeanine is the key . . . you've seen her name before." Through these rabbit holes, players eventually visited over thirty different websites that doled out segments of an elaborate, interactive story about the struggle for sentient robots' rights in the year 2142. While the complete narrative is too complicated to present here, by the time the game had concluded, players had held phone conversations with an in-game character and had taken part in rallies in New York, Chicago, and Los Angeles. And players had done all this without ever explicitly acknowledging that they had been playing a game.

ARGs like *The Beast* differ from other forms of gaming by incorporating narrative and physical elements that attempt to disguise the fact that a game is being played at all. This unique characteristic has come to be embodied as "This Is Not A Game," or TINAG. As David Szulborski, author of the book, *This Is Not A Game* (2005), wrote, "In an alternate reality game, the goal is not to immerse the player in the artificial world of the game; instead a successful game immersed the world of the game into the everyday existence and life of the player . . . The ultimate goal is to have the player believe that the events take place and characters of the game exist in his world, not an alternate reality. In a strange but very real way, the ARG creator is trying not to create an alternate reality, but change the player's existing world into the alternate reality."[11] Rather than employing narrative and gaming techniques to generate a sense of immersion within the game, ARGs use rhetorical techniques and provide interpretive frameworks similar to those of legends and occult texts that encourage players to engage in a performance of belief that the story itself is real and so can be affected by "real-world" actions. McGonigal comments that "one of the most intriguing and lingering effects of TING [TINAG] immersion tactics is a tendency to continue seeing games where games don't exist."[12] This parallels the observations made by some occultists: studying magic can result in identifying magical signs where none actually exist. McGonigal suggests that ARGs allow players a method of "transforming game to reality and reality to game, choosing the interface that best suits their current problem-solving needs and experiential desires."[13] As for the players' beliefs in the reality of the game, McGonigal writes: "The immersive aesthetics of the Beast inspired belief from its players, although certainly not a literal or naive belief that confused the 2142 A.D. fiction with present 'real life.' Rather, the game aroused an affective and self-conscious belief that enabled players to respond emotionally and viscerally to the needs and demands of each other and of the fictional world."[14] In other words, the performance of belief allows people to apply communally constructed interpretive frameworks tht encourage them to experience "reality" according to the logic provided by the game. As I've mentioned before, what separates legend-trippers from alternate reality gamers, as well as magicians, is that the latter are self-consciously aware of their performance and believe in the potency of their play. Legend-trippers, however, generally disavow that it is they who are the cause of the supernatural event. In order to ascribe a supernatural quality to an experience, agency must reside with the otherworldly.

McGonigal recorded several personal experience narratives from the Cloudmakers—players of *The Beast*—that describe the experience of their collective force as a phenomenon akin to the noosphere. One Cloudmaker describes an extreme feeling of communitas: "The 7500 + people in this group . . . we are all one. We have made manifest the idea of an unbelievably intricate intelligence. We are one mind, one voice . . . made of 7500 + neurons . . . We sit back and look at our monitors, and our keyboards . . . our window to this vast collective consciousness . . . we are not alone. We are not one person secluded from the rest of the world . . . kept apart by the technology we have embraced. We have become a part of it through the technology. We have become a part of something greater than ourselves."[15] McGonigal notes that for many Cloudmakers, this experience of an emergent collective intelligence was the highlight of the game. Another player mentions how *The Beast* "might, would, could produce what we've been wrangling with all along: an (admittedly low-level) sentient artificial intelligence . . . this would blow my mind - and completely blur the line between entertainment and philosophical and technological advances in our modern society."[16] Similarly, one player speculates that a distributed collective intelligence has emerged on the Cloudmaker message boards by stating, "Cloudmakers are organic, yet using their brains in a gigantic parallel-processing venture, like SETI@home on a wetware scale."[17] The awareness of their agentive social network was enough to inspire one Cloudmaker to suggest "real-world applications of their collective intelligence."[18] In 2002, some of the Cloudmakers discussed utilizing their mystery-solving skills to catch a serial killer in Washington, D.C., though the predator was caught before the Cloudmakers could contribute.[19]

Alternate reality gameplay has much in common with legend narratives entwined with legend-tripping behavior and occult texts outlining magical rituals: all are world-making venues that invite participants to search for and share experiential knowledge pertaining to specific imaginary content—to perform belief in worlds of plausibility to which the community gives breadth, coherence, and a sense of the real. In this context, world-making is an interactive quest for experiential knowledge governed by an emergent system or systems of communal rules. The generative collectivity that online environments afford, coupled with the idea that both these environments and communication itself are somehow magical or supernatural, can result in legend-trippers explicitly acknowledging their performances as such without damaging the efficacy of the ritual, thereby aligning their activities more with magicians, as we shall see.

Zine Culture

In her study of interpersonal relations developed through computer-mediated communications, Barbara Kirshenblatt-Gimblett described how the collaborative framework of the mail art movement both paved the way for computer networking and conceptualized interactivity as art through the use of hypertextual principles.[20] Mail art refers to the cooperative appropriation, alteration, distribution, and remediation of various mailed memorabilia. During the 1950s, it emerged as a response to the exclusivity of a High Modernist aesthetic culture that focused on individual expression. Among mail art are self-published magazines, or "zines," often created by and for fans of the science-fiction genre. Henry Jenkins and Helen Merrick have noted that the transmission of zines significantly contributed to the development of virtual or "imagined" and "imagining" communities "long before the introduction of networked computers."[21] These communities exhibit what Merrick describes as an "identifiable cultural and social identity, produced through unique narratives, lore, specialised language and iconography, expressed through a diverse range of texts, media, exchanges and rituals."[22] Essentially, such communities demonstrate coherent cultural transmission outside of close proximity or even in the absence of face-to-face relations, much like the Cloudmakers.

Some of the more subversive members of zine culture attempt to harness "memes"—self-replicating, parasitic units of cultural information.[23] Several also extol the practice of chaos magic, a type of metabelief in the *efficacy* of belief and imagination as tools for spiritual growth, illumination, and/or power. Chaos magicians frequently incorporate memes in their practice of manufacturing "sigils" and "hypersigils"—magically charged works of art, often designed as narratives, that focus magicians' wills to make them manifest in the real world; accordingly, the power of sigils directly corresponds to the number of people who embrace them.[24]

A colorful representation of zine ideology is illustrated in the following quote by Mark Frauenfelder, co-founder of the zine *bOING bOING*: "The decentralized, iconoclastic quality of zines is ideal for people interested in shucking prescribed realities in favor of designing their own worldview. The Church of the Sub-Genius, one of the first religions to use a zine to spread its own blend of particularly virulent memes, reminds us that truth and reality are subjective yet inescapable shams and the best course of action is to reject the reality tunnels thrust upon us by the corporate/political world and instead 'pull the wool over your own eyes.'"[25] This sense of collaborative world-making (equally a sense of collaborative world-unmaking, in which members of a community champion the ability to escape the constraints of ideology) is also forwarded in *Factsheet Five*, a zine about zines: "The zine readers reject consensus reality and, rather, peruse over the zines out there to create their own realities . . . what unites all zine readers is their passion for communication."[26]

From zine culture emerged the immersive online mystery known as both the "Incunabula Papers" and "Ong's Hat." This many-threaded, open-ended interactive narrative weds an alternate history of chaos science and consciousness studies to conspiracy theories, parallel dimensions, and claims that computer-mediated environments can serve as magical tools. Variously identified as one of the earliest Internet-based legends, a myth-making system, an ARG, and/or an elaborate hoax, the phenomenon of the Incunabula Papers demonstrates how supernatural legend complexes

and occult philosophies may generate supernatural experiences and interpretations of these experiences through game-like performances of belief
in mediated environments. The next four chapters focus on the narrative
and discourse of the Incunabula Papers chiefly as legend performances,
for once placed online, the Incunabula Papers began acting as a legend
complex inducting participants into different ways of thinking, acting,
and experiencing by way of a largely overlooked folk ritual—the legend-
trip.

The Incunabula Papers

The Incunabula Papers surfaced sometime during the late 1980s to early 1990s, while the legend-trip resulting from their online circulation started in the late 1990s and peaked in activity around 2001.[1] The first of these two enigmatic documents, entitled *Ong's Hat: Gateway to the Dimensions! A Full Color Brochure for the Institute of Chaos Studies and the Moorish Science Ashram in Ong's Hat, New Jersey*, was allegedly written by members of the Institute for Chaos Studies (or ICS), an underground, loosely affiliated group exploring "the enhancement of consciousness and consequent enlargement of mental, emotional, and psychic activities."[2] The ICS purportedly operated as an ashram in the Pine Barrens of New Jersey near the area once known as Ong's Hat, and this booklet details their history connecting them to a number of real and/or fictitious quasi-religious sects. *Ong's Hat: Gateway* also offers an alternative history of science, one in which extrapolations from chaos science and quantum physics splintered scientific thought into two distinct camps. Those championing studies in chaos science—such as the ICS—were forced underground by the dominant "determinists," for whom "chaos was the enemy, randomness a force to be overcome or denied." According to the text, the ICS's experiments in computer chaos applications, tantric exercises, biofeedback, and psychedelics resulted in the discovery of inter-dimensional time travel. Soon after this scientific breakthrough, the ICS began charting out parallel worlds. Most of these worlds are uninhabited, offering travelers the opportunity to live outside of societal rules, but some are inhabited by alien beings (often described as "lemurs") that reside alongside crumbling, ancient ruins of unknown purpose or design. While the ICS and other groups, such as the Garden of Forking Paths (or GFP), seek to liberate mankind by sharing their knowledge about traveling to other worlds, factions in positions of power—the Probability Control Force (or PCF), for example—actively repress this material. *Ong's Hat: Gateway* claims the document itself contains a series of embedded clues so that others may rediscover for themselves the means to travel to these undiscovered worlds.

Numerous "clues," many in the form of cryptic allusions, do exist within this document. "Garden of Forking Paths" refers to the 1941 short story written by Jorge Louis Borges, which presents a fictionalized layman's interpretation of the many-worlds theory everything that could ever possibly happen in our universe (but doesn't) happens in another. Another "clue" is the biography of the two founding members of the ICS—Frank and Althea Dobbs, twins who had lived among a UFO-cult commune in Texas chartered by their father. The allusion to Borges refers to quantum agency wherein an observer may shape the outcome of a quantum event merely by participating *as* an observer (thus, readers, according to this interpretive frame, are already participants). And those familiar with the Church of the Sub-Genius, what some would call a postmodern parody religion, know that its purported founder is J. R. "Bob" Dobbs, whose fictional biography describes how he founded a UFO cult in Texas. The allusion to the Church of the Sub-Genius offers a knowing wink to some readers, while goading others to seek out additional materials concerning the Dobbs twins that very well might eventually lead readers to writings concerned with the Church of the Sub-Genius. Invited to decipher a web of clues, allusions, and metaphors culled from science, history, pop culture, literature, and mail art culture, participants are encouraged to reinterpret their relationship to these texts. Like occult texts, *Ong's Hat: Gateway* assumes readers to be familiar with its many literary and thematic references and its many intuitive leaps; if they are not, it presents a considerable interpretive challenge.

The second document, *Incunabula: A Catalogue of Rare Books, Manuscripts & Curiosa—Conspiracy Theory, Frontier Science & Alternative Worlds*, was allegedly written by Emory Cranston, the proprietor of the catalogue. This document looks like a mail-order catalogue, but also provides an annotated bibliography of twenty-seven works, some real and some nonexistent, on a variety of subjects such as mail art, consciousness studies, magic, conspiracy theories, communications studies, quantum physics, and pulp fiction popular within the alternative reality tradition. One of the annotated works is the aforementioned *Ong's Hat: Gateway*. When the catalogue's annotations are read in their entirety, they reveal several paranormal, supernatural, and occult themes, and they readily supply a history of various cult activities, ideas, and conspiracies surrounding travel to other worlds, times, and dimensions. When *Ong's Hat: Gateway* and *Incunabula: A Catalogue* are read together, a far-reaching, open-ended narrative emerges that chronicles the efforts of several groups and organizations conspiring to either liberate or enslave man through the distribution or repression of technologies enabling travel to parallel worlds. The narrative manifests ideas championed within the mail art movement: liberation from oppression, the construction of utopia, and the creative principles behind world-making. The Incunabula Papers also symbolically portray what media theorist Douglas Rushkoff identifies as the agenda of countercultural media: "to create a picture of the world as a vast set of interdependencies that foster life and work naturally against those who seek a disproportionate share of power or control. The established powers, on the other hand, hope to isolate individuals by disconnecting them from these networks and preventing them from conducting any sort of feedback or iteration."[3] By offering a story about an antiestablishment commune of free-thinkers seeking to assist those wishing to empower themselves against oppression, the legend complex of the Incunabula Papers rallies like-minded individuals to come together to solve a mystery.

According to Umberto Eco (whose 1988 work, *Foucault's Pendulum*, plays a considerable role in the Incunabula Papers, as I discuss below), the descriptions of possible narrative worlds (such as those that arise from world-making) are only one of two critical factors in the production of meaning. The other is framing, the sequence of actions oriented toward describing other worlds, which we can consider to be determined in part here by which rabbit holes one uses to enter the narrative world(s) of the Incunabula Papers.[4] Should a conspiracy enthusiast happen across the Incunabula Papers while on a trusted website doling out various conspiratorial theories, he might be more inclined to initially accept the factuality of the narrative worlds the Incunabula Papers present, but a gamer who encounters the narrative of the Incunabula Papers through a website about alternate reality games will likely approach the narrative worlds presented by the documents in a considerably different way. Likewise, both will—should they begin to participate in the discourse surrounding the Incunabula Papers—begin to encounter and perhaps incorporate other people's interpretations. The sequence of action that frames immersion is critical, yet entirely open-ended and subject to change, just like legends. As specific legend complexes may bleed into one another and expand by sharing the same motifs, themes, stories, ideas, and material culture, so, too, can interpretations of these legend complexes; certainly, shared, open-ended interpretations allow for a kind of permeability of ideas and beliefs. Subjects commonly presented in supernatural legendry, such as magic, monsters, UFOs, and psychic powers, are not considered "real" by many people. When people believe some (or all) of these subjects to be actual phenomena, they have integrated these subjects into their world-view, at least in part. There are people who have no difficulties with this, and there are several communities that authenticate and normal-ize supernatural beliefs. The Internet—and, by extension, the Incunabula Papers—serves as an ideal environment in which such beliefs can become normalized and present a rich tapestry with which to begin weaving one's own interpretations of these subjects alongside others.

Legends of the Incunabula

The Incunabula Papers include a variety of supernatural themes, such as time travel, psychic powers, inter-dimensional or alien beings, and occult technologies, within commentary on physics, speculative sciences, and historic fact. It also vaguely outlines the curriculum developed by the ICS to train "cognitive chaotes," adepts of a futuristic transdiscipline that combine the technologies of science and magic to achieve fantastic, seem-ingly supernatural feats. *Incunabula: A Catalogue* presents several legend narratives within its annotations of allegedly "real" manuscripts (many of which don't actually exist). One such annotation focuses on the (nonexis-tent) work entitled *Poetic Journal of a Traveller; or, A Heresologist's Guide to Brooklyn* and offers a summary of this imaginary text as the account of the anonymous "X" who seeks knowledge of other worlds. Chronicling his various encounters with different informants, the annotation suggests "X" actually found the means to travel to Earth 2, one of many parallel worlds. *Incunabula: A Catalogue* also provides an annotation of the anony-mously written (nonexistent) work entitled *Folklore of the Other Worlds*, which it describes as a first-person account of life on alternative worlds that pays special attention to paranormal manifestations. *Incunabula: A Catalogue* suggests this manuscript is likely written by the same (nonex-istent) author of *Poetic Journal of a Traveller; or, A Heresologist's Guide to Brooklyn*. Other, "real" works, like James Gleick's *Chaos: Making a New Science* (Penguin Books, 1988), are also included, although in many cas-es, such as in the annotation of Gleick's work, the annotative narrative contextualizes these works within the legend complex of the Incunabula

Papers. For instance, *Incunabula: A Catalogue* inserts Gleick into the story by accusing him of being an agent for the PCF who has "embedded his text with subtle disinformation meant to distract the chaos-science community from any interest in 'other worlds.'"

In addition to fabricating many of its reference materials, the Incunabula Papers also borrow from, refer to, and provide materials for other legends and belief systems. For example, on the now-defunct Ong's Hat/Incunabula forum at the website *Darkplanetonline*, someone compared the "lemurs" depicted in the Incunabula Papers to the popular, human-abducting aliens described in considerable detail by modern UFO legendry:

By TemoralVelocity on Nov. 30, 2000—4:36 pm:

. . .

The so called 'Lemur' beings were named so apparently because of their large eyes. However could they also be a variation of the large-eyed 'gray' entities? Traditional grays have four fingers, greenish blood, partially scaly grayish-green skin, and no external reproductive organs nor working digestive system [they take in their food in liquid form through the skin and excrete it out the same way]. Do the 'Lemurs' possess such characteristics, or are they of an entirely different physical configuration?[5]

The contents of this post might strike some as a bit weird—this person is speaking about an apparently fictional creature with as much legitimacy and reality as popular culture has bestowed upon the "greys," a type of alien being discussed within ufology circles for some time. But the fact that the Incunabula's "lemurs" are somewhat similar to ufology's greys allows people to appropriate the ontological status that the greys have developed over multiple decades upon the lemurs. Here, correlation becomes evidence for some that the lemurs and the greys actually exist. Other websites containing various content associated with the alternative reality tradition, such as www.cassiopaea.org, which is based on channeled question and answer sessions with a group of benevolent aliens (the Cassiopaeans) then make reference to Ong's Hat.[6] Such legend complex grafting imbues each of these legends with a kind of referential authority and contributes to their increased circulation. Of course, numerous individuals also add content to the Incunabula Papers legend complex. On the forum of *The Deoxyribonucleic Hyperdimension* website, a poster named mooncat writes:

By mooncat on June 9, 2000—7:53 am:

> The travel cults are QUITE real,let me assure you.
> A certain pagan group in northern CA has been working on things like
> eggless travel and dimensional doorways for some time some members
> are well known.
>   One such test of eggless travel (sort of like one of Michael G.
> Coney's Invisible Spaceships) occurred at a major midwestern pagan
> gathering in 1988.[7]

Soon thereafter, another poster comments that he or she will be constructing a website to discuss inter-dimensional travel:

By btpete on June 14, 2000—06:36 pm:

> Two years ago I stumbled upon this site and read about interdimen-
> sional travel with great interest. Reading through the E.C. catalog
> was most entertaining, enhanced by the fact that I actually own a
> copy of one of the theoretical publications mentioned. While ac-
> cepting the possibility of interdimensional travel, I have no desire
> to achieve it by way of the magical mushroom. Since no documented
> research seems to be generally available, perhaps some here would
> be interested in starting some. I expect to bring a web site online
> within the next few days that could be used as the crude beginning of
> a collaborative project: www.interdimension.org. This is an exciting
> topic, one I would like to learn a lot more about.

Mooncat's post enlarges the world of the Incunabula Papers by including
northern Californian cults and leading others to explore the ideas behind
the works of Michael G. Coney, a British science fiction writer whose
work often explored ideas about autonomous communities. Btpete's post,
indicating the creation of a future website where "documented research"
will be available, bridges the first stage of the legend-trip with that of the
second: the uncanny journey. Claims and proof pertaining to the Incunabula Papers' veracity are key topics throughout these discussion forums,
just like other forums and websites devoted to supernatural subject matter, which are almost always intended to persuade, one way or the other.
These venues also attempt to expand upon supernatural narrative worlds
and perspectives. By adding to this legend complex, posters such as mooncat and btpete connect their activities to a larger secondary world, just

as occultists and magicians enact and contribute to occult texts, and just as legend-trippers experientially test legends and report their findings through other legends.

The theme of modifying perspectives, pervasive throughout the Incunabula Papers, also appears in the numerous fictional works that Incunabula participants regularly discuss, such as Robert Shea's and Robert Anton Wilson's *Illuminatus! Trilogy*, Umberto Eco's *Foucault's Pendulum*, and several stories by Jorge Louis Borges. By referencing these works, participants are indicating that their participation is itself a kind of magically charged ostensive play blurring fact, fiction, and even genres to such a degree that these labels become useless. Of course, these literary references and allusions serve to comment upon the very interpretive framework supplied by the Incunabula Papers legend complex. One anonymous posting, entitled "The Internet Cathedral," states:

> It can be said that one aspect of the Incunabula and Ong's Hat document structure is to create a "unifying" story - a story that will provide meaning and purpose greater than their collected individual stories, a story that will "create" Transcendent Meaning. But, there is a "flip" side to that aspect, as well. In Eco's <u>Foucault's Pendulum</u> we find a clear example of how our drive and desire to "find" meaning and "create" meaning often results in reaching conclusions where none actually exist.[8]
>
>   . . .
>
> Eco's editors in "Pendulum" randomly feed manuscript pages on hermetic thought into a computer. Incunabula and Ong's Hat may be derived from similar "cut up" methodology, but takes it to another level. In much the same way that Eco's character's begin to experience weird and unexpected events, after commencing what began as a terrific joke - "the Plan" assumed a life of its own.
> One must wonder at the similarities.

Comparing the activities surrounding the Incunabula Papers to the activities in Eco's novel, the above post succinctly demonstrates that participants are at times self-consciously comparing their activities presencing the realities outlined in the Incunabula Papers to fiction, essentially blurring fact and fiction and choosing to ascribe meaning to these events according to their own experiential desires.

The Challenge

The Incunabula Papers directly and indirectly challenge their readers much as occult texts and legends that incite legend-tripping performances, and they include materials culled from legend and occult narratives explicitly for this purpose. The fantastic is presented as plausible or actually existent in liminal realities that one must somehow access to apprehend (or apprehend to access). Like those legends that transform a dilapidated house into a haunted building, the Incunabula Papers converts its own narrative into an uncanny agent of esoteric knowledge—and those immersed within its narrative interpret their own online presence as being somehow otherworldly or supranormal. *Ong's Hat: Gateway* begins with the following passage:

> *YOU WOULD NOT BE READING THIS ARTICLE if you had not already penetrated halfway to the ICS. You have been searching for us without knowing it, following oblique references in crudely Xeroxed marginal samizdat publications, crackpot mystical pamphlets, mail-order courses in 'Kaos Magick' - a paper trail and a coded series of rumors spread at street level through circles involved in the illicit distribution of certain controlled substances and the propagation of certain acts of insurrection against the Planetary Work Machine and the Consensus Reality - or perhaps through various obscure mimeographed technical papers on the edges of 'chaos science' - through pirate computer networks - or even through pure synchronicity and the pursuit of dreams. In any case we know something about you, your interests, deeds and desires, works and days - and we know your address. Otherwise...you would not be reading this.*

This introduction speaks directly to readers, identifying them as central characters in the story, placing them into the role of participants regardless of their choice to participate. While those legends usually instigating legend-trips rely on some geographical site, structure, material artifact, or action, legend-tripping as a form of online immersion chiefly relies on narrative, so engaging participants through direct address is most prescient. After this introduction, the brochure presents a series of past happenings involving quantum agency, magic, conspiratorial intrigue, heterodox spiritualities, and the quest to discover possible worlds. The brochure then concludes with the following:

Meanwhile our agents of chaos remain behind to set up ICS courses, distribute Moorish Orthodox literature (a major mask for our propaganda) to subvert and evade our enemies ... We haven't spoken yet of our enemies. Indeed there remains much we have not said. This text, disguised as a sort of New Age vacation brochure, must fall silent at this point, satisfied that it has embedded within itself enough clues for its intended readers (who are already halfway to Ong's hat in any case) but not enough for those with little faith to follow. CHAOS NEVER DIED!

By incorporating the discursive conventions and subversive iconographies of the mail art community, it attracts audiences familiar with mail art lexicon and invites other readers into actively participating with the narrative as well. And by explicitly using the phrases "intended readers" and "those of little faith," the document forces readers to effectively choose which camp they belong to. The document says that its readers are "halfway to Ong's hat," implying that those who read this document have already begun a journey and have been—consciously or not—following the right rabbit holes or paths toward discovering the "truth" all along. Such rhetoric, found also in occult literature, challenges readers to unravel the mysteries in its texts to achieve secret knowledge and power. Like occult texts, this brochure makes authoritative claims based in special power (in this case, the knowledge of and ability to travel to parallel worlds). After offering an account of past happenings—a legend about the Institute of Chaos Studies and its magical and/or scientific discoveries—the brochure dares readers to explore its contents further, thus inciting an uncanny journey, the next stage of a legend-trip.

Incunabula: A Catalogue opens with a similar rhetorical appeal:

This catalogue has been put together with a purpose: to alert YOU to a vast cover up, a conspiracy so deep that no other researcher has yet become aware of it (outside certain Intelligence circles, needless to say!)- and so dangerous that the 'winding sheet' imagery in our title seems quite appropriate; we know of at least two murders so far in connection with this material.

Incunabula: A Catalogue then lists a series of annotated works, which, when read together, outlines an entire legend complex or secondary world that synthesizes a bricolage of ideas and stories about the quest to discover alternate realities gathered from fact and fiction. The annotations

comment on the truth status of many of these documents; some are proclaimed to be factual, while others (including *Ong's Hat: Gateway*) are
declared to be part of misinformation campaigns developed by the PCF.
Incunabula: A Catalogue ends with the following:

> The Conspiracy to deny the world all knowledge of the Many Worlds
> is maintained by both the forces active in the parallel universes Q the
> GFP and PCF both have their reasons for secrecy, evasion, lies, disinfor-
> mation, distortion and even violence [. . .] Remember: parallel worlds
> exist. They have already been reached. A vast cover-up denies YOU all
> knowledge. Only INCUNABULA can enlighten you, because only INCU-
> NABULA dares.[9]

We see again the glamour of danger and mystery, fantastic claims to
power, and esoteric knowledge all presented with a sense of urgency to
readers. The conspiracy within is offered as an ambiguous conflict without explicit motive, allowing readers to extrapolate analogies from their
real-world experiences. Because what they are being deprived of isn't
made clear, they must imagine what this knowledge consists of and how
to apply it.

Many mail art texts are conspiratorial in nature and by situating itself
within general conspiratorial discourse, as opposed to specific conspiratorial theories, *Incunabula: A Catalogue* remains indefinite enough to prevent
its exclusion from other discourses. Equally, it exploits the fact that conspiracy theories have become a part of mainstream culture (an example
of the popularity of conspiracy theory, Shea and Wilson's aforementioned
Illuminatus! Trilogy has inspired the production of various board- and role-
playing games). No longer exclusively associated with the thoughts and
actions of delusional or paranoid individuals, conspiracy theories now
attract a diverse multitude of individuals with rhetoric, which, according
to Véronique Campion-Vincent, "takes the form of play, mixing humor
and distance with paranoia and belief."[10] Such framing often necessitates
belief performances in addition to literal belief. As I described in chapter
2, the participants at Waverly Hills were seriously investigating claims
that the sanitarium was haunted, though this by no means excluded the
element of play. On the contrary, play behavior—acting "as if"—greatly
added to the legend-trip's efficacy.

Because both documents that constitute the Incunabula Papers present themselves as advertisements (one, an institutional brochure, the

other, a mail-order catalogue), this deception disrupts readers' expectations, as advertisements are, by definition, mediated persuasive forms of communication from an identifiable source. Similar to so many legends, the narrative's origins are obscured. The Incunabula Papers might have originally been a self-parody of the mail art movement and/or analogous to the Rosicrucian Manifestos, but once they began to be transmitted and contextualized in an online environment, communities formed by entering the fictional worlds they outline, performing belief in their contents, deciphering their clues, and engaging in a variety of ostensive acts.

Among legend-trippers, certain individuals stand out as active tradition-bearers—those who vigorously publicize and perpetuate the tradition. Just as the Louisville Ghost Hunters Society acted as the authorities on the supernatural phenomena surrounding Waverly Hills, so, too, are there experts on the Incunabula Papers, most notably Joseph Matheny, Peter Lamborn Wilson, and Nick Herbert.[11] Each of these individuals presents one or more interpretive frameworks with which to approach the Incunabula legend complex.

The Trickster/Culture-Jammer

Incunabula participants generally view Joseph Matheny, credited with first placing the Incunabula Papers on one of the earliest Bulletin Board Systems, the Well, as the most influential authority on this legend complex.[12] Matheny posted his ongoing investigations into the Incunabula Papers in the form of online journal entries as far back as 1992. In one of these entries, entitled "Advances in Skin Science: Quantum Tantra. An Interview with Nick Herbert by Joseph Matheny," Matheny recorded his alleged first meeting with Herbert, a physicist whose works (both real and nonexistent) appear in *Incunabula: A Catalogue*. Matheny claimed to have purchased a copy of *Incunabula: A Catalogue* from a group known as MediaKaos (which, incidentally, Matheny apparently was a member of). In this interview, Herbert explained that the Incunabula Papers reveal how consciousness operates, but that this revelation is hidden within numerous clues. Matheny's next journal entry stated that Herbert had left behind a telephone number written alongside the letters "EC." Matheny assumed this to be Emory Cranston, the name given in the *Incunabula: A Catalogue* as the mail-order company's owner, and phoned the number, contacting Cranston. He then provided a transcript of his interview with Cranston (the following is an excerpt):

> *EC: I'm not really running the catlogue anymore. It can't be suppressed -*
> *it's out there, it's circulating. But I'm not selling the books now. Those*
> *who need the books, get the books. I don't need the money, after*
> *all. Those who can really read the catalogue and figure out the next*
> *step...well, not everything in INCUNABULA is accurate, of course.*
> *But the clues are there. Follow the garden of forking paths. Ah, how*
> *many, you ask? I can tell you exactly. The answer is precisely 16*
> *people have followed the thread so far. We're aware of another dozen*
> *or so who are working on it. At a certain point in their researches*
> *they'll be helped...if possible. One may blunder, you see. Some tracks*
> *lead to the Minotaur, know what I mean? And some of those dozen*
> *or so are working for the wrong people. They won't be helped.*
> *JM: You mean INCUNABULA is located in "virtual space"?*
> *EC: As far as you're concerned, yes.*[13]

The term "INCUNABULA" here refers to either the mail-order company or the entire phenomenon surrounding the Incunabula Papers. Both are situated entirely within virtual space, which may be interpreted as cyberspace, the imagination, or both. The Incunabula Papers, as well as Cranston in the interview above, suggest that those who pursue knowledge of inter-dimensional travel will be assisted in their endeavors by those in the know, provided the seekers' quests are genuine and align with the philosophies of "chaotes." This echoes occult affirmations that "Ascended Masters" often appear to assist dedicated, worthy initiates on their paths to enlightenment.

Matheny often presents different versions of past accounts. In a book co-written with Peter Moon in 2002, entitled *Ong's Hat: The Beginning*, Matheny claims to have been given a copy of *Incunabula: A Catalogue* by Nick Herbert. According to this account, Matheny lived in Santa Cruz and associated with a semi-organized crowd known as the Formless Ocean Group (F.O.G.), which included a number of counterculture figures such as Terrence McKenna, John Lilly, Robert Anton Wilson, and Peter Lamborn Wilson (who is sometimes credited with writing and/or circulating *Ong's Hat: Gateway*). In this version, Matheny admitted to being on friendly terms with Herbert, who, he writes, has encountered other-dimensional beings and invented something called a Metaphase Typewriter, which acts like a random text generator able to be manipulated by discarnate entities (the idea of such a device is a major plot point in Umberto Eco's novel, *Foucault's Pendulum*). Matheny claims that he once told Herbert about playing with the idea of developing a "living book," and Herbert advised him to include human interaction and magic principles.[14] The idea of the Incunabula Papers as a "living book" is a fundamental motif in Incunabula-related legends and characterizes the importance of ostension in this legend complex. After the online discourse surrounding the Incunabula Papers grew exponentially, Matheny developed an e-book published on CD-ROM, entitled *The Incunabula Papers: Ong's Hat and Other Gateways to New Dimensions* (1999). Matheny claims the e-book includes a random text-generating program and when certain links are clicked at specific times, the program begins to operate, allowing the text a degree of quantum uncertainty and offering users an opportunity to contact a nonhuman or transhuman intelligence.

Matheny has been a guest on several talk radio programs and podcasts and has recounted differing versions of his involvement with the Incunabula Papers, thus performing a variety of ostensive acts. However, he has consistently reported that these documents might or might not describe factual events and he often expresses exasperation at people's inability to contend with paradox and move beyond thinking only in binaries of *fact/fiction, real/unreal,* and *true/false.*[15] Taking a cue from the archetypal trickster, Matheny's actions concurrently validate and annul nearly any sole interpretation of, or rabbit hole leading to, the Incunabula materials. In fact, he regularly professes to be a culture-jammer, one who subverts the mass media in efforts to attack commercialism and undermine authority.[16] Matheny seemingly reveals his motives for publicizing the Incunabula Papers in the following excerpt (here he mentions MediaKaos, which is his own business enterprise—other members of MediaKaos are referred to as the "ennercore"):

RKN: *Tell us about MediaKaos. What do you guys do aside from spending a lot of time at the photocopy machine?*

JM: *MediaKaos is a cultural experiment. What we're attempting to do is break down the predominant method used to transmit information. In the theatre there is something called the proscenium, the precise definition of that is "the area that separates the stage from the auditorium." We're attempting to bridge that sacred moat. The method of information or entertainment presentation in this culture is predicated on the stage, or many people focused and passively receiving from a mono-source of information. You see it everywhere, I call it the screen. It can be a newspaper or magazine page, the computer, the television, the cinematic screen, the stage, all have in common the passivity on the part of the audience and many people sitting or standing around focusing on one source of transmission. I see the by-product of this in the generation of passive consumers or passive receptors to information that we have in abundance now in this culture.*

DJB: *Can you tell us about MediaKaos, and outline some of the theory behind your concepts?*

JM: *We are influenced by things like the experiments in ethnomethodology conducted by Harold Garfinkle, The works of Situationist International, the Burroughs/Gysin cut up method, the guerrilla hi-jinks of people like Negativeland and the Cacophany society, the Immediast Underground, the Immediasm theories of Hakim Bey, to name a few. Basically anything that jams the signal or attempts to break the spell of the consensus reality.*

. . .

RKN: *So if MediaKaos is a break from passive entertainment, then it's more than just live performances?*

ennercore: *It's a combination of space and general vision. It's abstract and there is no set pattern to what we do or how we do it. It may be a live situation where the public is openly invited to participate one time, and another time the experiment may take the form of a media prank or some other sort of 'poetic terrorism,' to borrow a term from Hakim Bey. We don't always publicly acknowledge our actions.*[17]

Though Matheny doesn't explicitly reveal the Incunabula Papers and/or his investigations of them as a perpetrated hoax in the 1993 interview, many Incunabula participants have accused him of this; it should be said, however, that hoaxing, as well as accusations of hoaxing, are irrevocably part of ostension and supernatural lore.[18] Ten years later, in a 2003 interview with *New World Disorder Magazine*, Matheny provided yet another history for *Incunabula: A Catalogue*:

The Incunabula catalog is a culture jam, created by culture jammers. There is no "group" that existed previous to 1987, at least not as described in the brochure. 4 people got together in the 80s and 90s and put those documents together. NONE preceded their existence. However, many legends and synchronicities have occurred since. That is beautiful and indicative of a responsive universe.

One was an artist, who made beautiful, moving and otherworldly collages and pictures.

One was a poetic terrorist who could weave words together with an unparallel passion and vigor.

Another was a media and network hacker who could make the media pay attention to a bingo match in Poughkeepsie if he wanted them to.

One was a physicist with lots of friends in the Dancing Wu Li master circles and a wonderfully twisted sense of sexual humor.

They decided one day to take some pre-existing fiction bits, stir in some current pop science, parody of paranormal conspiracy literature and graffiti it on the walls of the noosphere. Boys will be boys after all. Over the years, others in certain academic circles were brought in to work on updating and upgrading the concepts employed and to integrate the lesson learned into other projects, some of which are currently underway.[19]

Undermining his earlier stories about discovering the Incunabula Papers, Matheny provides yet another account of past happenings, renewing the legend complex by adding a layer of ambiguity onto the narrative. Matheny's remark that "other projects . . . are underway" encourages audiences to continue looking for (or creating) new rabbit holes, actions which expand the world of the Incunabula Papers legend complex. As to the "lesson learned," Matheny states later in the interview that this is a method to access the "Meta Data of the human morphogenetic resonance field." This alludes to the work of Rupert Sheldrake, whose hypothesis of Formative Causation argues that ever more complex systems of self-organization and evolution arise from a shared collective memory, which supposedly exist as resonance fields not limited by time or space (Sheldrake's "morphic resonance" essentially resembles both Jung's concept of the collective unconsciousness and Teilhard's noosphere).[20]

The Mail Art Mystic

Many consider Peter Lamborn Wilson (also known as Hakim Bey) to be another expert on the Incunabula Papers; the influences of his philosophy and rhetorical style are evident in both documents. Besides this, in 1988 Wilson forwarded a copy of *Ong's Hat: Gateway* to the science-fiction zine *Edge Detector*.[21] Wilson, an essayist, cultural critic, and poet, is perhaps best known for his work, *The Temporary Autonomous Zone (T.A.Z.)*, written as Bey. *T.A.Z.* begins with the pronouncement "CHAOS NEVER DIED," and is a work of self-professed "ontological anarchy." Bey claims that mini-societies of like-minded freethinkers require transient self-governing spaces, or "pirate utopias." In *T.A.Z.*, Bey writes:

As a Cyberpunk fan I can't help but envision "reality hacking" playing a major role in the creation of TAZs. Like Gibson and Sterling I am assuming that the official Net will never succeed in shutting down the Web or the counter-Net—that data-piracy, unauthorized transmissions and the free flow of information can never be frozen. (In fact, as I understand it, chaos theory predicts that any universal Control-system is impossible.)[22]

He later continues with:

The TAZ is "utopian" in the sense that it envisions an intensification of everyday life, or as the Surrealists might have said, life's penetration by the Marvelous. But it cannot be utopian in the actual meaning of the word, nowhere, or NoPlace Place. The TAZ is somewhere. It lies at the intersection of many forces, like some pagan power- spot at the junction of mysterious ley-lines, visible to the adept in seemingly unrelated bits of terrain, landscape, flows of air, water, animals.

Bey's insistence that freethinkers need to develop temporary autonomous zones parallels one of the goals presented by the Incunabula Papers: locating and constructing utopian worlds. Just as the TAZ "lies at the intersection of many forces," so too does the symbol of Ong's Hat—within the nebulous nexus of legendry, conspiracy, fringe science, magic, and mystery. The confluence of genres constituting the Incunabula Papers results in gatherings of diverse groups and individuals seeking knowledge; specifically, esoteric experiential knowledge with which to access and manipulate a meta-reality. By affirming that the "TAZ is somewhere" within an ambiguous "intersection of many forces" that may be identifiable to the "adept," Bey references magical thinking—a kind of perception fashioned during the second stage of the legend-trip.

Wilson, an influential counterculture figure, is affiliated with the Moorish Orthodox Church in America, a syncretic religious tradition incorporating mystical beliefs and practices, such as Sufism and Tantra (interestingly, the church is located on Ong's Hat Road in Pemberton, New Jersey). In a 1994 article, entitled "Moorish Mail-Order Mysticism," he writes (as Bey):

*There's something magical about the mail—voices from the Unseen— *documents as amulets*—and something very american, democratic & self-reliant—mysterious urban folklore—old ad's for AMORC in crumbling yellow magazines—HooDoo catalogues, dreambooks—ancient* *spirits-of-places intersecting with modern communications networks that are placeless, spooky, & abstract. And the mail itself now seems antique—a lost modernity, 19th century, sepia, violet ink—a fitting medium for the transmission of secrets.*[23]

Bey's characterization of mail-order mysticism as inherently magical also marks the Incunabula Papers as magical by extension, offering readers a framework with which to interpret the many legends of Ong's Hat:

Literal belief in one or another of these mail-order revelations would destroy our ability to believe in all of them simultaneously, like a palimpsest of angelic alphabets, a field of magical "correspondence(s)", a conceptual transformation-space of mythic energies and mythopoesis. The *eros* of postal mysticism lies in the whole pattern it makes, rather than in one part or another, one "course" or another. Sometimes those who sneer the most ironically at this textual spiritism are secretly drawn by its imaginal sensuality, even while their rational brains reject it all as high weirdness & superstition. However, one can believe (or "believe") both/and, rather than either/or.

. . .

The modern media are by definition forces for alienation—and yet— they contain within them hidden & unplanned magical linkages which are IMmediate—or at least far more direct than reason would allow. No technology can leach itself clean of the residue of magic which lies at its source—and communication tech is the most "spiritual" of them all. The mail is full of gnostic traces—even of love. Why not initiation?

Bey's conceptualization of technology as both an alienating force and as conduit for magical thinking (which emphasizes interconnectivity) locates two seemingly incommensurable impulses in the same idea, thus presenting somewhat of a quandary to readers—a paradox they must somehow contend with. The performance of belief seems to be a means by which, according to Bey, people may transcend this paradox. In another of his essays, "Immediatism," Bey articulates how mediated environments are ultimately unable to supply an authentic (immediate) experience without situations in which these same environments transcend their nature as being mediators. For this to occur, he argues that the audience must become performers.[24] In a sense then, Bey locates the magic of technology at situational interstices that are initiative or transformative.

The Quantum Perspectivist and the Artist

Many consider Nick Herbert, the physicist introduced in Matheny's journal entry and an established figure within the field of fringe sciences and futurism, to have significantly influenced the Incunabula Papers. Herbert's work frequently incorporates speculative science fiction, especially the motifs of time travel, parallel dimensions, and esotericism. He has long advocated "quantum tantra"—a method of transforming consciousness by combining the practices of Western alchemy and Eastern tantra in order to commune with self and cosmos. Like Wilson, Herbert has another identity, that of "Dr. Jabir." In the aforementioned 1992 interview conducted by Matheny, Herbert describes to Matheny the metaphysical aspects of quantum theory:

> *"So, try and think of what the essence of quantum theory is," he continued, "Three adjectives: Randomness, thinglessness, and interconective-ness. Randomness I associate with the spontaneity that is within people. Uncertainty is the very essence of romance. It's what you don't know that intrigues you. Now, thinglessness is even more renunciatory." He went on. "The notion of treating people like possibilities rather than fixed structures is a healthy one, I think. Interconnectiveness is the most fantastic feature of Q.T. Things are connected in the quantum world in such a way that not only did we not think of it before the discovery of quantum mechanics, but I don't think we could have thought this way at all. It's so strange. The terrestrial belief system that comes the closest to quantum connectiveness is VooDoo."[25]*

Herbert's comments on randomness and his insistence that people be treated "like possibilities rather than fixed structures" align with the viewpoints of chaos magicians (mentioned in chapter 4) who promote exploiting the fact that identity is dynamic, always being reconstructed through everyday social life (Herbert's comments also echo Bey's assertion that people are symbolic and should be treated as real and unreal, equally—this notion comes into focus when examining a certain kind of ostensive role-playing promoted by the Incunabula Papers and enacted by Matheny, Herbert, and Wilson). Herbert's emphasis on interconnectivity, like Bey's, underscores the operation of sympathetic correspondences, and invites audiences to transform their perceptions of reality, the goal of the second stage of the legend-trip.

In the *New World Disorder Magazine* interview, Matheny said that four people were instrumental in the construction and distribution of the initial Incunabula Papers. While I have mentioned three experts that fit well within Matheny's descriptions, the fourth is most likely the artist James Koehnline, who designed the cover of the original *Incunabula: A Catalogue*. Koehline, an anarchist and surrealist collage artist, has long been a presence within the mail art movement, and his work appears within a number of CDs, books, and magazines that are part of the countercultural milieu (especially those published by Autonomedia). Koehline also provided the illustration for the cover of Bey's *T.A.Z.* and edited the book, *Gone to Croatan* (Autonomedia, 1994)—a historical examination of North American autonomous communities.

As experts on the Incunabula Papers, Matheny, Wilson, Herbert, and, to an extent, Koehline, have all left their mark: the many rabbit holes they've each created provide distinct content to audiences. Into these rabbit holes enter a diverse number of legend-trippers unified in their efforts to verify or otherwise explore the story of the Ong's Hat ashram and its scientific discoveries. And from conversations and actions, other rabbit holes appear, expanding and reconfiguring the materials presented by the original tradition-bearers (or tradition creators, as the case may be). In other words, the narrative becomes legend.

Accepting the challenge to decipher the Incunabula Papers demands investigating past accounts represented by the story, the actual origins of the text, and navigating through a multiplicity of rabbit holes, clues, texts, websites, and interpretations. These actions introduce participants to a wide variety of events, persons, and materials associated with the alternative reality tradition, including communication studies, theories of consciousness, magic, radical politics, quantum physics, psychedelics, and neuro-linguistic programming.[26] The languages of quantum physics and magic become tools with which participants simultaneously integrate and apply multiple information systems irrespective of labels such as *real/unreal, fact/fiction,* and *truth/lie.* In short, participants begin to perform belief. Becoming familiar with the corpus of materials directly and indirectly associated with Incunabula Papers, as well as the broader alternative reality traditions that they are a part of, can incite the process of interpretive drift, and those who begin realigning their perceptions according to the interpretive frameworks supplied by these materials begin their journey into uncanny territory.

Where Is Ong's Hat?

After being introduced to the accounts of past happenings described by a legend or legend complex, some members of the legend audience decide to investigate further, and these investigations usually involve traveling to a specific site or performing a series of prescribed actions depicted by the legend or legend complex as having some supernatural quality. The past accounts generate an affective excitement that translates to expectation. All of us at the Waverly Hills sanitarium anticipated some kind of extraordinary encounter similar to those we had heard about, and we all had prepared for our venture by sharing ghost lore, essentially "psyching ourselves up" for a supernatural encounter and initiating the first stage of interpretive drift.

Though I am focusing on a computer-mediated legend-trip, some participants have actually traveled to the Pine Barrens of New Jersey to investigate the numerous claims surrounding the Ong's Hat ashram. After one poster named King Tornado asks the *Dark Planet* message board users if anyone would like to come along, a few posters reply:

By DarkPlanetOnline on December 4, 2000—01:53 pm:

```
Re: Anyone Interested in Visiting Ong's Hat?
That would be a great time! Although our friends and family might
think us a bit odd or perhaps "over the edge". I wouldn't say I'm
a "true" believer but I would love to go all the same. It would be
interesting to meet everyone to see who's who and observe all of
your various mannerisms. I've always been curious as to what kind of
social dynamic Ongs Hat appeals to. If you people are like me then
we would have a fantastic time! Only one problem though, we'd all be
dead from over-consumption.[1]
```

By wookie x on December 13, 2000—06:59 pm:

> Ong's Hat: Report From the Front
> I have to say, I don't much care if there is anything out there to see
> or not. For me, it's the impact of the place itself. I'm not looking
> for enigmatic relics of a long gone commune. What I am looking for is
> a sense of place and time, something I think we all can relate to.

In these posts, we see the evolution of an online community gathered around an online legend complex begin to move into the space of the "real world." We also find commonalities consistent with the second stage of legend-tripping: the first poster isn't "a true believer," yet wishes to go to Ong's Hat to meet others interested in the phenomenon. This kind of hesitant, yet open-minded approach to belief in a legend fuels legend-trips much more often than does absolute conviction. The capacity for an extraordinary locale to allow for a shared extraordinary experience among like-minded people open to that experience is important to both these posters, just as it was to everyone at Waverly.

Numerous legends and rumors pertaining to the Pine Barrens are integrated into the overarching narrative of the Incunabula Papers, together with claims that Native Americans considered the area a gateway to other worlds. Participants sometimes even swap stories about how the ghost town of Ong's Hat got its name; according to one variant, a local Native American named Ong mysteriously disappeared from the location, leaving only his bloodied hat.[2] The Pine Barrens has long been an area particularly rich with supernatural legends: the Jersey Devil, the Black Dog, and the Black Doctor are but a few supernatural figures featured in the many stories passed down there. The sum of these legends confers more recent supernatural accounts coming out of or pertaining to the region with a certain intrinsic authenticity or validity, which the Incunabula Papers fully capitalize on. By invoking the icon of the Native American, the independent spiritual authenticity of Native Americans is, as Christopher Roth states, "vicariously absorbed into the American sense of self even as the people themselves fade from history."[3] The Incunabula Papers aggressively appropriate both the supernatural character of the Pine Barrens and ties to American Indian spirituality to construct an expansive and effective series of past accounts.

Though the second stage of legend-tripping usually involves travel to physical sites or use of material artifacts (such as mirrors or Ouija boards), the Incunabula Papers legend-trip has as its focus narrative immersion in an online environment, constituting the first phase of interpretive drift wherein frameworks are employed to procure a supernatural experience. At this point in the ritual, Incunabula legend-trippers begin to consciously use their imagination as a tool with which to augment their perceptions in the hopes of seeking experiential evidence of these realities; the journey into uncanny territory for many Ong's Hat participants *is* the process of interpretive drift, developing a means with which to alter perceptions and have supranormal experiences. Travel to the Pine Barrens isn't a requirement for this, though, and those who do go there seem to be few in number.

Like materials in the mail art movement and occult treatises, different world-making venues and legend complexes often refer to one another in order to develop authority. A consequence of this is that the transmission of these narratives occurs more frequently than they otherwise would. In online environments, the more these narrative worlds interconnect, the more likely people will encounter them through hypertextual linkage and search engine queries, practically guaranteeing that people will approach Incunabula-related materials from a variety of rabbit holes.[4] Web forums bringing Ong's Hat researchers together allow for past, present, and emergent communities of Incunabula Papers participants to share their thoughts and experiences and to perpetuate the legend complex as well as the legend-trip. Here, online participants also self-consciously discuss how ostension not only advances the believability of the legend complex but serves as a kind of magical practice, having the potential to transform fiction into fact, at least according to the frames provided by the Incunabula Papers. Searching for Ong's Hat then becomes an immersive journey toward developing unique perspectives on online storytelling and communication.

Seeking Alternative Worlds

The following series of posts demonstrate a collaborative journey toward narrative immersion that incorporates the language of quantum theory, magic, and the supernatural to call attention to what participants perceive to be the very uncanniness of the immersive experience. The narratives presented here all stress *transition*—from the usual to the unusual, from the everyday to the strange, from skepticism to believability.

One of the online forums for participants of this journey opened in 1999 and was entitled, "Deoxyribonucleic Hyperdiscussion: Deoxyribonucleic

Autonomous Zones: Hyperspace: Incunabula."[5] The page's description, "The Incunabula Research Center provides the background material for productively participating in this discussion," encourages online audiences to engage in a dialogue, which, for some, eventually transforms into a legend-trip. On this particular forum, the first post that appeared is the following:

By Thomas on December 14, 1999—10:19 pm:

> It is observable that consiousness (whatever it may be) arranges itself in a hyper-fractal pattern; myriad levels of perception that can animate and occur simultaneously with the introduction of certain biochemical reactions.
>   It is concievable that this excited state of perception is evolutionary in nature, like a new modification to the perception of reality in our species (or old and just coming to practical utilization).
> Still wanting to take a second bite of the apple.
> Do what thou wilt the stilt

Thomas offers propositions about the operations of consciousness and perception, and relates scientific observation and theory to mythical allusion and a magical maxim. Thomas's premise is that humanity naturally seeks to modify and expand its own consciousness, which is, as we shall see, the central motif within the Incunabula legend-trip. "Wanting to take a second bite of the apple" alludes to Christian mythology, and seems to be Thomas's way of relating his or her desire for esoteric knowledge (fruit from the Tree of Knowledge), while "Do what thou wilt the stilt" refers to the Law of Thelema as composed by Aleister Crowley—"Do what thou wilt shall be the whole of the law" (this phrase encapsulates Crowley's insistence that magicians must follow their "true will," or divine spark of being). With this progression (from science to myth to magic), the poster reveals a willingness to customize or otherwise combine different frames; this performance acts as a model for others to follow when encountering different interpretive systems. Such versatility with regards to different interpretive systems gives people a range of opportunities to name and rename experiences according to their needs and desires.

A few days later, another poster mentions travel to "E2+" (which stands for Earth Two and other possible parallel worlds discussed in the Incunabula Papers):

By Anonymous on December 19, 1999—01:52 am:

> it seems that inculabula is an incredible scientific and media phenom-
> enon which few have heard of. I would like a better perspective on the
> availability of the books on EC's list and a general better awareness
> of others people's quest to confirm the validity of travel to E2+!!

This poster moves the discussion to the very contents of the catalogue,
and by inviting others to share their own stories—framed as quests—the
poster implies this investigative process has mythological, transformative
aspects.

Some days later, another poster replies:

By Anonymous on December 23, 1999—04:36 pm:

> *In response to your message:*
> *"I would like a better perspective on the availability of the books on EC's
> list and a general better awareness of others people's quest to confirm the
> validity of travel to E2 + !!"*
> *There is a hyperlinked version of the catalog on-line at http://www.
> incunabula.org/ that has links to on-line booksellers that carry the avail-
> able titles.*

The uncanny journey phase of legend-trips commonly involves participants recounting the past accounts in the legend narrative to maintain
both a heightened sense of purpose and a shift in perspective. And, like
past accounts depicted in legends, www.incunabula.org also outlines an
interpretive frame for summoning the supernatural—in this case, use of
the updated version of the catalogue is promoted as a magical practice.
This poster initiates participants' immersion within the legend complex,
as the suggested site serves as a kind of surrogate legend-tripping expert—
a reference center with accumulated materials that, as of this writing,
include numerous media files, a graphic novel, and a link to "The Incunabula Catalogue: The Frequency Edition 2001-2012." This updated
version of *Incunabula: A Catalogue* randomly presents one of seventy-four
different pieces of media every time online users click its central icon, a
morphing I-Ching hexagram. "The Frequency Edition" claims this random
generator "combines bibliomancy and personal synchronicity . . . to bring
you closer in touch with the underlying principles of the Incunabula."[6]

About two months later, a poster named insect discusses the mechanisms of inter-dimensional travel. Here, the whole of insect's comments articulate the congruence between the second stage of legend-tripping and the first stage of interpretive drift:

By insect on February 26, 2000—02:31 pm:

```
eggless travel
these parallel universes exist in what could be called the 5th
dimension
 1-d cannot be sensed, there is nothing but itself
2-d sensed by touch(primarily)
 3-d sensed by eyes(primarily)
4-d sensed by memory


you must understand the relationship between you (body), self (con-
sciousness-metaphysical), and physical (external world)
all things can be expressed as being varying levels and patterns of
energy (quantum structures)
this energy is the same as Consciousness
when physical and metaphysical were first "formed" (percieved) they
took on opposite appearance in order to be percieved, but are still
connected as the same physical is made up of quantum sub-atomic par-
ticles, which are in turn made up of (nothing, another universe on a
level "lower" than this one, patterns and and shifting complexities
of energy reacting off of itself, where more complex masses are,
"things" are)
you must understand the relationship between you-r-self and these
waves and fields of quanta
```

Insect introduces a formula that can be applied to create an alternative cosmology. By recontextualizing "the real" within the infinitely small "fields of quanta," insect seeks to imbue the legend complex of the Incunabula Papers, which focuses on the emergence of chaos science and the chronicles of inter-dimensional travel, with both supernatural and scientific authority, thus bridging the technological and the metaphysical. The poster later continues with:

```
what is called the being by a majority of "people" is biological
the "self" is a result of the patterns of bio-electro-chemical
```

synapses in the brain, these "sensory perceptors" interpret consciousness which is in wave form) and alternately emit waves,
vibrations
this biological determination as well as memory create what makes
up the standard "person"
however these chemical interpretations can be altered, expanded,
through use of various psychotropic chemicals, namely lsd dmt and
psilocybin
psilocybin and dmt act upon the language centers in the mind, all
of the internal dialogue you exchange with certain entities, this
dialogue comes as a sort of "translingual objective thought pulse"
non word based, which can develop into an advanced communication
which will inturn create a higher consciousness existing between
beings--overmind
they also allow for exploration of vast mental continents
but that has nothing to do with travel, rather a progression of
consciousness
after all of the conditioning and programming has been stripped away
(lsd i find is great for this) your naked "soul" (the unpaved self-
consciousness wave) is awakened

Legend-trips demand a liminal, imaginative space where the performance
of belief can transpire. While this post may not, at first glance, strike some
as pertaining to the supernatural, it certainly does, especially when we
consider the supernatural as a shifting conceptual category for that which
we consider to be somehow outside of or beyond the "natural" (i.e., the
otherworldly, the supranormal, or, in the above post, the "overmind"). In
fact, insect's many comments touch upon the features of telepathy and
mysticism—communicative processes transcending conventional physical
and spatial boundaries. Such content commonly appears in supernatural
or paranormal tales involving ESP, as well as in tropes within speculative
science and science fiction. This poster acknowledges the importance of
the imagination—but more important, insect offers an interpretation of
the Incunabula Papers by insisting inter-dimensional travel isn't really
"travel" at all, but rather the "progression of consciousness" that may purportedly lead to the "exploration of mental continents," seemingly syn-
onymous with autonomous zones. This position ostensibly frames what
we consider to be the journey into uncanny territory of the legend-trip as
a mental exercise leading to an "awakening," but, according to insect, this
first requires participants to break free from existing "conditioning and

programming" that limit their awareness—participants must transform their receptive psychological states. Here insect's comments correlate well with the mechanisms driving legend-trips.

In the next excerpt of insect's post, the imagination is presented as a way to perceive the Fifth Dimension—taken here to represent a meta-reality, a kind of magical vantage point:

```
you will later become aware of this 5th dimension and learn how to
operate it
(my guess is it has something to do with the centers of the brain
dealing with imagination)
and you can "access" other parrallel physical universes
it is also possible to "access" alternate meta-physical universes
as the wave collapses to a particle an infinite of alternate particles
is formed by the act of observation and the nature of possibility,
as the folks at ong's hat were doing- riding the wave...
once all this is figured out, you can "walk" into another universe
everything becomes understood, and a higher level of complexity in
awareness and wave-consciousness is reached by the individual
this "individuality" is also a false concept, only an appearance,
by a false observer
nothing exists, nothing is everything as one
all-is-one
this is Chaos
```

Insect's post illustrates how narratives used to frame a legend-trip can be seen as both setting the stage for an experience to occur and as an explanation for why the experience will occur. The statement that operating in the Fifth Dimension "has something to do with the centers of the brain dealing with imagination" deviates from earlier commentary; at this point, insect's "guess" effectively presents conjecture as credible because it is embedded in a series of propositions. More so, this comment invites others to involve themselves by presenting their own theories, hypotheses, and ideas. Overall, insect's statements on "the centers of the brain dealing with imagination" present imaginal realities (intermediate domains bridging imagination and reality) as agentive metaphors—a major theme in the Incunabula Papers.

People's narrative immersion or uncanny journey within the Incunabula Papers manifests in several ways, most often in the form of research. The following excerpted post, archived at the *Dark Planet* website and supposedly written for an academic course, demonstrates the research participants often undertake:

By Hassan Sabbah on December 22, 2000—12:27 am:

Working off of the original available materials pertaining to the Ong's Hat mythos (i.e., "Incunabula Catalogue of Rare Books", and the "Ong's hat: Gateway to the Dimensions" full-color brochure), several figures are implicated as possible architects of the phenomenon. Although there is currently no validated consensus among researchers as to who exactly authored these texts, I believe it is still enlightening to point out those whom these documents appear to point to. I believe it is precisely the nature of these texts, and the phenomenon as a whole, that asks that these characters be brought into the myth. Many of the references are nothing less than blatant, and with Matheny's admittance to contriving many of the interviews, it is even more clear that there is definitely some form of ontological experimentation going on here. The question is, what exactly are the mythos engineers trying achieve with their experiment?

Upon first reading the "Institute of Chaos Studies and the Moorish Science Ashram" (ICSMSA) brochure one is immediately struck by its similarity to much of Hakim Bey's writings. In fact, you needn't read any further than the introduction to note the mimicry of style. The introduction reads just like a chapter out of Bey's own work, "Communiqu s of the Association For Ontological Anarchy". However, the similarities extend past mood and writing style, the content within this work of Bey's is extremely relevant to that which is proposed in the brochure. Likewise, one can find numerous "giveaways" in Emory Cranston's catalogue of rare books, "Incunabula". The catalogue is a list of science texts; some of which are fringe, complemented with obscure and out of print sci-fi titles, along with supposed Xeroxed journals and pamphlets belonging to members of various travel cults. In entry "27" of the catalogue, one finds a clear connection to Bey's "…Ontological Anarchy". The supposed text, Maze of Treason, by John Lorde (Red Knight Books, Wildwood, NJ, 198 , described as a "pornographic thriller", tells the story of Jack Masters, a member of a "spyforce of American patriots who jokingly call themselves the Quantum Police", who are out to regain control of the alternate dimensions with the pretense of applying reason and order and subverting the forces of chaos. Within his summary and description of the text, Cranston claims that "John Lorde not only knows about the conspiracy, he's been there". Within the story, the hero travels to "Si Fan", which Cranston claims is the author's name for "Hurqa-lya", a ruin of an ancient civilization which exists (within an alternate dimension) as a center-point for many "travelers". At the end of "Communiqu #2, The Kallikak Memorial Bolo and Chaos Ashram: A Proposal", Bey gives thanks to "the Grim Reaper & other members of the Si Fan Temple of Providence for YALU, GANO, SILA, and other ideas". (Bey, p.32, 1985) Just what exactly this means, and just who exactly are the members of the Si Fan Temple are anyone's guess. In the acknowledgments for Bey's T.A.Z.: The Temporary Autonomous Zone, Ontological Anarchism, and Poetic Terrorism, it is stated that the "Communiqu s..." were first printed by the Grim Reaper Press of New Jersey in 1985. That the Si Fan Temple, of New Jersey, is noted in a communiqu pertaining to a free love, zero- work ashram, consisting of Airstream trailers, in the Pine Barrens, is just too much to be coincidence. Another interesting connection can be found in reading Bey's "T.A.Z.: The Temporary Autonomous Zone". This work is a call for places where individuals can experience complete and total au-tonomy, free from governmental, religious, and societal restriction. The fact that there is not a square foot to be found on Earth that isn't owned or claimed by one faction or another is a sad fact of our time... there is no wild frontier left, and if one wishes to do his/her own thing, it must be done clandestinely. If one were to operate within a true Permanent Autonomous Zone, about the only place this could be achieved would be within an Alternate Dimension as proposed by the Ong's Hat Papers.[7]

This post employs extratextual, "real-world" references to frame the real-ity of the Incunabula Papers, guiding those unfamiliar with Hakim Bey to seek out his other writings (especially by questioning the meanings of unfamiliar terms—see the endnote for more on these terms). This in-troduces readers to Bey's philosophy, much of which includes explicit commentary on the magical potency of ostension and communication. Commenting that an "Alternate Dimension as proposed by the Ong's Hat Papers" would be about the only place where "individuals can experience complete and total autonomy," the poster makes the case for those in search of such experiences to seek out the city of "Hurqalya," the Persian word for "heaven," and the name alternative reality traditions sometimes use to signify a kind of imaginal reality reminiscent of the noosphere. This mental topography, framed here as the legend-tripping destination for those undertaking the uncanny journey, again reveals that people investigating the Incunabula Papers are seeking supernatural experiences in the form of altered perceptions.

Conflicting Frameworks

Conversations about parallel worlds, which appear throughout the Incunabula Papers legend-trip, sometimes arise between those who believe these worlds to be metaphors and others who follow a more literal interpretation (this often results in interpretive dilemmas or amalgams of these conflicting interpretations) as seen in this post from the *Dark Planet* message board:

By agentq3 on November 24, 2000—2:57 pm:

> Subject: Return Portal, Where will ong's hat people return?
> Maybe they do not want to return,but perhaps they would wish too ,where they return,is this based on where they left from or where the eggs are?would it be too hard for other humans and or higher advanced beings to find their particular parallel earth,for an energy signature that leads to them would have to exist,to find exactly where and when they went,Are their survivors going to be found and taken to the other earth?When the paramilitary attacked,were any people killed?How could any escape,from the paramilitary group?Would not thepeople just be interrogated,and killed?(I would think that is what the evil Shadow Gov. darklings would do)Matheny??????agentq3[8]

This focus on the actual plot of *Ong's Hat: Gateway* offers a literal reading of the text, bringing the narrative back into the "real world" by interpreting the motivations of, expressing concern over, and generally treating the events depicted by the ICS in *Ong's Hat: Gateway* as if they had actually occurred. Posts like these that return to the story of the Ong's Hat ashram act as countermeasures for other posts that lean heavily on theoretical speculations and keep the legend narrative firmly between plot and allegory.

By Unit 62 on November 30, 2000—8:52 pm:

> Subject: More Questions
> Maybe I missed something, but I've been going over this Incunabula
> info I can't seem to get a clear answer as to how they can control
> where they go. If every event has an infinite number of possibilities,
> then there are an infinite number of possible Earths. I'm just an
> amateur astronomer myself, but it seems to me that the majority of
> the alternate Earths would be uninhabitable. (No atmosphere, too hot,
> too cold, no water, etc...)Not to mention the alternate universes
> where there is no Earth or even a Solar system. I imagine that the
> safest way to travel would be in a pressurized space suit. It could
> be argued that the Tantric methods used to travel only open portals
> to Earths where life exists, but I have not seen anyone elaborate on
> this. Any help would be appreciated.

At first glance, this post might appear absurd, especially since it mentions that "the safest way to travel" to parallel Earths would involve the use of a "pressurized space suit." But underlying this post is the merging of Newtonian physics with quantum theory, and science with mysticism. Such combinations demonstrate that all the materials within the Incunabula Papers can't be fully integrated within any one paradigm or framework exclusively. Other readers and participants may see this post as a mental exercise in envisioning a literal interpretation of the Incunabula Papers' narrative, but, in actuality, it contains multiple interpretations in concert, which effectively dislocates any one reading strategy, and adds to the Incunabula's appeal as a particularly uncanny and challenging supernatural legend complex. More so, by comparing the logic of the narrative to scientific logic, this post presents an opportunity for readers to account for the apparent lapse in this possibility, thus offering audiences a chance to formulate their own interpretations. We must keep in mind that legend complexes potentiate infinite variations and resist final conclusions.

A poster named TemporalVelocity attempts to explain the mechanics of reality portrayed by the Incunabula Papers with a theory bridging the physical and metaphysical:

By TemporalVelocity on December 1, 2000—11:07 am:

> In Response to 'More Questions'
> My own personal theory on parallel realities is that some are solid-

material like ours, and others are quasi-material. Try to view the Metaverse as a temporal tree, you have the trunk which is the base of all reality as we know it. Then you have the main branches steming from the trunk, let's say there are seven of them, PRIME-ACTUALITY worlds.

Then let's say that from each of these prime actualities there are SECONDARY-PROBABILITY worlds, these would not be as solid or linear as the prime actualities which exist at the particle-matter extreme of the particle-wave field superspectrum, as opposed to those sub-realities which exist at the wave-energy extreme of the wave-particle field superspectrum.

Since the secondary probabilities exist more towards the wave-energy end of the spectrum you may find that in such worlds paranormal manifestations are much more common as psions are much more able to influence the matter-thought forms of such a reality because of its more multilinear nature. Generally, the more linear a reality, the more 'solid' it will be. If one were to create multiple paradoxes within a prime actuality for instance [that is if such paradoxes do not escape into alternate dimensions] then such a linear reality may begin to become multilinear and slightly dematerialized and more paraphysical in order to compensate for the paradoxes. This is why grossely irresponsible temporal projects such as those being carried out at Montauk may be very devastating to our timeline, and destroy the very nature of our linear reality as the multiple paradoxes begin to dematerialize our reality into one that might be likened to a cross between a physical reality and a dreamscape. In fact the Montauk crowd claims to have travelled to the future and to have seen this very thing occur, around the year 2012...

The secondary realities might be much more numerous than the pri-mary worlds, by the way, just as a main tree-branch separates into increasing numbers of 'finer' sub-branches.

The TERTIARY-POSSIBILITY worlds would be even more towards the wave-energy side of the spectrum, even more multi-linear, and like the finer branches of a tree even more numerous... you might call them dreamscapes or dream pools, ectoplasmic realities of phantasmical ghost-worlds, whereas the secondaries would be some sort of hybrid

between temporal-matter and ecto-matter. In other words the tertiary
worlds would be GASEOUS realities which may number in the billions or
near infinity, whereas the secondary worlds would be LIQUID realities
which may number in the thousands or millions, and the primary worlds
being SOLID realities which may number in the tens or hundreds, although nevertheless finite in number.

It would seem natural [I may be wrong], but the denser realities of
nature tend to be somewhat finite in number, whereas the finer realities of nature stem OUT FROM the denser realities and are more infinite
in number. So when speaking of parallel universes one might ask, are
there infinite parallel universes? The answer would be: Yes AND No.
Yes in regards to the ectoplasmic nonlinear wave field realities at
one end of the spectrum, and no in regards to the material linear
particle field realities at the other end of the electro magnetic
superspectrum.

Essentially, this post explains a very complex relationship between
waves and particles by way of elementary sciences one learns in primary
schools—the states of matter—solid, liquid, gas—and submits a formula
for the emergence of alternate realities not unlike theories forwarded by
nineteenth-century Spiritualists to account for manifestations of psychical substances and energies ("ectoplasmic realities of phantasmical ghost-
worlds"). According to TemporalVelocity, a thought has its own material
substance; this proposition provides for highly interpretive frameworks
with which to approach the Incunabula Papers story from multiple angles
seemingly limited only by one's creative capacity. The interpretive drift
that Incunabula participants begin to go through, when incorporating
TemporalVelocity's and others' explanations, doesn't focus on a supernatural experience so much as it does the production of perspectives that
allow one to create supernatural experiences.

TemporalVelocity makes reference to the "Montauk Project," a legend
complex about the U.S. Government's supposed covert use of acquired
alien technologies to travel to alternate dimensions and different time periods. Navigating through the Montauk Project legend complex, one may
uncover (or, as some say, one is mysteriously guided toward uncovering)
a conspiratorial narrative undercurrent that aligns quasi-historic facts,
locations, persons, and events that ostensibly support claims that our
military has developed technologies so advanced as to function as magic

(recently adding fuel to legends of the Montauk Project, an unidentified creature—coined "the Montauk Monster"—washed up on the shores on Montauk, New York, in July 2008). By bringing up the "Montauk crowd," those immersed in the Montauk legend complex (who somewhat notoriously make frequent claims that they were once psychics working with the military to explore alternate dimensions), as well as mentioning the year 2012, the poster both reinforces the believability regarding time/dimensional travel and conjures forth the plethora of prophecies relating to the end of the Mayan calendar, which some believe foretell the end of the world, and others that it will mark a significant shift in human consciousness. The sum of this high weirdness efficiently presents a surreal narrative landscape for Incunabula legend-trippers wherein they may appropriate any of these scenes and settings to expand upon and substantiate their own interpretations.

Bishop's Dilemma

The many interpretations that arise from narrative immersion, whether coming from the tentative ideas associated with the Incunabula Papers or from research into the documents' origins, often clash, resulting in participants finding themselves at odds with one another's readings. This seems to be common among legend-trippers. While preparing to enter Waverly Hills with other members of my group, it wasn't unusual to hear people debating different theories accounting for supernatural manifestations and discussing whether certain stories about the sanitarium were true; ideas regarding the usefulness of psychics in ghost hunting were an especially heated topic. Some degree of skepticism or conflict over the differing interpretive frames during this stage of the legend-trip is advantageous to the ritual's success, as this feeds into the ritual's overall ambiguity or liminality and allows for people to be introduced to and to play with various frameworks, modifying them as they deem necessary. Should everyone be in absolute agreement over how the ritual will transpire, the performance of belief becomes conviction, which significantly hinders, if not completely obliterates, any opportunity to presence the unknown. As a dramatic performance, the legend-trip requires conflict to advance the narrative. The following exchange among the posters Bishop, Anonymous, and Nergalus demonstrates the manner in which debates over different interpretations transpire:

By Nergalus on April 2, 2000—06:48 pm:

> INCUNABULA.org and its proported events and "conversations" is an
> online COMIC BOOK, nothing more. Polydimensional travel and multiple
> planes of existance are intriguing and highly probable, though.

Despite labeling the Incunabula Papers as a comic book to trivialize the
documents, Nergalus still claims to accept the possibility that certain spiritual technologies and highly speculative theories are possible or even
"probable," inviting others to respond:

By Anonymous on April 3, 2000—06:23 pm:

> Wrongo.
> Incunabula.org uses the graphic novel format to present *some* of
> it's information, but for the most part it is a repository of and
> portal to, ongoing investigations and new information resources
> concerning the very subject matter that this discussion area is
> concerned with.

Besides elevating the comic book status of the Incunabula Papers to that
of the graphic novel, Anonymous describes incunabula.org as a portal, a
term often used in fiction to mean a magical doorway or a point of passage that doesn't necessarily operate in accordance with logic or reason.

The next post comes from an avowed skeptic who nonetheless wishes
to participate. Skepticism functions within this stage of legend-tripping in
an adversarial role, against which legend-trippers, practicing for their upcoming performance of belief (which may culminate with a supernatural
experience), cooperatively gather to formulate countermeasures:

By Bishop on May 25, 2000—07:39 am:

> Hello,
> I have just recently stumbled upon the Incunabula and find it very
> entertaining (Would make a great movie). Dont get me wrong, I am a
> seeker of truth and the concepts within the texts are interesting
> but... There is no real formula presented, no math or hard sci-
> ence. Sure there is alot of talk about chaos theory, string theory,
> particle physics, fractals, alternate dimensions and pretty words

of sudo science but nothing tangible. I could rattle on about how
these concepts work (as some have tried) and come off as someone who
"might" know what there talking about as could everyone else in this
forum. Lets not waste our time. If someone has something to add to
these very interesting theories than let it be based on and explained
in real scientific terms. And if your going to bother going that far
then include the math! I am as intrigued about this as the rest of
you but lets start bringing facts to the table. If anyone is involved
with this project and is actively participating within a cell please
bring your knowledge of these matters to this forum. I have heard
your group speak of wanting to get some of this information out and I
would be willing to dedicate some time altering my web page for your
needs. I am a graphic designer and digital media artist and would
love to help you out.(IF YOU EXIST)Please dont hesitate to contact
me by e-mail so that we may discuss this topic in detail. Now that
I sound like a complete flake I should go...Take care!

Expressing frustration over the lack of theories "based on and explained in
real scientific terms," Bishop seems opposed to frameworks that privilege
imagination. Bishop is later criticized because he/she doesn't appear to
realize that becoming an active participant in the Incunabula Papers demands altering perspectives of what is possible. What Bishop fails to realize is that some of the more pervasive frameworks within the Incunabula
legend-trip forego conventional dichotomies of *fact/fiction* and *true/false*.

Oftentimes skeptics declare a legend's past accounts to be the results
of hoaxing. After someone suggests Matheny has perpetuated the entire
Incunabula phenomenon as an elaborate prank, the following appears:

By Eggnog Octopus on May 25, 2000—10:46 am:

Here's the funny thing about 'pranks':
Because, as we all now know, a single butterfly flappin' it's lips
can alter the course of Russian politics, so called 'pranks' can
actually have the effect of monumental social and economic upheval
given enough time.

    . . .

Point is: there's no such thing as a 'prank', because somewhere,
somehow, all things will one day be true.

In this post we see a recurrent theme in many discussions about this legend complex, namely, that narrative immersion renders obsolete the story's factuality. Drawing upon concepts from chaos theory (such as the "Butterfly Effect" and the "Many-worlds interpretation"), some participants begin to consider all possibilities as "real," which is a beginning point for generating alternative realities. This is actually the function of the second stage of legend-tripping—to alter the perceptions of all participants so that they might be more able to perceive the extraordinary and supernatural.

Shortly after this post, Bishop again requests evidence and, in doing so, exemplifies a level of skepticism similar to those scientists who actively attempted to debunk (or demystify) paranormal manifestations at séances. Because Bishop seems to detract from interest in formulating ideas about how human perception can lead to an evolution in consciousness, others question Bishop's involvement:

By N N on May 26, 2000—07:22 am:

> you want numbers, but are prepared to DO the numbers....there Is no scientific explanation exactly..as you describe....well maybe there is but....it is in the wrong hands...you don't want conspiricy, but there it is staring you in the face...what you going to do about it ? take another sip of your rum?....the is No Disinformation, only outlines of something, that has been constructed of various parts.... disinformation...is coming at us from all sides, all the time, no quantum theory covers all the bases....there is no quick fix to the time travel issue....out of fantasy comes facts and out of facts, we cycle the fantasy again and again in order to Do the myth, (MATH).... keeping sipping your Rum...contemplating the mysterys, turning over data and thoughts sifting the surface images until you have an AHA experiance...then it will slowly come into focus, don't be so one sided and demand immediate solutions to complex problems... time travel is not something to do a science project on; it demands certain ferquences of thought vibration, everything has to be prepared slowly like an alchemists retort...magick is the secret to time travel. but those whom abuse it are traveling in the rong direction....how do you abuse it? well that's for each practitioner to find out....happy hunting!!!
> P.S. sorry if you in your scientific knowhow don't like this explanation...but there it is....

N N argues that the importance of the Incunabula Papers lies in audiences' relationships with it, and identifies personal experience (the "AHA experiance" [*sic*]) as a legitimate source of knowledge (presumably acquirable only through a process congruent with interpretive drift—"turning over data and thoughts sifting the surface images"). Such experiences are extremely important to the participants of this (or any) legend-trip, for experiential knowledge is the primary means with which one may validate—or enter the reality of—the legend. The comments made by N N here reinforce participation in the Incunabula Papers as a magical process whereby labels such as fact and fiction become outmoded.

Days later, Stseamonelmo critiques Bishop's adamancy for objective proof:

By Stseamonelmo on June 14, 2000—04:12 pm:

Your quest for the absolute truth is your greatest weakness. It helps
explain your dislike of religion too. "There are absolutely no absolutes!" to borrow a religious "truth". IS the quantum object a wave,
or IS it a particle? The problems arise when we confuse our semantic
models with objective reality. Why read as journalism what should
be read as allegory, metaphor, parable? jesus spoke in parable, why
should we believe the rest of the bible is any different? A story
which means something else. "I never let the truth interfere with a
good story," as Sam Clemens liked to say. Does it make a difference
to us today if 2000 years ago jesus actually walked the earth, died
on a cross, and was resurrected three days later? Not really. But
does the lack of tangible evidence make any of what he said less
"true"? Not really. Read a little deeper into symbolism and mythology
before you go poking around the annals of magic and expect them to
make any sense at all. Moses approached Pharoh, demanding to "Let my
people go!" Our understanding now is that the Jews were being used
as slaves to construct the pyramids. Stop for a minute, clear your
mind, and think. How do these words from several thousand years ago
(or so the story goes) apply to me? What pyramids? Turn over a dol-
lar bill! Who are the "chosen people"? A symbol for you and me! WE
are the slaves working away to build the pyramid of Gross National
Product and heirarchial control systems.
How does any of this apply to the whole incunabula mess? Demonstra-
tion of methodology. If I remember correctly (it has been a few
years since I last purused the incunabula files) the last part is

a transcript of an interview with Nick Herbert. Does it matter if
this interview actually took place or was just a literary creation
of an especially creative individual (or group of individuals)? No,
not really. But in the interview, Nick gives away the secret. Don't
be rigid when subtlety works better. (or something to that effect)
You chase away the intangible element such delicate work requires.
We live in a quantum world, like it or not. If this world is built
up from quantum principles, as modern science assures us, then this
world works on quantum principles. Popular convention claims we
do not see the effects of quantum wierdness because we exist on a
macroscopic scale, and these quantum jitters have miniscule effect
here. The only time they have any tangible physical effect is on the
quantum scale. As I said, this is popular conception. I disagree. The
reason we don't see quantum effects here, resides in the idea that
quantum particles are unbound by temporal constraints. As soon as
quantum jitters make a new possibility actual, the quantum world in-
stantaneously (to our macroscopic perception) adjusts itself so that
was how it always happened. The ineffable wave-form cthulhu beast
lurking just outside of perception's reach condensed to a quantifiable
form when measured (but only for the traits measured for, and still
subject to uncertainty - so as precision of one increases, precision
of the opposite decreases), only to rebound to existing in all possible states as soon as observation ceases. AND, let us not forget
the effect of observation itself. In a quantum world, the observer
changes the parameters of the event. The photons of light recorded
by the observing instrument (maybe just your own eye) exist along
their entire history, so even after the fact of your observation,
they can go back and change the event.
"As above, so below." This is the quantum world as described by
modern physics. Why should we think this world of everyday events
is any different? Psychedelic substances open us up to these situations by breaking down our rigid perceptual grids and allowing us to
see thru a different set of lenses for a while. Or a few sets - thus
explaining quick changes in observed reality. Any claim that use of
these substances invalidates the observations of the observer seems
ridiculous once you understand the mental process involved. Such an
argument taken to its most absurd logical conclusion would invali-
date anyones observations, because nobody will observe a situation
in "exactly" the same way.

Stseamonelmo's response somewhat mirrors a conversation I remember from my Waverly Hills excursion. While preparing to enter the sanitarium, the group talked for some time about how ghosts might be a kind of "psychic residue" imprinted in the fabric of reality, pure conscious energy, or perhaps psychokinetic projections of a group mind. In hindsight, it's evident that we were all practicing for our upcoming group belief performance to make the prospect of encountering ghosts seem more plausible. In the above post, Stseamonelmo outlines how the "delicate work" of magic and storytelling can create transformational quantum events (as can various psychedelic substances, according to the poster). These comments operate similarly to those discussions at Waverly, offering legend-tripping participants the chance to communally cultivate different ideas as to how the supernatural will manifest. When Stseamonelmo tells Bishop, "You chase away the intangible element such delicate work requires," this echoes those statements offered by nineteenth- and twentieth-century mediums to scientists who impeded upon séances. We can compare this poster's opinion of Bishop to audiences' initial reception to the wrestler Elijah Burke during the *Ghost Hunters* Halloween special, for both Bishop and Burke are viewed as skeptics whose presence seems to hamper the spooky atmosphere desired by legend-trippers (though having some skepticism present in legend-tripping performances benefits the ritual). As for Stseamonelmo's allegory for the quantum wave-form—the "cthulhu beast"—this again insinuates that the Incunabula material is beyond logic, it is *uncanny*, and can only be comprehended experientially (though the poster, by referring to Lovecraft's writings, implies that such knowledge can be perilous). This experiential knowledge is only obtainable when conditions are favorable (i.e., when overbearing doubt and skepticism are absent from the ritual "space").

Bishop's critiques of the Incunabula Papers then take a decided turn:
By Bishop on Wednesday, May 31, 2000—09:47 pm:

. . . If you are a part of some ultra secret time travel-dimensional travel group and your traveling to some utopia with sparce human habitation (and you wish to keep it that way)then why do interviews at all? Rather than makeing me mystified it just adds one more nail in the coffin of the Incunabula story. I do not take the story seriously but it makes for some great entertainment. I am puzzled however as there are some interesting bits of fact invovled in the case. My hats off to the creators of this new internet mythos! Youve obviously spent

a good deal of time creating this situation. The interesting thing
about the case is that it has a self proliferating knowledgebase.
Information is added through rumor and conjecture by use the users.
We are the Incunabula ...[9]

Though some participants seem to view Bishop, like Elijah Burke, as a
skeptic whose company threatens the legend-trip, Bishop's proclama-
tion, "We are the Incunabula," demonstrates to others that Bishop has
started his or her own journey into uncanny territory, a "new internet
mythos." By acknowledging different readings of the Incunabula, Bishop,
like Burke, assumes the role of convert, providing a kind of testimony to
the transformative power of the legend complex.

Hypersigils, Fiction Suits, and Ostension

In the last chapter, Matheny, Bey, and Herbert—three key figures affiliated with the Incunabula Papers—were introduced, as was the fact that
each of them often assume alternate personas, engaging in prolonged
ostensive role-play to perpetuate certain storylines and narratives, even
going so far as to become characters in these narrative worlds. In the following post, Mr. Nowhere comments on this kind of ostensive action:

By Mr. Nowhere on December 29, 2000—6:16 pm:

Fictional accounts as a means of drawing in the reader and bypass-
ing the rational mind or the usual "screens" we utilize to filter our
perceptions and instill separate and yet curiously entwined levels
of meaning...All the great storytellers down thru history employed
this simple, subtle, downright subversive method to impart wisdom to
the masses. The internet as a medium is no different by any means,
except for the fact that disinformation is as widely circulated as
the aforementioned, if not moreso. And while disinformation could
be thought of as an "anti-story" in that sense (in that it imparts
no great truths but lies and half-truths meant to confuse and cloud
one's thinking), it could also be thought of as a form of "roleplaying"...To take the role of a disseminator of informatiom and then
to do the opposite, and then to pretend to be doing the opposite of
that while saying "not so" and providing beside-the-point replies
when asked about intent and content for that matter...And yet there

is something to be gained from "treading the labyrinth" as it were, a literary or even multimedia labyrinth straight out of one of Borge's lucid dreams...Perhaps all such cognitive struggling ultimately leads to a more refined sort of "roleplaying" in the end, but I'll leave that for you to decide.[10]

The lives, actions, and writings of many occultists, including the afore-mentioned Carlos Castaneda and G. I. Gurdjieff, as well as Matheny, Bey, Herbert, and some Incunabula participants exemplify the kind of role-playing Mr. Nowhere refers to. Prolonged ostensive peformances perpetu-ate occult and legendary realties by inciting others to participate in a sustainable world-making enterprise. By assuming the identity of an Ong's Hat researcher, Matheny steps into the legend, so to speak, becoming able to retool it from the inside. Herbert, albeit a real person, nonetheless be-comes a central fictional character in the Incunabula Story. And Wilson's writings as Bey have significantly contributed to the Incunabula Papers' milieu. The ease in which online personas can be constructed to interact with and influence the Incunabula narrative hasn't gone unnoticed by participants, all of whom have created online identities.

Many Incunabula legend-trippers consciously utilize memes, sigils, fic-tion, and ostension to advance their collective perception-altering play performances. Artist and magician Austin Osman Spare popularized the magical act of sigil-making among contemporary magicians (although the emblem books and alchemical imagery developed in the late Medieval period to the Renaissance also demonstrate use of sigils). Sigils are any written symbol, work of art, or other creation that magicians construct to affect reality. One pervasive trend among chaos magicians is that of creat-ing hypersigils—more elaborate works of art, performance, and stories. Legend engineering, or the construction and transmission of a fabricated legend-like narrative, may be considered a type of hypersigil if created to goad people toward particular beliefs, actions, and/or ideologies. Argu-ably, the Incunabula Papers began as an engineered legend, and, when analyzing engineered legends, it is critical to remember that audiences may consider such fictions as anonymous compositions after they are transmitted through multiple channels and performances; engineered or constructed legends have the capacity to become traditionalized. Hyper-sigils and memes might become less abstract for some readers when com-pared to Bill Ellis's characterization of the legend as "part of a complex process in which information systems respond cautiously to foreign ideas . . . either as the invader or as an individual's or community's response to an invasion."[11] Viewed in such a way, memes and hypersigils, like more "traditional" legends, offer a potent means with which to commence belief-related ideas and ostensive performances that attack or defend other worldviews.

Tlon's post below presents the idea that the Incunabula Papers constitute a hypersigil. Prior to the excerpt provided, Tlon included materials from Grant Morrison's website to argue that any type of creative world-making process is inherently magical. Morrison, a well-known chaos magician and writer, has publicly stated that his popular comic book series, *The Invisibles*, is a hypersigil intended to circulate the idea that humanity must do away with conventional cognitive frameworks in order to access its full evolutionary potential, which Morrison equates with the ability to live paradoxically. After comparing Morrison's own work to the Incunabula Papers, Tlon writes:

By Tlon on March 15, 2001—8:38 pm:

> Interesting parallels with what Joseph (and possibly the original author or authors) has done with the Incunabula material. Fact and fiction are combined in creating a character (or an entire hypernarrative), who is then projected out into the physical world via method acting, magick, memetics etc. If everything goes correctly, the character manifests as a "real" person (or the hypernarrative begins to manifest/write itself onto the physical plane/consensus reality).[12]

Incunabula participants may self-consciously engage in ostensive performances to become part of the story, so to speak, through ostensive role-playing—what some call wearing a "fiction suit." The website deoxy.org defines a fiction suit as:

> A fictional persona which one wears like a suit. Coined by writer Grant Morrison.
>
> A fiction suit can be used to interact with fictional / historical characters. For example in The Invisibles Morrison uses the character King Mob as a fiction suit. He soon discovered that whatever happened to his fiction suit would happen to the "real" him. One can easily see how this can be extremely advantageous - and perhaps dangerous.
>
> A fiction suit can also be used in consensual reality. When worn in this fashion, a fiction suit becomes similar to the idea of a reality

tunnel. One constructs the fiction suit, with all of the persona's passions, prejudices, quirks and perspectives and then "puts it on", essentially becoming it.

This can be used to test a model of reality, experiment with various modes of social interaction or as a method of testing and refining a "beta version" of an aspect of the gestalt personality / mind-body that is being considered for an upgrade.[13]

Wearing fiction suits or engaging in deliberate ostensive role-play not only allows people to embody a fictional character, or personify part of a legend narrative, but also permits them to actually exist within fictional realities. Certainly, experiencing the self as another might perhaps be among the most uncanny experiences one can have.

Morrison himself discussed writing *The Invisibles* as a hypersigil (referred to below as a "kind of super-sigil") in an interview given in 2002:

So, roundabout in 1997 I decided I would really serious turn this thing in to some kind of super-sigil and it was based on the idea of - if you look at cave-art, the first art was done, the first writing was done basically as art, and if someone wanted to make something happen like if you were some fucked-up caveman in the caves somewhere, moaning about your dinner, what do you do? You draw a bison on the wall, stick some spears in it, go out and the bison dies filled with spears. And "Hey man!" we can make this happen. Slowly those things become letters, they become words, they become reduced to abstractions, complexes of meaning, and you can take that basic idea, people like Austin Osman Spare, the magician from the early part of this century, or Crowley, or the chaos magicians from the 80s who were a big inspiration on me . . . The sigil will work, you can project desire in to reality and change reality. It works! This is verifiable. People have been telling us about this for thousands of years. Even the Tibetans have been telling us about this, the Mesopotamians have been telling us about this, and why has it been made occult? Because Coca-Cola have got the secret, these people know what we're talking about here because what you do is you create a sigil, Coca-Cola is a sigil, the McDonalds 'M' is a sigil, these people are basically turning the world in to themselves using sigils. And if we don't reverse that process and turn the world in to us using sigils, we're going to be living in fucking McDonalds! Magic is accessible to everyone, the means of altering reality is accessible to everyone, and when everyone starts doing

it we're going to see our desire manifest on a gigantic scale. Everyone's
desire. What happens when everyone's desire becomes manifest?[14]

Many writers have claimed that their works of fiction have somehow
manifested in the real world. Morrison alleges to have once met King
Mob—one of the principle characters in *The Invisibles* (and purportedly
an occasional fiction suit for Morrison). The writer Alan Moore, who also
draws upon magical philosophies for his graphic novels, reported an encounter with his fictional creation, John Constantine. And Jack Parsons,
often considered the "James Dean" of the occult world, made a similar
claim after his ritual to summon a demon lover—the "Scarlet Woman"—
resulted in the appearance of Marjorie Cameron, his future wife. These
accounts invest magically oriented creative acts with supernatural authority—one can have a supernatural experience by *interacting* with fiction.

Tlon's moniker alludes to the potency of hypersigils by referencing
Jorge Louis Borges's short story, "Tlön, Uqbar, Orbis Tertius." Written in
the first person, this tale recounts how the narrator, a fictional Borges,
stumbled onto an immense mystery upon hearing about a peculiar nation called Uqbar. Some years later, he discovers a book, entitled *A First
Encyclopedia of Tlön. Vol. XI,* which describes Tlön, a planet mentioned
in Uqbarian mythology, and the Orbis Tertius, one of Tlön's regions. The
fictional Borges begins to suspect that this work is part of a vast conspiracy—an intellectual hoax, but both he and the rest of the world begin to
uncover ever more evidence that Tlön actually exists. Eventually, by the
end of the story, the earth has actually become Tlön. What was once a
conspiracy of ideas becomes, over time, an actuality. Borges's exploration of mind-dependent worlds resonates strongly with chaos magicians
and others invested in quantum folk metaphysics and alternate reality
traditions.

Earlier I stated that legend-trippers, unlike magicians, don't usually
acknowledge their activities as ritual performances. But as Tlon and the
poster below demonstrate, some Incunabula legend-trippers are extremely
aware of their performances as gateways to the imaginal.

By M. Nasruddin on March 29, 2001—10:21 pm:

    How random is random? The game of life as perceptual cut-up is not
    a new idea, certainly John Cage was experimenting with chance and
    indeterminacy in music, the Dadaists were pulling poems out of hats
    and the Surrealists were making "Exquisite Corpses" long before Bur-
    roughs appropriated the Cut-Up from Gysin

. . .

Of course, the flip-side to these experiments in altered perception through cut-up was the discovery of the much heralded "Third Mind", the creation of an "other" through interaction between self and the tools one uses for achieving cut-up techniques. The Surrealists called it "The Marvelous", when the incongruous meetings of chance achieved a kind of poetic reverie or meaning that reverberated out of nowhere. Burroughs talked about messages from the future. Gyisn talked about magick, as did Crowley when referring to the use of the "Book of Thoth" (ie. Tarot cards).

. . .

Mr. Morrisson's use of the comic-book format as a "hypersigil" to effect change on a grand scale through the use of unfolding narratives and discoveries about the "universe's programming language" accessed through manipulation of word and image bears mentioning as well, in light of your comments Harla and a previous thread on "fiction suits". Here we see the cut-up applied directly to magickal intent, through feedback and iteration on a "triple-loop", between creator and created, between created and audience, and between audience and society.

M. Nasruddin comments that magic involves abilities to perceive the ordering principles within any given reality or moment (all of which, according to magic, are ultimately connected) and to utilize those principles to direct the chaotic potential of desire. The facility to manipulate randomness then offers up special noetic features or ideational opportunities for Incunabula participants, just as it did for Burroughs, the Dadaists, and the Surrealists; these opportunities include communicating with or experiencing the supranormal.

Incunabula participants utilize the language of quantum mechanics and magic to lend scientific and mystical credibility to their readings of the Incunabula Papers, which locate the alternative universes pursued by the Ong's Hat ashram within states of mind. Immersion within the Incunabula legend complex leads some into co-constructing an exegesis that recognizes their own contributions as integral to the materialization of these realms. And once participants situate their activities within the narrative of the Incunabula Papers, they become primed to experience manifestations of the supernatural.

Supernatural Experiences

Contact with the supernatural is the peak of the legend-trip, for the ritual's main purpose is to initiate a supernatural event congruent with that described by the legend(s). With regard to the Incunabula Papers, contact with the supernatural occurs when people perform the belief, or literally believe, that the Incunabula Papers have some supernatural or initiatory quality and when they begin interpreting events or perceptions as supranormal. We can begin to understand what happens during this stage by examining personal experience reports. Many scholars grapple with how to approach these types of narratives, let alone the experiences they describe, but Donald Ward offered perhaps the best advice when he said, "The folklore scholar . . . need not concern himself with the question of the existence or non-existence of paranormal phenomenon. The folklorist is interested . . . in the reality of the supranormal experience and not in the reality of paranormal phenomenon."[1] Ward's hypothesis, namely that supranormal experiences arise from an "incredible, innate human facility"—the imagination—has been critiqued by Bill Ellis, who argues that, should Ward be correct, "the supernatural experience thus becomes little more than an aesthetic puzzle to be solved."[2] While this debate is too complex to be presented here in its entirety, Ellis's concerns over the dismissal of supernatural phenomena is well founded. Those who do have unaccounted for experiences they consider to be the result of some supernatural, external agency face considerable obstacles when attempting to make sense of them, especially when challenged by people whose own interpretive processes uphold the assumption that the supernatural *cannot* and *does not* exist. Since this work is concerned with those supernatural experiences reported to arise from legend-trips, it locates these experiences within the domain of the creative imagination. Thus, the

112

scope of this investigation only goes so far. With regard to such experiences stemming from some kind of artistic method, many participants of the Incunabula Papers see their experiences as originating exactly this way, resulting from a surrealist perspective in which "the real and the imaginary . . . are not perceived as contradictions."[3] Deciphering between the two doesn't concern Incunabula legend-trippers, as both are seen as equally valid sources of experiential knowledge.

To qualify any experience as supernatural is contingent upon what we or anyone else believes the supernatural to be. If a legend complex identifies dreams about owls as implanted "screen memories" that mask an alien abduction experience, and if someone adheres to this particular analytical frame, then should they have a dream about an owl, that dream might be considered supernatural. If someone chooses to believe that investigating the Incunabula Papers results in acquiring supranormal perceptions, they too can interpret any number of actions and observations as being supernatural. When analyzing personal reports of supernatural encounters, we should bear in mind that, as David Hufford states, "Another's experience is always a reconstruction to be inferred rather than a 'fact' to be directly observed."[4] Such reports do, however, advance the legend.

Interestingly, the memorates shared by Incunabula participants describe experiences not unlike those purportedly had by the Elizabethan mathematician John Dee, best known for having transcribed the Enochian Keys, a system of magic allegedly revealed by angelic spirits to the medium Edward Kelley. Years before working with Kelley, Dee had become fascinated with the idea of conversing with spirits—particularly angels—but considered himself to be a rather poor medium. After several failed attempts to contact the spirit world, Dee began to have a series of haunting dreams that led him to search for someone who might communicate on his behalf. Despite Kelley's reputation as a necromancer, Dee enlisted his services from 1582 until 1587. During this period, Dee, through Kelley, communicated with various supernatural beings, especially angels who told him they wished to impart the very knowledge they had once given to the biblical Enoch—knowledge about other hidden realities.

The material Dee and Kelley compiled eventually caught the attention of other magicians and occultists, and the popularity of Enochian magic endures to this day. Occult lore holds that Enochian magic, based upon the very language of the angels, is so dangerous that to verbally utter it invites disaster. According to Dee, while translating Kelley's conversations, the spirits presented this material backward, as to ensure that neither man would inadvertently speak it aloud. Some wonder whether the angels Dee and Kelley associated with where those who had fallen—the Watchers—whose taboo knowledge, once shared with humanity, led the biblical God to flood the Earth. Enochian magic is not the only legacy of John Dee's to be discussed among Ong's Hat enthusiasts, however. Matheny and others have mentioned Dee's treatise, *Monas Hieroglyphica*, published in 1564. This esoteric work on symbolic language proposes that if readers carefully meditate upon the glyph (or sigil) Dee provided within it, they may grasp the innermost mysteries of existence.

Many supernatural motifs in Dee's story appear to have been only slightly updated for the modern era, for Incunabula participants report bizarre dreams, the presence of spirits, communicating with seemingly superhuman forms of consciousness, and developing potent sigils with which to both create and experience currents of magic. Participants use these reports to make sense of their own anomalous experiences and to validate those interpretive frameworks in which these experiences occur. While the previous legend-tripping stage emphasizes constructing and exploring various interpretive frameworks, this stage stresses applying these frames to generate altered perceptions, which aligns with the second phase of interpretive drift.

The Domain of Dreams

In many magical traditions, practitioners strive to become lucid dreamers, those able to consciously guide the content of their dreams. Occult lore holds that the soul leaves the body during sleep, so if one retains consciousness while dreaming, one may engage in astral travel to different nonphysical supranormal or numinous realities and access mystical information encoded in these environments.[5] But the ties dreams and dreaming have to supernatural experiences aren't only depicted within occultism, for supernatural legends also describe a gamut of experiences occurring within the province of sleep (such as some encounters with "The Hag"). Strange dreams that befall legend-trippers after their ordeals may be interpreted as evidence of supernatural contact, and sometimes dreaming itself can be the goal of a legend-trip; the ancient practice of visiting sacred sites to sleep there in the hopes of receiving divine dreams still exists. The Incunabula Papers legend complex asserts that dreamers have the ability to visit alternate realities during lucid dreams and that their dreams even have the power to manifest in material reality. The next two posts present dreams as possibly constituting "real" experiences

in another reality. After DarkPlanetOnline shares his own "first Ong's Hat
related dream," Pahana enters the discussion:

By Pahana on May 8, 2001—04:10 am:

Dreams are fun ain't they?

Its interesting you mentioned the place which was a mish mash of
places you'd visited. I used to get them a lot. One place I used to
go to was one I nicknamed 'Astral Brisbane', in that it was like Brisbane (nightclubs, city life, street life etc) but had parts of the
topology taken from another town Rockhampton (and other yet weirder
parts which were constructs of my own imagination). Another place
which I call the Hanging Gardens is apparently a shared place where
other people have also been. Its supposed to have existed in ancient
Sumeria pretty similar to what it looks like now. I don't know about
the library though (although Assurbanipal loved his books).

One other interesting dream feature is books which contain the secrets of the universe (which you understand perfectly in the dream,
but forget promptly upon waking) and books containing 'past life
experiences' (for those who call them that).

I once even had a dream (not since repeated) in which 3 of us - me
and 2 friends - shared the same dream and scenery and could confirm
details down to the appearance of others in the dream. It was especially meaningful. To have something like that (or shared dream
experiences in the Hanging Gardens) happen is to know that the dream
world is not entirely caused by senses internal to your body and
influences from another level or continuum of stuff is influencing the
subject being dreamt of.[6]

Pahana distinguishes between dreams arising out of an individual's consciousness and those manifesting by some other, additional operation
("influences from another level or continuum of stuff"), offering group experiences in a "shared place." Such a location (what Pahana identifies as
the "Hanging Gardens" of ancient Babylon) operates as an astral environment, a setting accessible through non-ordinary states of consciousness,
which, according to the historian Alex Owen, occultists regard as "alternative media in which to continue their occult activities."[7] In this setting,

Pahana reports availing him- or herself to books that readily supply "the secrets of the universe," although the knowledge gained from reading them dissipates upon returning to the waking world (thus demonstrating an example of acquiring state-specific knowledge that can't be retained in full after leaving that state of consciousness in which it was gained).[8] The proposition that this dreaming space is somehow objectively real implies the poster believes dreams may act as gateways into "parallel realities" constructed only in part by one's own experiences and thoughts.

Crusoe then shares his or her own dream experiences with people who don't seem to the poster to be constructs of his/her own imagination, but rather real persons able to enter Crusoe's own dreaming space:

By Crusoe the painter on May 8, 2001—08:51 am:

Mine is a mish-mash of Cincinnatie, Covington Ky, East Lansing Michigan, and other places.

I've never had a shared dream though in this one, my companions seemed to be other people rather than parts of 'me'.

Never had dreams of a hanging garden.

Once when I was 12, or 13, living in Ohio, I sat up in bed and was looking at a young man in a grey jumper who smiled back at me. He looked a lot like me. I saked him who he was. He smiled and said he was my grand-son, and he was a time traveller.

I was skeptical and said "prove it". He held out his hand. I climbed out of bed, and grabbed it, and we stepped through a shimmering grey ring. I found myself in St. Louis in my aunt and uncles house, in their kitchen. I walked lightly on their hardwood floor, trying to avoid waking up there yippy dog. If it was a dream, it seemed incredibly REAL.

He then asked for my hand again, and this time, we were somewhen else, instead of somewhere else. This was the future, dark and beautiful, in some major city. Lights illuminated large skyscrapers/ arcologies. Cars flew by in the air. We were just kind of floating there, looking.

He told me to never doubt my life, that he helped to perfect time-travel,
and that I helped to build this future in some way.

He smiled, and I woke up in bed, with that weird wonderous feeling stick-
ing with me the rest of the day. And wondering if it were all real.

While Crusoe hasn't visited the "Hanging Garden" Pahana speaks of, Crusoe does mention communicating with people who aren't figments of the
dream: time-traveling future relatives able to enter his/her dreams. This
particular incident correlates to supernatural and magical tales about traveling in dreams to nonphysical realities and being visited by beings with
supernatural powers while one is asleep; as a subjective experience, the
event was "real" in that Crusoe was left with "a wonderous [sic] feeling."
This post demonstrates that even past events may be reinterpreted according to present frameworks, essentially transforming a previous dream
experience into a supernatural encounter.

Supernatural Entities and Shifting Perceptions

Incunabula participants sometimes report witnessing black streaks, blobs,
or dark silhouettes of humanoid figures in their visual peripheries. Many
legend complexes and heterodox belief systems describe these "shadow
entities" as spiritual beings, although no consensus exists as to whether
they are benign, hostile, or indifferent to human affairs. One popular
explanation for shadow people is that they are beings somehow trapped
or traveling between the parallel worlds of the multiverse, thus they only
appear as shades to us in our reality. This kind of supernatural entity has
grown in popularity largely through the paranormally themed late-night
talk show *Coast to Coast AM*, though the souls of the dead have been
described as shades in the underworld by religions coming out of the
Ancient Near East for millennia. Harla Quinn, the moderator of *Harqalya*
message board, writes on the *Dark Planet* Ong's Hat discussion forum:

By Harla Quinn on May 21, 2001—03:45 pm:

I've been receiving lots of mail and inquiries about "shadow entities" such as the Shadow People and other ancient archetypes which

```
are reputedly dimensional in nature...and perhaps even malevolent.
Other than those which Castenada writes about and Gurdjieff "hints"
at, I'd like to hear some other accounts.
Thanks,
Harla⁹
```

Mentioning Carlos Castaneda and G. I. Gurdjieff directs participants to an unsettling idea advanced by both these men: some unknown, nonhuman force has succeeded in enslaving humanity by implanting in mankind a kind of defective organ—a spiritual appendage that shackles us to the limiting illusion of material reality. Only by studying spiritual sciences and tending to our imaginative powers can we break free from this imprisonment.[10] Of course, this is a striking analogy for what some participants see as the repressive constraints of scientific materialism and rationality, but it also reinforces the idea that modifying one's perceptions is, in itself, a supernatural event. Harla Quinn's statement that she's "been receiving lots of mail" regarding "shadow entities" quite possibly provokes others to begin to construe any perceptual anomalies as shadow entities, and by announcing that she'd "like to hear some other accounts," she prompts others to share their theories and personal experience reports. Taking cue, DarkPlanetOnline relates his own experiences:

By DarkPlanetOnline on May 21, 2001—04:04 am:

```
Seriously though, I have been seeing more "black streaks" or visual
distortions than usual. Most often between 2 and 3 AM. But this
truly could be because my eyes are overexposed to monitor radiation.
What is the supposed nature of these black streaks, blobs, shadow
people?
```

DarkPlanetOnline's description quickly offers up a more "down-to-earth" explanation, possibly to counter any criticisms, common within memorates of supernatural experiences.[11] One might hardly consider "monitor radiation" to be a mundane explanation, but the fact that it seems to be for DarkPlanetOnline, and that the visual distortions he reports are viewed as considerably more odd, reveals that he is recounting experiences beyond his normal frame of reference. This is contextualized as possibly resulting from researching the Ong's Hat material, though this in no way limits incorporating different etiologies for shadow entities. Such borrowing actually reinforces the agency, authority, and validity of the Incunabula Papers as a supernatural conduit. Since Harla Quinn and DarkPlanetOnline each run their own respective forums on the Ong's Hat phenomenon and frequently post on this subject, many see them as experts; their comments on shadow entities might readily influence others equally interested in the Incunabula Papers to begin seeing these supernatural entities.

By Rythmaning on May 22, 2001—05:51 pm:

> As for shadow people? Is that shadowy entities, formless beings
> which sort of "shadow" people, excesses in our perception or what?
> Sounds so vague, I could tie it to any number of experiences or
> ideas and it wouldn't really have much meaning. I'd say that when
> subtle or intangible things start appearing it's an indicator that
> something's happening, maybe it's 'reality shifting' or maybe it's
> you shifting and your perception is changing. Then again, it could
> be higher-dimensional beings preparing us for the coming wave of
> consciousness-evolution

Although Rythmaning says that the appearance of shadow entities can mean practically anything, the poster still identifies their presence as an indicator that those who witness them have altered their perceptions of reality in such a way as to see other dimensions. The poster also implies that the Incunabula Papers are somehow a part of a paradigm shift, which Rythmaning describes below:

By Rythmaning on May 23, 2001—05:12 pm:

> A little more on the shifting thing I said yesterday. During times
> of shifting a given (person, community, collective conscious) is
> in a state of transition, less attached to any particular ideal or
> perceptual filter, hence being more open to seeing/experiencing things
> they wouldn't otherwise, even after an ascension-style transition.
> A question to tack on to this musing is whether or not something
> along the lines of RAWs "pseudo-schizophrenia" or or assimilating
> multiple simultaneous perceptions could be an attempt to keep this
> transition-state receptiveness on all the time?

Rythmaning's previous post suggests that contact with the supernatural is caused by a change in perception. The post above describes the state of being open for such contact as a "state of transition, less attached to any particular idea or perceptual filter" (i.e., liminality). Rythmaning also mentions RAW (Robert Anton Wilson, coauthor of the *Illuminatus! Trilogy*), who forwarded the idea that a kind of self-induced schizophrenia is necessary to counter an increasingly chaotic, inane world. Wilson often wrote about "reality tunnels," those beliefs, ideologies, philosophies, and information systems through which we encounter the world and interpret events. He proposed that an awareness of these tunnels and the performance of belief—rather than literal belief-in these tunnels (or multiple tunnels at once—"schizophrenia") would release one from the ideological constraints they had unknowingly fastened themselves to. Wilson's relevance here is that his material is incorporated into the Incunabula Papers legend complex and is presented as a technology with which others may access differing, multiple "realities"; Wilson is one of the few writers mentioned in discussions about the Incunabula Papers who describes not only alternate "dimensions" but also provides a thinkable means of self-transport. In effect, he translates a version of "the egg" in a more easily understood way to folks unable or unwilling to engage in strenuous performances of belief in something like a time traveling device. By "assimilating multiple simultaneous perceptions," according to Rythmaning, people increase their "receptiveness" to the supernatural.

Some individuals, like the following poster, who claim to have experiences with spiritual entities identify these beings as the Watchers. This exemplifies the content variability of supernatural legendry, forcing people to interpret for themselves the nature of the supernatural (in this case, whether noncorporeal beings are benign or malicious):

By who cares on February 20, 2001—07:59 am:

> i want to know why people make references to stuff in my life that hasn't happened yet while they continue to pretend to be 'normal'. we all want.
> i want to know why my 1943 copper cent got stolen just as i began to look into time-travel and Montauk related events.
>
> are 'they' trying to make me believe i'm special - would this serve them ?
> are they pulling a CigSmokeMan on me ?
> do they want me to believe i am protected ? or under survelliance ? or both - for maximum mind-rape ?

are they alien scum who can't believe i can be both aware of them
and indifferent to their insanity - so must keep in occult contact
with me ?
i don't know for sure.
all i know is that i am heavily spied upon by peoples who aren't
interested enough to actually ask me for whatever it is they want,
but are interested enough to keep raping my mind.

at the least, i suppose i at least have actual important reasons for
being interested in 'conspiracy' topics : i want to know why English
is such a difficult language for the watchers to learn. i picked it up
quite quickly as a youngster - i knew that if i wanted to communicate
with others then i'd have to learn their language.
why is it so hard for the penny-pinchers to learn English and talk
to me ?
i don't know, but it obviously is.
they would rather play a silly game in which i am supposed to perform
certain tasks in order to recieve my 'reward' - which they took.
there is a failure in the connections in their own brains : they
have yet to realise that abusing magick / magic holds no curiosity
for me. i don't care if they can fly. i don't care if they can steal
my cent from miles away and years before.
such things do not impress me at all.

ooh, real life X Files. And i've seen spooky lights. oo-oo.

i am impressed by truly rare qualities, such as honesty, integrity, trustworthiness. if you can add magick to that lot then you
may as well be crowned King, or Queen, or Juggernaut (Lord of the
Universe).[12]

This disjointed, tortured post by the cynically named "who cares" resonates with rejection. By blaming his or her mental anguish on the Watchers ("pulling a CigSmokeMan" refers to the enigmatic, yet often hostile
actions performed by the character "The Cigarette Smoking Man" on the
television show, *The X-Files*) and on exploring the inter-dimensional conspiracy known as the Montauk Project, this poster offers other participants a cautionary tale told by a narrator whose life seems negatively impacted by "occult contact" with supernatural beings. The persecution this
poster claims to suffer from isn't unlike that of people who "play" with

Ouija boards and come to believe that they have inadvertently gathered the attention of malevolent supernatural spirits. An earlier post reporting mistreatment by magical powers appears below:

By Stseamonelmo on Tuesday, June 13, 2000—03:28 pm:

. . .

consider, just for a moment before denying it outright, the possibility of mental "breaking and entering" if you will. what would stop
a high powered occult organization that pries into interdimesional
travel from temporarily co-habitating your own body, pushing you
aside, you photographing your own work, then sending the roll out
to their own agents, before restoring you to your seat of concsious-
ness? can you account for every second of every day? ??I only ask
this because i've witnessed it happening in myself. my increasing
awareness of their activites drove them crazy, but when they finally
realized I didn't have what they wanted, they mysteriously vanished.
??or maybe that's just what they want me to believe?[13]

Since so much of the subject matter proffered throughout this legend-trip subverts practical, commonplace notions of reality, it can appear schizophrenic, even psychotic, to unfamiliar readers and might present a risk to those who are particularly fantasy-prone, highly suggestible, or to those who suffer from any number of dissociative illnesses. Thus, warnings and pleas for caution are sometimes well founded. The poster Rythmaning revealed on the *Dark Planet* message boards in February 2001 that he/she is schizophrenic, which led the poster danteBot to comment upon discerning spiritual perceptions from delusions:

By danteBot on February 27, 2001—06:05 pm:

. . .

You might want to talk to Harla about your ability to perceive things
in varied ways simultaneously. She experiences this and there is a
name and physical cause for it.

Don't get confused in the mystical hype - there are things that can be
attributed to spirituality and there are things that can be attributed

to science. What we don't understand we tend to lump in with the former - regardless of the applicability of that category.[14]

. . .

Discriminating the supernatural from from symptoms of mental illness, and even fact from fiction, are part of the complex contextualization of altered perspectives arising from interactions with supernatural legends and occult lore. Applying these schemata can certainly present interpretive dilemmas, but the reverse also holds true: sometimes employing these same schemata rectifies interpretive dilemmas arising from spontaneous anomalous experiences. People in the midst of intense spiritual experiences or undergoing extremely disturbing anomalous perceptions need to make sense of them. For example, the framework encompassing the esoteric philosophy and practice of kundalini awakening has served to alleviate interpretive dilemmas triggered by anomalous perceptions had by several individuals.[15]

On the same forum that Rythmaning posted his comments about shadow people, someone by the name of DW remarks that the human brain might be capable of perceiving "creatures and or experiences" within parallel worlds, and that this might also explain déjà vu (an experience named by psychical researcher Émile Boirac in which a person senses a new situation or environment as strangely familiar). This prompts a response from a poster named Line Walker:

By Line Walker on June 2, 2001—07:42 pm:

> Yes, that is a very interesting way to view the phenomenon(percieving beings of other worlds) and I actually think It may have some merit behind it. However, I'm not sure how that would explain deja-vu.
>
> I tend to appoint deja-vu more to the following: I am a firm believer that there are those(like myself) who have a strong connection with beings which has accended to a higher level of spirituality/ conscienceness(sp.). These beings or spirits if you will, have infinite knowledge of everything that has been and all that is to come due to the fact that they exist at all points in time at once. Deja-vu is mearly an uncontrolled link(a controlled one being like what a "psychic" does) to one of these beings which causes said person to catch a glimpse of some past or something to come.[16]

This explanation transforms the sensation of déjà vu into evidence of a psychic link with advanced supernatural beings, and is a perfect example of how a range of impressions, sensations, and other feelings are reinterpreted as confirmation that supranormal realities can be accessed by altering human consciousness.

Goals of the I.C.S.

Whereas most legend-trippers don't explicitly acknowledge that they are engaging in a ritual performance (albeit an open-ended one), many immersed in the Incunabula Papers do. For them, contact with the supernatural comes about because they are aware that they are the architects of the experiences they seek. Some, like Harla Quinn, attempt to convey this to others.

By Harla Quinn on March 7, 2001—06:10 am:

. . .

Now that we have the original template utilized by the I&OH architects, have a fairly broad understanding of "jamming the noise ratio", and can appreciate that "higher intelligences" come in all sizes and flavors just like our favorite brand of prophylactic, the next transcendent layer of gloss applied is found within Robert Anton Wilson's "Cosmic Trigger". Here lies the "key" (or "keys" as we shall soon see) to understanding the entire palimpsest structure. To say that Incunabula and Ong's Hat is an "experiment" or even an experiment in reality architecture is a gross understatement and only a part of its quantum equation. It is "model" in metaprogramming, i.e., a memetic process of *"deliberately induced brain change"* to quote RAW; a process developed from a long history of initiatory practices derived from sources as diverse as Sufism, western hermetic traditions, behavioral psychology and consciousness studies. It is the "open conspiracy" as defined by Pauwels and Bergier in Le Matin de Magiciens, "The Morning of the Magicians", the transmutation of matter and the human mind. Or perhaps, the "transubstantiation of matter"?[17]

Harla Quinn identifies the Incunabula Papers as an "open conspiracy," a creative effort to beneficially change society by transforming peoples' perceptions of reality.[18] Harla Quinn's post is then followed by dante's:

By dante on March 11, 2001—00:59 am:

. . .

The "egg" is a modern Koan - haven't you got that?
There IS no "explanation" for it because the explanation is the answer. The answer, like the Tao, cannot be taught or shared but has
to be understood and experienced...
...what is going on here is exploring all the aspects to entrain
the mind to be capable of making the blind intuitive leap to
understanding...
...the Inc is the Tao Te Ching of the Western world - the guide to
entraining the mind to understand in a culture that is far different
from the Eastern mind...
...why do we relate everything that is in here to the core
"egg"...
...because it all relates...

Both dante and Harla Quinn characterize the peak of the legend-trip as
the realization that subtle, natural laws exist that most don't understand.
In other words, for them, contact with the supernatural manifests as experiencing illumination.

Below, Pahana suggests there is no need to qualify anything as supernatural or supranormal, which is reminiscent of Spiritualists' claims that
the supernatural is only that which we currently don't understand.

By Pahana on March 23, 2001—10:34 am:

. . .

There is a real bio-energy that flows through our body in the nervous
plexuses, the movement of the cerebro-spinal fluid, and the cells of
the body. There is no need to suggest a 'mystical' explanation for
the aura or other such phenomena - the idea of the Eastern and other
religions stands as it is: we are centers of force, surrounded by
other centers of force, who's continuous interaction (both action
and reaction) evolve the set of multiverses we live in. As such, it
is our duty to live our lives in such a way as we see fit, to use our
energies wisely, and take our liberties with emotion, pleasure and
other such things as we see fit. Such a philosophy when seen in its
true light does not create what we (reactionarily) call 'evil' - for

activities such as anger and violence can be seen as useful only if
they produce a useful and satisfying effect to effect our situation.
Usually they do not.

I look forward to peoples comments on their view on how well this
synchronises with Ong's Hat and how it relates to our hoped goal of
realising at least some of the goals of the I.C.S.[19]

Pahana frames the Incunabula legend-trippers' goals as being identical to
those of the Institute for Chaos Studies (members of the purported Ong's
Hat ashram): exploring "the enhancement of consciousness and consequent enlargement of mental, emotional and psychic activities." Viewed
this way, those supranormal experiences and perspectives reported by
some Incunabula legend-trippers confirm for them that they are consciously evolving, liberating their minds from limiting conceptual frameworks. Like more conventional legend-tripping participants who discuss
whether they've proved the legend, those enmeshed in the quest to find
Ong's Hat collectively decide whether they've succeeded in achieving the
"goals of the I.C.S."

8. INTENSE DISCUSSION AND THE
PROCESSING OF EVENTS

Making Sense of High Weirdness

During the final stage of legend-tripping, participants discursively attempt to make sense of the entire ordeal. This process might seem to signal the ritual's "end," but it actually renews the legend complex and parallels the third stage of interpretive drift wherein interpreted events justify the very frameworks that instigated them. Involvement can be prolonged and can last indefinitely. Since the computer-mediated environment in which the Incunabula Papers legend-trip unfolds isn't governed by the immediacy of face-to-face interactions, the negotiations of meaning are preserved as an archive of "accounts of past happenings." Other forms of legend-tripping also convert the communal discussions of what transpired into narratives that become part of the accounts of past happenings, but online, conversations about the legend-trip are verbatim the documentation of the legend-trip. The postings below include various analyses of the Incunabula Papers and constitute "closing remarks" forever open to reinterpretation.

By Harla Quinn on March 28, 2001—5:27 pm:

> It's been a busy month - running down the remaining leads, interviewing lots of *key* figures as well as former culture jammers, authors, psychologists, cultural anthropologists, engineers, physicists, and generally tying up the remaining up loose ends. Whew! Like Chinese macrame', the information is so densely interwoven that it is practically impossible to separate it into different *threads* (pun intended) without losing meaning. Thus, a careful and articulate dissemination is required so as not to sound rambling and incoherent.

There are a few final areas which require further examination and discussion and I respectfully request everyone's assistance and input.

I. The Magical Tool

The first of these are the way in which Incunabula and Ong's Hat can be viewed as a "magickal tool". We've begun similar discussions on prior occasions but always gotten lost inside the very fabric of magick, itself. Many of those on this board and who "lurk" here are well versed in hermetic studies. Rather than expound on your own degrees of expertise, let me attempt to break it down into areas which I humbly request your insight and commentary.

(1) The Akasa "egg" and its symbolism. Also, the alchemenical "cur-curbite" (or "Egg Philosophic" as defined by Regardie).[1]

(2) Kabbalistic correspondences, if any.

(3) Whether or not I&OH acts as a type of Neophyte initiation toward development of inner knowledge and enhanced perceptual cognition.

(4) I&OH as a type of "great work" in and of itself. Outline the framework as to the ways in which it acts as sort of a "ritual" and discuss the possible objectives both to the initiate and to the I&OH architects. (Please don't get too immersed in the LHP/RHP aspects.) Does our *conscious* efforts toward studying and researching I&OH create an intended synergistic force?[2]

(5) Karmic ramifications. Should you reach an individual determina-tion that I&OH has been used as a type of intiatory memetic device to further the awakening of the "higher self" existing within us all - does doing so without our awareness bode any Karmic ramifica-tions? What is the psycho-spiritual effect in doing so without proper "protection" being afforded the unwitting?

Many of you have written to me to discuss the "wierdness" which you suddenly begin to experience while studying and researching aspects of I&OH and for which you seek some explanation. In most cases I have responded that the experiences are merely an indication of in-creased perceptual *awareness*. However, that answer, in itself, is

not sufficient. Thus, I must humbly counter that I truly don't know
and certainly won't hazard a guess. I realize that many of these
unexplained phenomena are embarrassing to discuss because they are
unfamiliar and unbalancing occurrences and fit neatly into the "text-
book definitions" of psychosis, neurosis and delusion. For most, the
subconscious connections between the wierdness and I&OH is simply too
outrageous and implausible an explanation. We have given insufficient
individual attention to these disturbing results. My apologies if I
have given the incorrect and untenable impression that we are little
more than scientific "eggheads" and that this course is not without
psychological and spiritual risk.[3]

Harla Quinn's speculations clearly reference others' supernatural experience reports, acknowledging them as valid whether or not she has had
similar experiences. This openness to or acceptance of the reality of another's experience seems to be a hallmark of legend-tripping, for should
legend-trippers doubt or criticize one another's experience, the communitas falters, as does the affect of the ritual. Harla Quinn's invitation to others to discuss these events further, as well as her question as to whether
everyone's collaboration results in "an intended synergistic force," suggests she is aware of the importance of communitas and performance in
this legend-trip, as well as the significance of other perspectives: she understands that people are presencing their experiences, though she states
that she is unable to analyze just what is being presenced.

Pahana then answers Harla Quinn's request for additional input:

By Pahana on March 28, 2001—9:06 pm:

"Give me the end of a golden thread,
But wind it in a ball,
It will you in at Heaven's Gate
Built at Jerusalem's Wall"

To Blake, gold symbolised man's rational and intellectual faculty,
while Jerusalem represented Liberty - complete freedom to do one's
true will (see S Foster Damon - "A Blake Dictionary"). Truly that is
exactly what we've been doing - following the golden thread :), and
I wonder whether you're aware of the connotations there.
It's interesting you posted this last night Harla - I was beginning
to get worried about the level of quietude on this forum (the 3 day

lull). Just last night I was working on the conclusion to my own 4 part series on Incunabula and the Mystery Traditions. I'll be interested to see how closely our views match up.

At the same time, no matter what happens I'll be dissatisfied with my work. I feel that no matter how far one goes, there is always more threads to follow. When Ariadne gave Theseus the ball of thread to make the journey inward to the Minotaur, we never knew how many winding passages there would be on our way to the center. I guess because of the broad scope of the subject matter we might never fully exhaust our researches.

I think we are making good headway toward a place to start practical researches from. Researches which may not be related to the original Ong's Hat, but could develop into a similar kind of project. What are your thoughts on an eventual attempt at a group practical effort at something like this? Anyone who has an opinion on this, I'm up for it.

Pahana claims that the Incunabula participants are at least beginning to understand what has transpired through their collective conversations and experiences: the hero's journey. The suggestion that other participants might consider producing "a similar kind of project" sounds like the conversations I heard after spending the night at Waverly—people developed tentative plans to visit other legend-tripping sites, such as the Mansfield Reformatory in Ohio. People who successfully legend-tripped together (and who have enjoyed the ordeal) seem to be able to easily repeat their performances in various settings. Most ghost-hunting enthusiasts frequently go "out in the field" with the same colleagues. As explained by interpretive drift, once a framework is validated by people's experiences, people can more easily apply that framework in the future.

A few months later on the *Harqalya* message boards, Djinn N' Tonic considers the framework woven together by enthusiasts of the Incunabula Papers as a shared enterprise to expand human potential:

By Djinn N' Tonic on June 16, 2001—6:26 pm:

If I had to choose a direction for all of this, I'd say it was about directly applying memetics on a grand cultural canvas to help accelerate evolution. Like a survival tool. Once we apprehend the connections that underly all out false social and psychological constructs, the ones that inhibit our ability to "see", will the

resulting shift in perception cause us to make those intuitive leaps
necessary towards a more holistic existence? While I don't claim this
to be an absolute by any means (and are there really any absolutes
nowadays?), I do think such memetically-inspired intuitive leaps are
in our near-future. Call it a gut feeling if you like.[4]

During the "discussion of events" stage, people attempt to integrate their
interpretations with their personal philosophies. Seeking to explain their
ordeal to others and to themselves, they incorporate their experiences into
their hopes, desires, and dreams, thereby expressing or expanding their
worldviews. This passage in particular recalls the manner in which some
ghost hunters' anxieties about life after death became reduced after they
reflected upon their legend-tripping experiences (proving for them that
one's personality remains regardless of mortality), as Djinn N' Tonic's own
contemplation of his or her experiences seems to have remedied anxieties
over a fragmented present by offering hope for a more "holistic" future.

On the *Dark Planet* message board, the poster Tungsten portrays the
Incunabula Papers as "an infinite game." Important here are the poster's
comments on how others may acquire experiential knowledge of the Incunabula Papers:

By Tungsten on February 14, 2001—10:26 am:

Since there is no goal to this experiment other than the goal of
perpetually discovering new forms and new ways of perceiving, it
is an infinite game. An infinite game is played for the purpose of
continuing play, as opposed to a finite game which is played for the
purpose of winning or defining winners. It is an act of free will. No
one can "play" who is forced to play.

This work endeavors to escape the constancy of numerical boundaries. Whenever persons may walk on or off the field of play as they
wish, there is such a flux of participants that none can emerge as a
clear victor.

The traditional format of the book is one that dictates a posture of
passive reception on the part of the reader. The author is deliver-
ing a monologue (much like the one delivered here) and the reader
is the receiver or passive audience. Even bold experiments like the
cut -up can become an exercise in monologue. To be effective or to

> have real relevance to the reader cut-up must be an act on the part
> of the reader. To discover new ways of perceiving is the responsi-
> bility of the individual. To make it truly experiential cut it up
> yourself! This is not to say that the cut-up discoveries of others
> cannot be a valuable source of information, but why stop there. This
> act could move the reader into a position of becoming a co-author
> or co-conspirator in the process of creation. To conspire literally
> means "to breath together".[5]

Tungsten's statement regarding "co-conspirators in the process of creation" echoes the fact that legend-tripping participants are on equal foot-
ing, each having the potential to share with others their own interpretations, thereby adding their own voices and opinions to the significance of
the narrative and their experiences with it. Here Tungsten seems to fully
acknowledge the value in the final stage of legend-tripping: collectively
ascribing meaning to the experience, however tenable that meaning may
be. The poster claims that this particular form of participation operates
like the Dadaists' cut-up technique, presenting participants with the opportunity to penetrate the marvelous.

Most legend-trips never conclude with an absolute consensus on what
has exactly transpired, though this doesn't quell legend-trippers efforts to
name the experience and to articulate what attracts them to the legend:

By Thyrsus on July 17, 2003—8:15 pm:

> i think the thing as a whole brings with it its own sense of realism,
> wether the event actually took place or not.. for whatever reason,
> as i read the data at deoxy for the first time, i ran abruptly up
> against the very real feeling that these guys had done something...
> just the way they talk about it, there seemingly knowledgeable
> blending of fringe tech and esoteric meditation... like if you can
> describe a thing to that degree and with that amount of precision,
> either its about to burst forth from your mind ufo-like, or you've
> actually acheived it.[6]

Effectively merging the language of "fringe tech" with "esoteric meditation," the Incunabula Papers, according to Thyrsus, presented a bricolage
of ideas in such as way as to effectively give people the tools to presence
the realities depicted therein. And since this bricologe was presented in
such a complete fashion—as an immersive world, the reality of these

ideas seems for the poster not only coherent but also appealing. By describing the Incunabula Papers as being either real or bursting forth "ufo-like," Thyrsus relies on other participants' familiarity with the idea that in its evolution, human consciousness—individual and collective—strives for wholeness (many countercultural thinkers view the UFO phenomenon as an intentionally designed enigma that forces those who study it to resolve its seemingly diametrically opposed attributes, thus forcing the mind toward overcoming its own limitations). Comparatively, this notion echoes the goals of occult writers to successfully create ideational works and the capacity of supernatural legends to successfully describe otherwise indescribable areas of existence (essentially bringing them into being).

A similar theme appears in Joseph Matheny's 2002 book, *Ong's Hat: The Beginning*, wherein the author ascribes an ideational function to the Incunabula Papers:

> *The Incunabula and Ong's Hat are a great mystery. From a different perspective than the Montauk Project saga, they allude and sometimes point directly to truths that demonstrate there is a body of scientific information, which, if accessed and understood, will raise the consciousness of individuals to where they can reach well beyond the constructs of ordinary human consciousness. The description of the books and literature in the Incunabula catalog are designed to raise people's expectations but, more importantly, their curiosity and interest to such matters. Ideally, it will make one ask questions they had not thought of before and make them think, grow, and expand. The documents were not handed out on a platter although they provide a springboard for those seeking further knowledge. Everyone is encouraged to carry out their own investigations of such matters.* [7]

Peter Moon also presents a comparable summary of the Incunabula Papers in his 2004 book, *Synchronicity and the Seventh Seal*. He describes the *Ong's Hat* brochure as a "mythological analogy of different events and circumstances," and considers the *Incunabula* catalogue to be "too big and complex to be dismissed as an ordinary hoax." [8] In the end, Moon identifies the Incunabula Papers as a magical operation with a specific intent. He writes:

> *If man is going to evolve, he has to account for quantum realities and all possibilities that are before him. But, it is not enough to just consider all possibilities at once. That can jam one's mind with too much information*

and will cause an overload that cannot be processed. Insane asylums are filled with beings that cannot process and integrate information. Sometimes those creatures have the right information, but they cannot relate it properly to their current environment. Others refuse to integrate with ordinary reality . . . As Mankind makes its quantum leap, or is forced to cope with the times ahead, he will be dealing with all possibilities and probabilities. At the very least, this means opening the door a little bit to chaos.[9]

Like Djinn N' Tonic, Moon argues that it is necessary to understand complexity—even paradox—in order to adapt to a near future potentially overburdened with information. Moon seems to have some of the same anxieties other participants demonstrate: fears concerning information overload and the uncertainty that the future will bring. And like other Incunabula legend-trippers, Moon too seems to address this angst by collaborating in the circulation of legendry.

A Final Report from the Front

After a prolonged discussion lasting several days, Pahana finally shares answers to the questions, "What can we learn about the Incunabula documents? Most importantly perhaps, what do they insinuate for us and what possibilities do they open to us for action?"

By Pahana on March 30, 2001—11:24 am:

As a result of looking at the documents in the light of some aspects of the older Mystery Traditions we have developed themes and lines of thought that diverge towards a conclusion, one which is continuously evolving. In sort it goes something like this:

• Life is a dynamically evolving system in continuous flux, where all systems have a chance of affecting remote systems directly or indirectly. The ancients recognised the process of the renewal of Nature through death, for example the process of composting. Thus they constructed ideologies including (for example) one interpretation of the Ouroborous serpent - Gurdjeff's Trogoautoegocrat (Eating Myself, I am Renewed). The philosophical ramifications of ideas such as these put human concepts of morality and emotional ideas of 'good' or 'evil' into perspective, as personal tastes and preferences.

• The human mind-body-spirit complex is capable, by its unique method of design, of multiple talents. Yet we use surprisingly few of them, and rarely to their full potential. This is because the human organism is squashed into a box of social constraints and a mistake form of 'education' in order to pass on our knowledge. By creating stability in our lives in this manner, we limit the forward motion that can occur. As creative evolution can only occur as the result of the synthesis of 2 dissimilar ideas, it takes the eternal rebel, the archetypal Prometheus, to bring about many changes.

• The lack of full potential is also due to a poor understanding of the proper way of interfacing the different parts of the human being together. Mystery Schools in the past have traditionally taught concepts on how to obtain non ordinary states of perception, maintenance of the bodies, and subjugation of the body to the inhabiting force we call mind and consciousness. The greater the understanding we have both scientifically and intuitively of the process of life happening inside us, the more we can apply these ideas with the Will to acheiving our results.

These principles are applied in the light of some other facts - first, the teachings of the traditions on refining the attention faculty and modifying the effects of the Will or perception via various methods. Secondly, our desire to reach a specific goal - whether it be a Siddha or simply good health.

But there is more to it than this. Concepts such as 'desire demands the other', sex as a tool to higher consciousness rather than a degradation of it, and so on. In a way the authors of these documents, whether they wanted to or not, opened up a Pandora's box when they wove the many counter-culture elements together within it. In the vast world of routers, switches and hubs it has developed a life of its own. What I see in it may differ from yours, mileage may vary.

What I see is an invitation to a unification of science, religion, culture and such. Unification into a new 'uncommon sense' where Truth and truth are wed. Our science has a lot it could teach spiritualism, and vice versa, spiritualism has a lot it could teach materialism. All that is required is an unbiased outlook and a desire to learn what tangible phenomena we are talking of when we say 'energy' or 'aura' or 'vibe' (for example).

. . .

In summary, I think its become clear what the goal of Incunabula is
and now its time to implement and live it. Whether or not this is
merely a reflection of my own inner state I don't know, but it certainly feels to be correct. The need is to unify science, religion
and culture and redefine the way we interact to become more liberating
rather than restricting, according to our own tastes. Liberation has
been a continuous theme in the mysteries, and perhaps the Masons can
be forgiven by us for helping the Luciferian forces, for co-creation
with the all powerful Fire is exactly our goal.[10]

Pahana focuses on two themes adult legend-trippers commonly discuss at
the culmination of a legend-trip: the philosophical implications of the experiences, and the differences and similarities between the interpretations
participants have. Through a process of negotiation, participants in this
or any other legend-trip regularly incorporate each other's explanations
to achieve a synthesis of ideas pertaining to the nature of events occurring during the ritual. This isn't to say that everyone who posted on the
message boards in which the Incunabula legend-trip occurs shared in this
sense of community. But those who posted regularly and who interacted
with other posters usually demonstrated an openness to others' conclusions, regularly even borrowing others' ideas.

Rather than represent an end to the Ong's Hat research, the posts I've
gathered here show that the final stage in legend-trips can renew the
entire process. However, just as the popularity of many legends rise and
fall with the tides of need and desire, the Incunabula Papers eventually
receded for a time, undermined by the arrival of the ARG.

9. CONCLUSION

A Majestic End

On July 31, 2001, a commercial alternate reality game called *Majestic*, inspired by the "Majestic 12" documents allegedly written by a highly secretive insider group privy to information regarding the U.S. Government's relationship with UFOs, made its debut. As part of the effort to conceal the fact that it was a game, *Majestic* incorporated real conspiracy-based websites in its gaming narrative. It also developed fictional materials that real-world conspiracy theorists absorbed into their own narratives, not realizing these materials had been designed for an ARG. The summer of 2001 also introduced *The Beast,* and some Incunabula participants were concered that these new, interactive yet commercialized forms of storytelling appeared to mimic the very nature of the Incunabula legend complex. This struck Incunabula enthusiasts as antithetical to their own endeavors:

By Harla Quinn on May 4, 2001—8:28 am:

. . .

```
Here are a few related topics that I would like to see bounced around
to get a better overall perspective.

[1] Viral Marketing Campaigns
As if the Majestic spoof/conspiracy game scenario isn't "lame" enough
in its creation of hoax web-sites and the spread of disinformation of
false conspiracies on an already overloaded disinfo network we call
the "World Wide Web", now we have the latest scam from none other
than the Hollywood crowd who has finally "caught up" with the meme-
meisters - viral marketing memes disguised as interactive/immersive
games and conspiracy theory based on Bayseian network theory.
```

As a part of one of the "most complex viral movie marketing campaigns ever created", nearly 40 fake websites are devoted to promoting "revolution" and the liberation of artificial intelligence "slaves" (formerly known as Robby Robots) and the related murder of a man named Evan Chan. But the sites aren't linked to a cult or militia group but to a new movie soon to be released entitled "AI" which was originally devised by Stanley Kubrick of "2001 A Space Odessey" fame.

. . .

Here's the scary part:
"But what's so amazing is that the websites seem to be changing their narrative to interact with us. They're watching us, and they know what we're doing."

So, Dante was quite correct in his assessment that the use of Beyesian theories have now been appropriated by the marketing crowd. Everytime you view one of these sites, not only do you get "cookies", your IP information and who knows what other information which can be gleaned about you is being accumulated and stored. What's the upside and the downside? Worst case scenario? Is it too outlandish an idea that through the use of this information they are seeking to, in effect, give 'sentience' to an AI/bot of their own creation?

. . .

What we've been hitting hard over and over again is the use of memes, conspiracy theories, cut-ups, etc. to "entrain the brain" to achieve altered states of cognitive perception and to expand consciousness to a higher state of awareness. I think for most of us, the means to achieve a greater self awareness and self-realization. Conversely, the use and effectiveness of this burgeoning methodology is nothing short of mind control.

The immersive adventure surrounding the Incunabula Papers constitutes a folk practice of a rather small group of people. When the techniques of this practice appeared to be usurped by corporate institutions without an interest in the expansion of consciousness, many Ong's Hat enthusiasts considered it sacrilege. This isn't unlike the frustration experienced by Spiritualists when their séances became solely a source of entertainment or even the indignation expressed by various ethnic groups when adherents of "New Age" beliefs freely borrow their religious customs.

A few days after *Majestic* officially launched, Incunabula-related message boards received the following post from someone claiming to be Matheny:

By Matheny on August 9, 2001—3:32 am:

```
Open letter to conspiracy community
Nick and I decided today to publicly announce in the near future
that the Ong's Hat Project has now concluded. We will be contacting
Peter L. Wilson as well and see if he'd like to make a statement. I
think it would still make a good book from a cultural anthropology
perspective, your call.
My program has finished running and I am being recalled from duty.
I think we were successful in laying the groundwork for the coming
change. The gateways are open now.
I am glad to finally be myself again: 7:37 PM PST.
PS: This is not a joke.
The Real Joe Matheny
AKA/ Michael Kelly¹
```

An "Official Statement" soon followed this post:

August 14, 2001—11:47 pm:

```
Ong's Hat Tantric Egg Research Center
was a necessary ruse for deflecting
attention from our real project--
to open up your conduits, brother and sisters,
to rip off the confining condom of language and
to Fuck Nature Unprotected.
Doctor Jabir
Public Relations
Quantum Tantra
Huh? I think I was mind controlled...
What eBook?
Joseph Matheny
Incunabula Research Center
Fuck Off!
Peter L. Wilson
AKA
```

```
Hakim Bey
Don't, don't!
Don't unplug me!
EmoryBot 3.0
(unplugged)
Permission to repost
Copyleft 2001
```

By calling an end to this "project," Matheny actually adds yet another
layer to the legend complex, having become a central character in the
legend himself. Together with the second post, the "Official Statement,"
purportedly signed by the very people once thought to have been most influential in the early stages of the phenomenon (including EmoryBot 3.0,
which, according to Peter Moon, was an artificial intelligence program),
Matheny's statement elicited the following responses.[2]

By Rev. Justin on August 15, 2001—00:51 am:

```
Gee
IT
dIdn't
work...
```

By Parsifal on August 15, 2001—1:07 am:

```
That's it?!?? I was hoping the official statement would tell us fi-
nally, once and for all, who(individual, group, or interdimensional
entity) wrote the pamphlet!????!!
```

By Rev. Justin on August 15, 2001—1:12 am:

```
Not only that, old Joe or whoever didn't seem to "Fuck nature un-
protected" in my book. Basically if that is the end of the whole
Incunabula phenomenon then with the selling of the e-books, Joe is
nothing more than a profitable Macroteleport. Offering nothing more
than "art"! Disappointing...[3]
```

By Parsifal on August 15, 2001—1:30 am:

```
It ain't the "end of the whole Incunabula phenomenon". I am still
holding a few aces up my sleeves, anybody else holding cards who
```

wants to continue playing the "game"? We could keep this "game" going
forever. Hell, it will keep going by itself forever anyway.

By Sparky on August 15, 2001—3:26 pm:

I'm still in. Still holding onto my pat hand.
However, comma, I still have no idea who the 'Deep Throat' char-
acter is in this game. He has introduced some new twists into the
adventure.
To me, the game is still on!
Who needs Majestic?
This is one hell of a game!

By Djinn N' Tonic on August 15, 2001—5:50 pm:

The game is still on, the empire never died, the egg is neither here
nor there (not until the observer opens his/her eyes) & I once knew
the secrets of the universe & all of creation until the acid wore
off. Who wants to cut the deck? Who wants to deal?

By Caustic Gnostic on August 15, 2001—10:17 pm:

Hey Sparky,

I'm with ya. Alternate worlds are out there. What I think is being
missed here is how the vortex influxes aether into space-time causing gravity. But what is moving in the vortex is consciousness - a
baseline phenomena present throughout the universe.

The question is really how one breaks the light speed barrier and
figures how to thus move matter from one light speed barrier (or dimension) to the next, as well as how to navigate outside space-time.

This may not require extra technology to pull off; it may be possible
in body. Perhaps technologically speaking what is needed is a way to
affect matter via sympathetic resonant vibration. What do ya think?

By Mooncat on August 16, 2001—6:24 pm:

and now its time to abandon and nuclear destruct all the magick
modules and return our ships to commercial service
commercial towing vehicle Mooncat reports final jettisons

By Harla Quinn on August 17, 2001—00:17 am:

> Interesting responses....I'm amazed...Parcifal still has a few
> "cards" up his sleeve; Sparky is still holding a pat hand; Djinn's
> looking for a dealer; Caustic Gnostic knows about alternative uni-
> verses????? OK... tell me more.... GO Fish....(hehehe)
>
> Hey, no matter what everyone's interpretation of the "official state-
> ment", the themes and science have a helluva lot of validity - I think
> EVERYONE here knows that which is why you are HERE and not joining
> in the chorus line elsewhere - and my efforts toward untangling the
> quantum entanglement question for me doesn't end with an 'announce-
> ment'. As Djinn probably knows (though I'm not trying to speak for
> ya, babe) there's a LOT going on beneath the surface and the "best"
> we can hope for from the recent exodus is that there won't be anymore
> disruption underfoot. (Jeez....I was hoping that until I got hit with
> all thse bugs...) The Majestic gamers will look for their clues and
> move on to the next level. The newbies and naysayers will point and
> laugh and pat themselves on the back that they "got it". (snicker)
> All that serves to clear the board - which is fine by me.
>
> Djinn, you termed it very well: "..the current change" is upon us...
> and there's more to come.
> . . .[4]

Most of the immediate responses to the "Official Statement" argue for continued research into the Incunabula Papers, a shared practice with specific
rules governed by an online community. Harla Quinn quickly addresses
many of the participants by their screen names, claiming that the only
people who will take the "Official Statement" to heart are the "Majestic
gamers"—those who don't really understand the dynamic undertaking of
Incunabula Papers research. Rather than view the "Official Statement" as
detrimental, Harla Quinn announces that it will have a positive effect: it
will remove those who don't fully appreciate and participate in this "open
conspiracy," leaving unfettered those community members who continue
to practice authentic research by seeking out noble spiritual truths.

Though Matheny's posts did little to interfere with the legend-trip,
what did have an adverse effect was the popularity of ARGs. Shortly after
the general public caught wind of *The Beast* and *Majestic*, *Dark Planet's*
message boards closed down and were archived, and Incunabula-related

conversations on *The Deoxyribonucleic Hyperdimension* and *Harqalya* sites all but stopped. The fact that many began to assume they had been playing an ARG without realizing it lead to a disinterest in pursuing what was previously promoted to be a life-changing immersive mystery but what suddenly seemed to be little more than an outlet for entertainment, or perhaps a greed-motivated hoax. A few of the more dedicated Incunabula participants did continue to seek out the philosophies and magical ideas promoted by the legend complex, although growing efforts to actively debunk the Incunabula Papers as an ARG all but ruined participants' efforts to collectively presence and sustain the environment within which the legend could expand. Some, like Denny Unger (a.k.a. DarkPlanetOnline), attempted to put together a defense against the idea that the phenomenon was little more than an ARG, rallying around the factuality of the legend complex, much like Spiritualists gathered to defend spirit photos:

> *Ong's Hat/Incunabula has always been about levels of understanding. As you research each aspect of the story you are presented with a challenge. That challenge is usually based on twisting and distorting your belief systems. For example: You find a piece of compelling info that takes you down one path only to find that its a invalid path but wait . . . it turns out that the path you thought was a false path is actually the correct path and so on, and so forth. This is the dance of the Incunabula. Destroying rational assumptions of what is true and what is false.*[5]

Regardless of the efforts put forth by Unger and others, the Ong's Hat and Incunabula message boards were slowly abandoned.

The Living Book Shows Signs of Life

While the Incunabula Papers faded from the spotlight, the legend complex of the Montauk Project began to grow in popularity, due in part to the writings and lectures of Preston Nichols and Peter Moon, and through the publications of Moon's company, Sky Books Publishing (their adage: "Where Science Fiction Meets Reality"). While the Montauk Project contains many thematic similarities to the Incunabula Papers, including the existence of alternate dimensions and the enhancement of perceptual abilities, it also included more specifically political material. The Montauk Project explicitly accuses the U.S. Government of concealing an extraterrestrial existence and of conducting mind-control experiments at the Fort

Hero Air Force Base in Montauk, Long Island. Eventually, the Montauk Project narrative began to incorporate ever more references to the Ong's Hat story, which, after a time, introduced and reintroduced people to the Incunabula Papers.

By Anonymous Poster #833 on August 10, 2005—1:12 pm:

> I was super-into Incunabula maybe 4 or 5 years ago, but dropped it
> when I read the debunking solution, but now I'm back after having
> read the first 2 Montauk books (Montauk Project and Montauk Revisited)
> and I'm not 100% sure what to make of it.[6]

Some people began to see the Incunabula Papers in a different light, and others, like the poster below, happened upon the vestiges of the Incunabula Papers message boards, lurking about them much as they would a haunted house:

By abernathy #841 on January 5, 2006—8:09 am:

> I've only just found this site. I'm fascinated, drawn and completely
> aghast. I obviously need to catch up further on the topics involved,
> realising now, that many of you have spent a considerable amount
> of time and effort involved in it. I make no judgement, only in my-
> self for not having any of the background knowledge to keep up with
> such incredible claims and speculations. Some of the contributors
> seem pseudo-scientific, some pseudo-spiritual (even zealots) There's
> purported links with space-time, the military, satanists, god and
> countless dead people whose lives and truths are, quite possibly,
> corrupted wholesale by the depth of un-substantiated cross referenc-
> ing and speculation. Are we in control? Should god (whatever that is)
> be in control, have you done too many trips and can we time travel in
> a diamond-shaped craft with Crowley and crew? Phew, guys and gals!
> that's tortuous. Interdimensional, psycho-spiritual soap wars, I
> love it. Off now to do some background.[7]

Many contemporary legend complexes are constructed and transmitted via websites that combine various subjects like the supernatural, magic, psychic phenomena, and conspiracy theories under a common heading: "the unexplained." The Incunabula legend complex persists online through archives, but just as other legends change over time, it has transformed through the years, merging with other legend complexes. Its influences can be seen today, especially on online forums devoted to the unexplained, where conversations about alternative realities, memes, and myth-making systems are increasingly commonplace. This community supports and contributes to publishing houses like Sky Books which promote the interpretation of everyday experiences in accordance with the frameworks provided by legends.

Some Final Thoughts

Legend-trippers concurrently discover and create, or perhaps more correctly, *perform into being,* liminal realms bordering between fantasy and reality. Through these performances, people may enter what the anthropologist Charles Whitehead has called "a theatre of mind," a reflexive vantage point permitting play with constructs of belief.[8] When legend-tripping, people draw upon various interpretive frames tailored from supernaturalism to occasion non-ordinary or extraordinary experiences. Anyone may see strange lights in the sky, glimpse a shadow moving in the corner of an old abandoned house, hear odd noises coming from the attic, or even feel mystically interconnected online. But once such an experience is recounted, and once this telling draws upon supernatural legendry to contextualize the experience during a legend-telling performance, it then immediately becomes part of a broader legend complex. In the case of legend-tripping, experience is instantly and irrevocably part of the tradition that instigated it.

New configurations of media and communication technologies facilitate diverse modes of framing and transmitting both experience and tradition. For instance, supernaturally themed entertainment, notable with films such as *The Blair Witch Project, Paranormal Activity,* and *The Fourth Kind,* exploits the presentational form of legends to engage audiences. These films are introduced as portrayals of actual events, though their plots and characters are entirely fictional (the first two films deal with demonic powers, the third, alien abductions—*The Fourth Kind* is actually a fictionalization of a fictionalization claimed and marketed as real). Furthermore, fictional websites developed as marketing campaigns support the films' ostensible realism (in the case of *The Blair Witch Project* and *The Fourth Kind*) to offer audiences an immersive experience; sometimes these films and their accompanying marketing tactics lead people to actually believe that the reality presented is factual. Legends have long provided thematic content for entertainment media, but now their presentational qualities increasingly supply the form of entertainment as well. Conversely, entertainment media have long produced supernatural characters and plots and have long publicized hoaxes and fabrications that become incorporated into legend-telling events.[9]

One finds within the labyrinth of UFO tales numerous legend reconfigurations and ostensive acts, which are at least partially due to the fact that UFO legends comprise the most thoroughly mediated form of legendry. Beginning in the early 1940s, subscriptions to the pulp magazine *Amazing Stories* soared after its editor, Raymond A. Palmer, began including allegedly "true" stories written by Richard Shaver, who claimed to have once been imprisoned by the "deros," a race of degenerate aliens living deep under the earth in honeycombed, antediluvian tunnels. According to Shaver, deros traveled in spaceships and took great delight in abducting and torturing humans; they also plagued mankind by projecting three-dimensional holograms of terrifying images. After Shaver's stories were published, an avalanche of unsolicited letters reporting personal experiences with the deros crashed upon the *Amazing Stories* office. Many of these letters were printed in the magazine, and the "Letters-to-the-Editor" section beccame a medium for ongoing communal storytelling sessions that were often ostensive in nature. Below is one such contribution, originally printed in 1946:

Sirs:

I flew my last combat mission on May 26 [1945] when I was shot up over Bassein and ditched my ship in Ramaree roads off Chedubs Island. I was missing five days. I requested leave at Kashmere [sic]. I and Capt. (deleted by request) left Srinagar and went to Rudok then through the Khese pass to the northern foothills of the Karakoram. We found what we were looking for. We knew what we were searching for.
For heaven's sake, drop the whole thing! You are playing with dynamite. My companion and I fought our way out of a cave with submachine guns. I have two 9" scars on my left arm that came from wounds given me in the cave when I was 50 feet from a moving object of any kind and in perfect silence. The muscles were nearly ripped out. How? I don't know. My friend has a hole the size of a dime in his right bicep. It was seared inside. How we don't know. But we both believe we know more about the Shaver Mystery than any other pair.
You can imagine my fright when I picked up my first copy of Amazing Stories and see you splashing words about the subject.[10]

This account is similar to so many other contemporary memorates that pervade and promote legends and legend complexes; by testifying to the truth of the legend while concurrently warning others of the dangers inherent in this truth, others become thrilled by the legend, leading them to further investigate it. Legends about UFOs and their occupants continue to evolve principally though cottage-industry publishing houses, esoteric specialty magazines, television shows, radio programs, and websites. What's more, people now promote various methods—from devising technological instruments, to visiting specific sites, to conducting elaborate magical rites and meditations—to induce alien contact.

Legend-tripping is more about exploiting the affective qualities of ostensive performances than proving the objective existence of the supernatural. The process of interpretive drift that occurs throughout the stages of legend-tripping is important because it moves participants toward belief in the legend. This doesn't imply that people always end up literally believing in the story or the legend's past accounts—what it does mean is that by ostensively participating in the legend, people, at the very least, contribute to and believe in the legend's reality as a social phenomenon. Technologies of communication have contributed to a cultural condition in which such ostensive acts no longer merely invite a supernatural experience, but instead supply artifacts that give breadth to legend complexes. Records of ostensive performances endure through photographs, audio and video footage, message boards, and the printed word—these artifacts add dimensions to legend complexes and can be recontextualized for future legend complexes. Whereas supernatural legends once depicted the intrusion of supernatural realities into the everyday, now they equally convey the incursion of the everyday into the supernatural. Communication technologies allow us to see more clearly how the reciprocity between experience and tradition results in the ongoing construction of what we call the supernatural.

With this present work, I've attempted to showcase not only online legend-tripping, but the synergy between experience and tradition; and the creative impulses, both individual and communal, behind supernatural folklore. Undoubtedly, as innovative technologies continue to present new mediated environments and new platforms for entertainment, the forms and functions of legend-trips will continue to evolve.

Two of the following appendices consist of *Ong's Hat: Gateway to the Dimensions! A Full Color Brochure for the Institute of Chaos Studies and the Moorish Science Ashram in Ong's Hat, New Jersey* (Appendix 2) and *Incunabula: A Catalogue of Rare Books, Manuscripts & Curiosa—Conspiracy Theory, Frontier Science & Alternative Worlds* (Appendix 3). Both of these anonymously written documents emerged out of the mail art movement sometime in the late 1980s to early 1990s.

Each of these documents can be found on numerous websites. Versions of the documents presented here were gathered from *The Deoxyribonucleic Hyperdimension* (www.deoxy.org) on December 4, 2005. Grammatical errors are left "as is," and I've only reproduced the text of these documents, not the few accompanying illustrations. I'd recommend any party interested in these works to look at different online sources for possible variation in both texts and contexts, as well as refer to Joseph Matheny's 2002 book, *Ong's Hat: The Beginning.* The rich assortment of content within the following works is futuristic, bewildering, inspiring, nonsensical, and, at times, poetic.

Key to "Incunabula Papers" and "Ong's Hat" Referents

Incunabula Papers: Collectively refers to both the *Ong's Hat: Gateway to the Dimensions! A Full Color Brochure for the Institute of Chaos Studies and the Moorish Science Ashram in Ong's Hat, New Jersey* document, and the *Incunabula: A Catalogue of Rare Books, Manuscripts & Curiosa—Conspiracy Theory, Frontier Science & Alternative Worlds* document. Also refers to the discourse and performance surrounding these documents.

Incunabula: A Catalogue: Shorthand for *Incunabula: A Catalogue of Rare Books, Manuscripts & Curiosa—Conspiracy Theory, Frontier Science & Alternative Worlds*.

The Incunabula Papers: Ong's Hat and Other Gateways to New Dimensions: 1999 CD-ROM electronic book written by Joseph Matheny.

Ong's Hat: Refers to the Incunabula Papers as well as the discourse and performances surrounding these documents. Also the name of the ghost town mentioned in the legend complex.

Ong's Hat: Gateway: Shorthand for *Ong's Hat: Gateway to the Dimensions! A Full Color Brochure for the Institute of Chaos Studies and the Moorish Science Ashram in Ong's Hat, New Jersey*.

Ong's Hat: The Beginning: 2002 book written by Joseph Matheny.

ONG'S HAT: GATEWAY TO THE DIMENSIONS!

A full color brochure for the Institute of Chaos Studies and the Moorish Science Ashram in Ong's Hat, New Jersey.

YOU WOULD NOT BE READING THIS ARTICLE if you had not already penetrated half-way to the ICS. You have been searching for us without knowing it, following oblique references in crudely xeroxed marginal samizdat publications, crackpot mystical pamphlets, mail-order courses in "Kaos Magick"—a paper trail and a coded series of rumors spread at street level through circles involved in the illicit distribution of certain controlled substances and the propagation of certain acts of insurrection against the Planetary Work Machine and the Consensus Reality—or perhaps through various obscure mimeographed technical papers on the edges of "chaos science"—through pirate computer networks—or even through pure synchronicity and the pursuit of dreams. In any case we know something about you, your interests, deeds and desires, works and days—and we know your address. Otherwise...you would not be reading this.

Background

During the 1970s and '80s, "chaos" began to emerge as a new scientific paradigm, on a level of importance with Relativity and Quantum Mechanics. It was born out of the mixing of many different sciences—weather prediction, Catastrophe Theory, fractal geometry, and the rapid development of computer graphics capable of plunging into the depths of fractals and "strange attractors; "hydraulics and fluid turbulence, evolutionary biology, mind/brain studies and psychopharmacology also played major roles in forming the new paradigm. The slogan "order out of chaos" summed up the gist of this science, whether it studied the weird fractional-dimensional shapes underlying sworls of cigarette smoke or the distribution of colors in marbled paper—or else dealt with "harder" matters such as heart fibrillation, particle beams or population vectors. However, by the late '80s it began to appear as if this "chaos movement" had split apart into two opposite and hostile world-views, one placing emphasis on chaos itself, the other on *order*. According to the latter sect—the Determinists—chaos was the enemy, randomness a force to be overcome or denied. They experienced the new science as a final vindication of Classical Newtonian physics, and as a weapon to be used *against* chaos, a tool to map and predict reality itself. For them, chaos was death and disorder, entropy and waste. The opposing faction however experienced chaos as something benevolent, the necessary matrix out of which arises spontaneously an infinity of variegated forms—a pleroma rather than an abyss—a principle of continual creation, unstructured, fecund, beautiful, spirit of wildness. These scientists saw chaos theory as vindication of Quantum indeterminacy and Godel's Proof, promise of an open-ended universe, Cantorian infinities of potential...chaos as *health*.

Easy to predict which of these two schools of thought would receive vast funding and support from governments, multi-nationals and intelligence agencies. By the end of the decade, "Quantum/Chaos" had been forced underground, virtually censored by prestigious scientific journals —which published only papers by Determinists. The dissidents were reduced to the level of the *margin*—and there they found themselves part of yet another branch of the paradigm, the underground of cultural chaos—the "magicians"—and of political chaos-extremist anti-authoritarian "mutants".

Unlike Relativity, which deals with the Macrocosm of outer space, and Quantum, which deals with the Microcosm of particle physics, chaos science takes place largely within the Mesosphere—the world as we experience it in "everyday life," from dripping faucets to banners flapping in the autumn breezes. Precisely for this reason useful experimental work in chaos can be carried on without the hideous expense of cyclotrons and orbital observatories. So even when the leading theoreticians of Quantum/Chaos began to be fired from university and corporate positions, they were still able to pursue certain goals. Even when they began to suffer political pressures as well, and sought refuge and space among the mutants and marginals, still they persevered. By a paradox of history, their poverty and obscurity forced them to narrow the scope of their research to precisely those areas which would ultimately produce concrete results—pure math, and the mind—simply because these areas were relatively inexpensive.

Up until the crash of '87, the "alternative network" amounted to little more than a nebulous weave of pen-pals and computer enthusiasts, Whole Earth nostalgists, futurologists, anarchists, food cranks, neo-pagans and cultists, self-publishing punk poets, armchair schizophrenics, survivalists and mail artists. The Crash however opened vast but hard-to-see cracks in the social and economic control structures of America. Gradually the marginals and mutants began to fill up those fissures with the wegs of their own networking. Bit by bit they created a genuine black economy, as well as a shifting insubstantial "autonomous zone", impossible to map but real enough in its various manifestations. The orphaned scientists of Q/C theory fell into this invisible anti-empire like a catalyst—or perhaps it was the other way around. In either case, something crystallized. To explain the precipitation of this jewel, we must move on to the specific cases, people and stories.

History

The Moorish Orthodox Church of America is an offshoot of the Moorish Science Temple, the New World's first Islamic heretical sect, founded by a black circus magician named Noble Drew Ali in Newark, New Jersey in 1913. In the 1950s some white jazz musicians and poets who held "passports" in the M.S.T. founded the Moorish Orthodox Church, which also traced its spiritual ancestry to various "Wandering Bishops" loosely affiliated with the Old Catholic Church and schisms of Syrian Orthodoxy. In the '60s the church acquired a new direction from the Psychedelic Movement, and for a while maintained a presence at Timothy Leary's commune in Millbrook, New York.

At the same time the discovery of sufism led certain of its members to undertake journeys to the East. One of these Americans, known by the Moorish name Wali Fard, traveled for years in India, Perisa, and Afghanistan, where he collected an impressive assortment of exotic initiations: Tantra in Calcutta, from an old member of the Bengali Terrorist Party; sufism from the Ovayssi Order in Shiraz, which rejects all human masters and insists on visionary experience; and finally, in the remote Badakhshan Province of Afghanistan, he converted to an archaic form of Ismailism (the so-called Assassins) blended out of Buddhist Yab-Yum teachings, indigenous shamanic sorcery and extremist Shiite revolutionary philosophy—worshippers of the *Umm al-kitab,* the "Matrix Book." Up until the Soviet invasion of Afghanistan and the reactionary orthodox "revolution" in Iran, Fard carried on trade in carpets and other well-known Afghan exports. When history forced him to return to America in 1978, he was able to launder his savings by purchasing about 200 acres of land in the New Jersey Pine Barrens. Around the turn of the decade he moved into an old rod & gun club on the property along with several runaway boys from Paramus, New Jersey, and an anarchist lesbian couple from Brooklyn, and founded the Moorish Science Ashram. Through the early-to-mid-'80s the commune's fortunes fluctuated (sometimes nearly flickering out). Fard self-published a series of xeroxed "Visionary Recitals" in which he attempted a synthesis of heretical and antinomian spirituality, post-Situationist politics, and chaos science.

After the Crash, a number of destitute Moors and synpathizers began turning up at the Ashram seeking refuge. Among them were two young chaos scientists recently fired from Princeton (on a charge of "seditious nonsense"), a brother and sister, Frank and Althea Dobbs. The Dobbs twins spent their early childhood on a UFO-cult commune in rural Texas, founded by their father, a retired insurance salesman who was murdered by rogue disciples during a revival in California. One might say that the siblings had a head start in chaos—and the Ashram's modus vivendi suited them admirably. (The Pine Barrens have often been called "a perfect place for a UFO landing.") They settled into an old Airstream trailer and constructed a crude laboratory in a rebuilt barn hidden deep in the Pines. Illegal sources of income were available from agricultural projects, and the amorphous community took shape around the startling breakthroughs made by the Dobbs twins during the years around the end of the decade. As undergraduates at the University of Texas the siblings had produced a series of equations which, they felt certain, contained the seeds of a new science they called "cognitive chaos." Their dismissal from Princeton followed their attempt to submit these theorems, along with a theoretical/philosophical system built upon them, as a joint PhD thesis. On the assumption that brain activity can be modeled as a "fractal universe," an outre' topology interfacing with both random and determined forces, the twins' theorems showed that consciousness itself could be presented as a set of "strange attractors" (or "patterns of chaos") around which specific neuronal activity would organize itself. By a bizarre synthesis of Mandelbrot and Cantor, they "solved the problem" of n-dimensional attractors, many of which they were able to generate on Princeton's powerful computers before their hasty departure. While realizing the ultimately indeterminate nature of these "mind maps," they felt that by attaining a thorough (non-intuitive and intuitive) grasp of the actual *shapes* of the attractors, one could "ride with chaos" somewhat as a "lucid dreamer" learns to contain and direct the process of REM sleep. Their aborted thesis suggested a boggling array of benefits which might accrue from such from such links between cybernetic processes and awareness itself, including the exploration of the brain's unused capacities, awareness of the morphogentic field and thus conscious control of autonomic functions, mind-directed repair of tissue at the cellular/genetic level (control over most diseases and the aging process), and even a direct perception of the Heisenbergian behavior of matter (a process they called "surfing the wave function"). Their thesis advisor told them that even the most modest of these proposals would suffice for their expungement from the Graduate Faculty—and if the whole concept (including theorems) were not such obvious lunacy, he would have reported them to the FBI as well.

Two more scientists—already residents of Ong's Hat—joined with Fard and the twins in founding the Institute of Chaos studies. By sheer "chance" their work provided the perfect counterparts to the Dobbs' research. Harold Acton, an expatriate British computer (and reality-hacker, had already linked 64 second-hand personal computers into a vast ad-hoc system based on his own I Ching oriented speculations. And Martine Kallikak, a native of the Barrens from nearby Chatsworth, had set up a machine shop. Ironically, Martine's ancestors once provided guinea pigs for a notorious study in eugenics carried out in the 1920s at the Vineland NJ State Home for the Insane. Published as a study in "heredity and feeblemindness," the work proclaimed poverty, non-ordinary sexuality, reluctance to hold a steady job, and enjoyment of intoxicants as *proofs* of genetic decay—and thus made a lasting contribution to the legend of bizarre and Lovecraftian Piney backwoodspeople, incestuous hermits of the bogs. Martine had long since proven herself a *bricoleuse,* electronics buff and back-lot inventor of great genius and artistry. With the arrival of the Dobbs twins, she discovered her *tre metier'* in the realization of various devices for the implementation of their proposed experiments.

The synergy level at the ICS exceeded all expectations. Contacts with other underground experts in various related fields were maintained by "black modem" as well as personal visits to the Ashram. The spiritual rhythms permeating the place proved ideal: periods of dazed lazy contemplation and applied hedonics alternating with "peak" bursts of self-overcoming activity and focused attention. The hodgepodge of "Moorish Science" (Tantra, Sufism, Ismaili esotericism, alchemy and psychopharmacology, bio-feedback and "brain machine" meditation techniques, etc.) seemed to harmonize in unexpectedly fruitful ways with the "pure" science of the ICS. Under these conditions progress proved amazingly swift, stunning even the Institutes founders. Within a year major advances had been made in all the fields predicted by the equations. Somewhat more than three years after founding there occurred **the** breakthrough, the discovery which served to re-orient our entire project in a new direction: the Gate. But to explain the Gate we must retrace some steps, and reveal exactly the purposes and goals of the ICS and Moorish Science Ashram - the curriculum upon which our activities are based, and which constitutes our *raison d'etre*.

The Curriculum

The original and still ultimate concern of our community is the enhancement of consciousness and consequent enlargement of mental, emotional and psychic activities. When the Ashram was founded by W. Fard the only means available for this work were the bagful of oriental and occultist meditational techniques he had learned in Central Asia, the first-generation "mind machines" developed during the '80s, and the resources of exotic pharmacology. With the first successes of the Dobbs twin's research, it became obvious to us that the spiritual knowledge of the Ashramites could be re-organized into a sort of preparatory course of training for workers in "Cognitive Chaos." This does not mean we surrendered our original purpose - attainment of non-ordinary consciousness - but simply that ICS work could be viewed as a prolongation and practical application of the Ashram work. The theorems allow us to re-define "self liberation" to include physical self-renewal and life-extension as well as the exploration of material reality which (we maintain) remains *one* with the reality of consciousness. In this project, the kind of awareness fostered by meditational techniques plays a part just as vital as the *techne'* of machines and the pure mentation of mathematics. In this scenario, the theorems—or at least a philosophical understanding of them—serve the purpose of an abstract *icon* for contemplation. Thus the theorems can be absorbed or englobed to the point where they become part of the inner structure (or "deep grammar") of the mind itself.

In the first stage, intellectual comprehension of the theorems parallels spiritual work aimed at refining the faculty of *attention*. At the same time a kind of psychic anchor is constructed, a firm grounding in celebratory body-awareness. The erotic and sensual for us cannot be ritualized and aimed at anything "higher" than themselves—rather, they constitute the very *ground* on which our dance is performed, and the atmosphere or *taste* which permeates or whole endeavor. We symbolize this first course of work by the tripartite Sanskrit term *satchitananda*, "Being/consciousness/ bliss" - the ontological level symbolized by the theorems, the psychological level by the meditation, the level of joy by our "tantrik" activity.

The second course (which can begin at any time during or after the first) involves practical instruction in a variety of "hard sciences," especially evolutionary biology and genetics, brain physiology, Quantum Mechanics and computer hacking. We have no need for these disciplines in any academic sense—in fact our work has already overturned many existing paradigms in these fields and rendered the textbooks useless for our purposes—so we have tailored these courses specifically for relevance to our central concern, and jettisoned everything extraneous.

At this point a Fellow of the ICS is prepared for work with the device we call the "egg." This consists of a modified sensory-deprivation chamber in which attention can be focused on a computer terminal and screen. Electrodes are taped to various body parts to provide physiological data which is fed into the computer. The explorer now dons a peculiar helmet, a highly sophisticated fourth-generation version of the early "brain machines," which can sonically stimulate brain cells either globally or locally and in various combinations, thus directing not only "brain waves" but also highly specific mental-physical functions. The helmet is also plugged into the computer and provides feedback in various programmed ways. The explorer now undertakes a series of exercises in which the theorems are used to generate graphic animations of the "strange attractors" which map various states of consciousness, setting up feedback loops between this "iconography" and the actual states themselves, which are in turn generated through the helmet simultaneously with their representation on the screen. Certain of these exercises involve the "alchemical" use of mind-active drugs, including new vasopressin derivatives, beta-endorphins and hallucinogens (usually in "threshold" dosages). Some of these tinctures are simply to provide active-relaxation and focused-attention states, others are specifically linked to the requirements of "Cognitive Chaos" research.

Even in the earliest and crudest stages of the egg's development the ICS founders quickly realized that many of the Dobbs twins' PhD thesis predictions might be considered cautious or conservative. Enhanced control of autonomous body functions was attained even in the second-generation version, and the third provided a kind of bathysphere capable of "diving down" even to the cellular level. Certain unexpected side-effects included phenomena usually classified as paranormal. We knew we were not hallucinating all this, quite bluntly, because we obtained concrete and measurable results, not only in terms of "yogic powers" (such as suspended animation, "inner heat," lucid dreaming and the like) but also in observable benefits to health: rapid healing, remission of chronic conditions, *absence of disease.*

At this point in development of the egg (third generation) the researchers attempted to "descend" (like SciFi micronauts) to the Quantum level.

Perhaps the thorniest of all Quantum paradoxes involves the "collapse of the wave function"—the state of Schrödinger's famous cat. When does a wave "become" a particle? At the moment of observation? If so does this implicate human consciousness in the actual Q-structure of reality itself? By observing do we in effect "create?" The ICS team's ultimate dream was to "ride the wave" and actually experience (rather than merely observe) the function-collapse. Through "participation" in Q-events, it was hoped that the observer/observed duality could be overcome or evaded. This hope was based on rather "orthodox" Copenhagian interpretations of Quantum reality. After some months of intensive work, however, no one had experienced the sought-for and expected "moment"...each wave seemed to flow as far as one cared to ride it, like some perfect surfer's curl extending to infinity. We began to suspect that the answer to the question "when?" might be "never!" This contingency had been described rigorously in only one interpretation of Q-reality, that of J.Wheeler - who proved that the wave function need never collapse provided that every Q-event gives rise to an "alternating world" (the Cat is both alive and dead).

To settle this question a fourth generation of the egg was evolved and tested, while simultaneously a burst of research was carried out in the abstruse areas of "Hillbert space" and the topology of n-dimensional geometry, on the intuitive assumptions that new "attractors" could thereby be generated and used to visualize or "grok" the transitions between alternate universes. Again the ICS triumphed...although the immediate success of the fourth-generation egg provoked a moment of fear and panic unmatched in the whole history of "Cognitive Chaos." The first run-through of the "Cat" program was undertaken by a young staff-member of great brilliance (one of the original Paramus runaways) whose nickname happened to be Kit—and it happened to take place on the Spring Equinox. At the precise moment the heavens changed gears, so to speak, the entire egg vanished from the laboratory. Consternation would be a mild term for what ensued. For about seven minutes the entire ICS lost its collective cool. At that point however the egg reappeared with its passenger intact and beaming...like Alice's Cheshire Cat rather than Schrödinger's poor victim. He had succeeded in riding the wave to its "destination"—an alternate universe. He had observed it and—in his words—"memorized its address." Instinctively he felt that certain dimensional universes must act as "strange attractors" in their own right, and are thus far easier to access (more "probable") than others. In practical terms, he had not been dissolved but had found the way to a "universe next door." *The Gateway had been opened.*

Where is Ong's Hat?

According to Piney legend, the village of Ong's Hat was founded sometime in the 19th century when a man named Ong threw his hat up in the air, landed it in a tree and was unable to retrieve it (we like to think it vanished into another world). By the 1920s all traces of settlement other than a few crumbling chimneys had faded away. But the name appealed so much to cartographers that some of them retained it—a dot representing nothing in the midst of the most isolated flat dark scrub-pines and sandy creeks in all the vast, empty and perhaps haunted Barrens. W.Fard's acreage lies in the invisible suburbs of this invisible town, of which we are the sole inhabitants. You can find it easily on old survey maps, even trace out the old dirt road leading into the bogs where a little square represents the decrepit "Ong's Hat Rod & Gun Club," original residence. However, you might discover that finding the ICS itself is not so simple. If you compare your old survey map with the very latest, you will note that our area lies perilously close to the region infamous in recent years, the South Jersey Nuclear Waste Dump near Fort Dix. The "accident" that occurred there has made the Barrens even more empty and unpopular, as any hard-core Pineys fled the pollution melting into the state's last untouched wilderness. The electrified fence shutting off the deadly zone runs less than a mile above our enclave. The Accident occurred while we were in the first stages of developing the fourth-generation egg, the Gate.

At the time we had no idea of its full potential. However all of us, except for the very youngest (who were evacuated), had by then been trained in elementary self-directed generation. A few tests proved that with care and effort we could resist at least the initial onslaught of radiation sickness. We decided to stick it out, at least until "the authorities" (rather than the dump) proved too hot to endure.

Once the Gate was discovered, we realized the situation had been saved. The opening and actual interdimensional travel, can only be effected by a fully trained "cognitive chaote;" so the first priority was to complete the course for all our members. A technique for "carrying" young children was developed (it seems not to work for adult "non-initiates"), and it was discovered that all inanimate matter within the egg is also carried across with the operator. Little by little we carted our entire establishment (including most of the buildings) across the topological abyss. Unlike Baudelaire who pleaded, "Anywhere! - so long as out of this world!" we knew where we were going. Ong's Hat has indeed vanished from New Jersey, except for the hidden laboratory deep in the backwoods where the gate "exists." On the other side of the Gate we found a Pine Barrens similar to ours but in a world which apparently never developed human life. Of course we have since visited a number of other worlds, but we decided to colonize this one, our first newfoundland. We still live in the same scattering of weather-gray shacks, Airstream trailers, recycled chicken coops, and mail-order yurts, only a bit more spread out—and considerably more relaxed. We're still dependent on your world for many things—from coffee to books to computers—and in fact we have no inclination of cutting ourselves off like anchorites and merely scampering into a dreamworld. We intend to spread the word.

The colonization of new worlds—even an infinity of them—can never act as a panacea for the ills of Consensus Reality—only as a palliative. We have always taken our diseases with us to each new frontier...everywhere we go we exterminate aborigines and battle with our weapons of law and order against the chaos of reality. But this time, we believe, the affair will go differently—because this time the journey outward can only be made simultaneously with the journey inward—and because this bootstrap-trick can only be attained by a consciousness which, to a significant degree, has overcome itself, liberated itself from self-sickness—and "realized itself." Not that we think ourselves saints, or try to behave morally, or imagine ourselves a super-race, absolved from good and evil. Simply, we like to consider ourselves awake when we're awake, sleeping when we sleep. We enjoy good health. We have learned that desire demands the *other* just as it demands the self. We see no end to growth while life lasts, no cessation of unfolding, of continual outpouring of form from chaos. We're moving on, nomads or monads of the dimensions. Sometimes we feel almost satisfied...at other times, terrified.

Meanwhile our agents of chaos remain behind to set up ICS courses, distribute Moorish Orthodox literature (a major mask for our propaganda) to subvert and evade our enemies...We haven't spoken yet of our enemies. Indeed there remains much we have not said. This text, disguised as a sort of New Age vacation brochure, must fall silent at this point, satisfied that it has embedded within itself enough clues for its intended readers (who are already halfway to Ong's hat in any case) but not enough for those with little faith to follow.

CHAOS NEVER DIED![1]

INCUNABULA

A Catalogue of Rare Books, Manuscripts & Curiosa
Conspiracy Theory, Frontier Science & Alternative Worlds
Emory Cranston, Prop.
Incunabulum / cocoon / swaddling clothes / cradle /
in-cunae, in the cradle / koiman, put to sleep / winding-
sheet / koimetarium (cemetery)/ printed books before
1501, hence by extension any rare & hermetic book ...

No book for sale here was actually printed before 1501, but they all answer to the description " rare and hermetic"—even the mass market pa-
perbacks, not to mention the xeroxes of unpublished manuscripts, which
cannot be obtained from any other source!

The symbol INCUNABULA was chosen for our company for its shape—
cocoon, egg-like, gourd-like, the shape of Chaos according to Chuang Tzu.
Cradle: beginnings. Sleep: dreams. Silken white sheets of birth and death;
books, white pages, the cemetery of ideas.

This catalogue has been put together with a purpose: to alert YOU to
a vast cover up, a conspiracy so deep that no other researcher has yet become aware of it (outside certain Intelligence circles, needless to say!)—
and so dangerous that the "winding sheet" imagery in our title seems
quite appropriate; we know of at least two murders so far in connection
with this material.

Unlike other conspiracy theories, such as Hollow earth, Men In
Black,cattle mutilation, UFO, Reich & Tesla or what have you, the INCU-
NABULA Theory harmonizes with genuine frontier quantum mechanics
and chaos mathematics, and does not depend on any quack nostrums,
pseudoscience or ESP for proof. This will become clear to anyone who

takes the trouble to read the background material we recommend and offer for sale.

Because of the unprecedented nature of the INCUNABULA File we have included short descriptions of some of the books, pamphlets, fly-ers, privately-circulated or unpublished manuscripts, ephemera & curiosa available through us. Some of this is highly inflammable and sexual in nature, so an age statement must be included with each order.

Cash (or stamps) only. No cheques or money orders will be accepted.

Thank You, Emory Cranston, Prop.
1. Wolf, Fred Alan.
Parallel Universes: The Search for Other Worlds
(New York, Simon & Schuster, 1988) cloth; 351 pp.; $25

Written by a scientist for non-scientists, simplistic and jokey, makes you feel a bit talked-down-to. Nevertheless Wolf uses his imagination (or other scientists imaginations) so well he seems to hit accidentally on certain truths (unless he knows more than he reveals). For example: the parallel universes must have all come into being simultaneously "at the begin-ning" in order for quantum uncertainty to exist, because there was no observer present at the Big Bang, thus no way for the Wave Function to collapse and produce one universe out of all the bubbles of possibil-ity (p.174). If an electron can disappear in one universe and appear in another (as suggested by the Everett/Wheeler material), a process called "quantum tunneling", then perhaps information can undergo a similar tunneling effect. Wolf suggests (p. 176) that this might account for cer-tain "psychic phenomenon, altered states of awareness," even ghosts and spirits! Actual travel between worlds must of course involve tunneling by both electrons AND information—any scientist would have predicted as much—but the mention of "altered states" of consciousness is extremely revealing! Elsewhere (p.204), Wolf speculates that a future "highly devel-oped...electronic form of biofeedback" will allow us to observe quantum effects in the electrons of our own bodies, making the enhanced con-sciousness and the body itself a "time machine" (which is what he calls a device for travel between universes). He comes so close to the truth then shies away! For instance (p.199) he points out that the Wave Function has a value BETWEEN zero and one until it collapses. If the wave func-tion does not collapse, the "thing" it describes exists in two universes simultaneously. How strange of him not to mention that fractal geometry also deals with values between zero and one! As we know the secret of travel between worlds is rooted in the marriage of quantum and chaos, particularly in the elusive mathematics of fractal tesseracts (visualize a 4-dimension Mandelbrot Set—one of the simplest of the trans-dimensional "maps" or "catastrophic topologies"). Wolf appears so unaware of this, we must sadly conclude that he's not part of the conspiracy.

Particularly interesting—and not found in any other material- are Wolf's specualtions about schizophrenia. Are schizophrenics recieving information from other worlds? Could a schizoid observer actually observe (in the famous double slit experiments) a wave becoming two particles and then one particle? Or could such an observation be made by an extremely blank and simple-minded watcher (a sort of zen simpleton perhaps)? If so, the perfect subject for parallel-worlds experiments would be a paradoxically complex simpleton, a "magnetized schizophrenic" who would be aware of the split into two worlds which occurs when a quantum measurement is made. Oddly enough, such a mental state sounds very close to the "positive schizophrenia" of certain extreme psychedelic experiences as well as the meditation-visualization exercises of actual travelers between worlds.

Despite it's flaws, an essential work.

2. Herbert, Nick.
Quantum Reality
(NAL, 1986) Cloth, $40

A masterful and lucid exposition of the different versions of reality logically describable from various interpretations of quantum mechanics. The Everett/Wheeler Theory is here given it's clearest explanation possible in lay persons terms, given the authors awareness (at the time) of experimental verification.

3. ibid.
Faster Than Light: Superluminal Loopholes in Physics
(NAL, 1988) cloth, $30

Some of the theorists who touch on the Many-Worlds "hypothesis" place too much emphasis on time distortions and the implication of "time travel". These of course seem present in the theorems, but in practice have turned out (so far) to be of little consequence. Chaos Theory places much more emphasis on the temporal directionality than most quantum theory (with such exceptions as R. Feynman and his "arrow of time"), and offers strong evidence for the past-present-future evolution that we actually experience. As K.Sohrawardi puts it, "the universe is in a state of Being, true, but that state is not static in the way suggested by the concept of 'reversibility' in Classical physics. The 'generosity' of Being, so to speak, is becoming, and the result is not reversibility but multiplicity, the unmeasurable resonant chaos-like fecundity of creation. " Nevertheless, Herbert's second book is a brilliant speculative work—and it led him directly to a certain circle of scientists and body of research concerned with dimensional travel, rather than "time travel," with the result that his third book (see next item) finally struck paydirt.

4. "Jabir ibn Hayaan" (Nick Herbert).
Alternate Dimensions
(publication suppressed by Harper & Row, 1989); bound uncorrected galleys, 179pp. $100. (We have 5 sets of proofs for sale, after which only xerox copies will be available at $125)

While working on *Faster Than Light* Herbert came into contact with one of the "travel cults" operating somewhere in California, perhaps one with a sufiistic slant ("Jabir ibn Hayaan" was a famous 10th century sufi alchemist); according to the preface of *Alternate Dimensions*, which is irritatingly vague and suggestive, this group seems to have trained him and sent him on at least one trip to America2. Herbert suggests that he already had so much experience of altered states of consciousness and ability to visualize complex space/time geometries that only a minimum of "initiatic" training proved necessary.

In any case, despite it's vagueness and brevity, this book is the most accurate and thoroughly-informed work on travel between worlds in our entire collection. So far we have been unable to obtain any deep theoretical work, and only a few papers dealing with practical aspects - but Herbert provides a magnificent overview of the entire field. Written for the lay person, with his usual clear and succinct approach to theory, Herbert's is the first "popular" study to make all the basic links: the Everett/Wheeler hypothesis, Bell's Theorem, the E/R Bridge, fractal geometry and chaos math, cybernetically-enhanced biofeedback, psychotropic and shamanic techniques, crystallography, morphogenetic field theory, catastrophe topology,etc.

Of course he's strongest in discussing the quantum aspects of travel, less sure when dealing with the math outside his field, and most inspiring when describing (pp.98-101) visualization techniques and "embodied ecstasy" (ex-stasis, "standing outside" the body; hence embodied ecstasy paradoxically describes the transdimensional experience).

Herbert makes no claim to understand the traveling itself, and goes so far as to suggest that even the (unnamed) pioneers who made the first breakthroughs may not have completely understood the process, any more than the inventor of the steam engine understood Classical physics (p.23). This definitely ties in with what we know about the persons in question.

Unfortunately the six illustrations promised in the table of contents are not included in the galleys—one of them was a "Schematic for a Trans-dimensional Express" which might be worth killing for!—and the publishers claim that Herbert never supplied the illustrations. They refuse to say why they suspended publication of Alternate Dimensions and in fact at first denied ever having handled such a title! Moreover Herbert has apparently dropped out of sight; if he hasn't met with foul play, he may have returned permanently to Earth2.

We regret having to sell copies of a flawed book for such an outrageous price; we'd like to publish a massmarket edition affordable by all—but if Harper & Row ever find out what we're doing, we'll need the money for court costs and lawyers' fees! So get it while you can—this is THE indispensable background work for understanding the Conspiracy.

5. Thomsen, Dietrick E.
A Knowing Universe Seeking to be Known
(Xerox offprint from *Science News,* Vol.123, 1983); $5

Unwittingly demonstrates the resonance between quantum reality theory and the Sufism of (for example) "the Greatest Shaykh" Ibn'Arabi, who discusses in his *Bezels of Wisdom* a saying attributed to God by Mohammad (but not in the Koran): "I was a hidden treasure and I wanted (lit.'loved') to be known; so I created the universe, that I might be known."

5a. We also have a few offprints (at the same price) of Thomsen's witty *"Quanta at Large: 101 Things TO DO with Schrodinger's Cat"* (op.cit, 129, 1986).

6. DeWitt, Bryce S. & Neill Graham.
The Many Worlds Interpretation of Quantum Mechanics
(Princeton, NJ, 1973); cloth, $50

The standard (and far from "easy"!) work on the Everett/Wheeler hypothesis—a bible for the early pioneers.

7. Cramer, John G.
Alternate Universes II
(Analog, Nov. 1984)

A popularization of the Theory by a prominent physicist—no knowledge of the Conspiracy is detectable. We're selling copies of the SciFi mag itself for $10 each.

8. Greenberg, D.M., ed.
New Techniques & Ideas in Quantum Measurement Theory
(Vol. 480 *Annals of the NY Academy of Sciences,* 1986); cloth, $50

Contains the valuable if somewhat whimsical article by D.Z. Albers, *"How to take a Photograph of Another Everett World"*. Also the very important *"Macroscopic Quantum Tunneling at Finite Temperatures"* by P.Hanggi (we suspect him of being a Conspiracy member).

9. (Anonymous).
Course Catalogue for 1978-79,
Institute of Chaos Studies and Imaginal Yoga (no address);
xerox of mimeographed flyer, 7pp, $15

An in-house document from the Institute where the first breakthrough was attained (probably in the late winter or early spring of 1979)—therefore, although it makes no overt mention of Travel or the Egg, the catalogue is of prime importance for an understanding of the intellectual and historical background of the event.

According to an unrelaible source (see ESCAPE FROM EARTH PRIME!, #15 in this list), the Institute was located somewhere in Dutchess County, New York, where the founder and director, Dr. Kamadev Sohrawardi, was employed by IBM in the 1960's, "dropped out" and began investigations into "consciousness physics"; it is also claimed that Sohrawardi was a Bengali of mixed English, Hindu and Moslem origin, descended from an old sufi family, and initiated into Tantra. All this disagrees with clues in other sources and is perhaps not to be trusted. Other groups take credit for the Breakthrough, and sohrawardi may have been a fraud—but we're convinced that the catalogue is authentic and Sohrawardi's claim the most certain.

At first glance, the Catalogue appears an example of late-hippy/early-New-Age pretentiousness. Thus there are courses in "Visions of Color &

Light in Sufi Meditation," "Inner Alchemy in Late Taoism," "Metaphys-
ics of the Ismaili 'Assassins,'" , "Imaginal Yoga & the Psychotoplogy of
the Imagination," "Hermetic & Neo-Pagan Studies," (apparently based on
Golden Dawn teachings), "Visualization Techniques in Javanese Sorcery,"
"Stairways to Heaven: Shamanic Trance & the Mapping of Conscious-
ness," "Stirner, Nietzsche & Stone age Economy: An Examination of Non-
Authoritarian Hunter/Gatherer Societies,", and—interestingly enough! -
"Conspiracy Theory".

The "shamanic" course may have been a blind for research in psychotropic drugs, including such exotica as ayahuasca (yage, harmaline),
ibogaine, yohimbine, Telepathine and Vitamin K, as well as the more
standard psychedelicatessan of the late 70's.

However, the Catalogue also contains amazing courses in frontier science, any combination of which could have provided the key or final
puzzle-bit to the Breakthrough: apparently Sohrawardi taught or super-
vised most of them. Thus "The Universe in a Grain of Sand" promised
information on models of brain activity, cybernetically-enhanced feedback, Sheldrake's morphogenetic field theory, Rene' Thom's Catastrophic
Theory as applied to consciousness, lucid-dreaming research, John Lilly's
work on "altered states" and other mind-related topics. Then in "Strange
Attractors & the Mathematics of Chaos," Sohrawardi discussed matters
unknown outside of the margins of academia till the mid-80's,and made
the astounding prediction that Chaos in the macroscopic world somehow
be found to mirror Uncertainty in the microscopic or Quantum World, a
truth still unrecognized in "official" scientific circles today.He felt that
n-dimensional strange attractors could be used to model the quantum
behavior of particles/waves, and that the "so-called collapse of the wave
function" could actually be mapped with certain bizzare ramifications of
Thom's catasrophic topology. Making references to work by Ilya Prigogine
which was still being circulated in private "preprint" or samizdat form at
the time, Sohrawardi suggests that "creative chaos" (as opposed to "deterministic" or entropic chaos) provides the link that will unify Relativity,
Quantum, Complexity and consciuosness itself into a new science.

Finally in his "Advanced Seminar on Many Worlds," he states baldly
that the alternative universes predicted by Relativity (Black Hole Theory)
are the same as the many worlds predicted by Quantum, are the same as
fractal dimensions revealed in Chaos! This one-page course description is
the closest thing we have to an explanation of why travel to other worlds
actually works. Hence the Catalogue is an indespensable document for the
serious student of the Conspiracy.

10. Beckenstein, J.
"Black holes & Entropy"
(xerox offprint from *Physical Review,* Vol.D7, 1973; 28pp), $15

An early (pre-Breakthrough) speculation with suggestive hints about
quantum and chaos-as-entropy—although no knowledge of actual Chaos
Theory is demonstrated. This paper was referred to in an in-house memo
from the Inst. for Chaos Studies & Imaginal Yoga, believed to have been
composed by K.Sohrawardi himself (see #9).

11. Sohrawardi,Dr Kamadev.
"Pholgiston & the Quantum Aether"
(Offprint from the *J. of Paranormal Physics,* Vol.XXII, Bombay, 1966),
$40

An early paper by Sohrawardi, flooded with wild speculations about
quantum and oriental spirituality, probably dating from the period when
he was still working for IBM, but making visits to Millbrook, nearby in
Dutchess Co., and participating in the rituals of the League of spiritual discovery under Dr. Timothy Leary, and the psychedelic yoga of Bill Haines'
Sri Ram Ashram, which shared Leary's headquarters on a local million-
aires estate. The basic insight concerns the identity of Everett/Wheeler's
"many worlds" and the "other worlds" of sufism, tantrik Hinduism and
Vajrayana Buddhism. At the time, Sohrawardi apparently believed he
could "prove" this by reviving the long-dead theories of phlogiston and
aether in the light of quantum discoveries! (Phlogiston Theory—based on
the thinking of the sufi alchemist Jabir ibn Hayaan—the original Jabir—
was propounded seriously in the 18th century to unify heat and light
as "one thing".) Totally useless as science, this metaphor nevertheless
inspired Sohrawardi's later and genuinely important work on alternate
realities.

12. ibid.
"Zero Work & Psychic Paleolithism"
East Village Other, Vol.IV #4 (Dec.1968)
xerox reprint, single sheet 11 1/2 x 17 $5

Unfortunately no scientific speculations, but a fascinating glimpse into
the political background of the inventor of Travel (or rather, one of the
inventors). Making reference to French Situationist and Dutch "Provo"

ideas which helped spark the "Events" and upheavals of Spring '68 all over Europe and America, Sohrawardi looks forward to a world without "the alienating prison of WORK," restored to the "oneness with Nature of the Old Stone Age" and yet somehow based on "green technology and quantum weirdness."

Wild and wooly as it is, this text nevertheless poses a fascinating scientific question in the light of the author's later accomplishments—a question still unanswered. All the "First Breakthroughs" we know of with any degree of certainty (those in New York, California, and Java—the actual sequence is unclear) without exception entered parallel worlds without human inhabitants, virtual forest-worlds. Most science fiction predicated other worlds almost like ours, populated by "us," with only a few slight differences, worlds "close" to ours. Instead-no people!

Why?

Two possible explanations:

1. We cannot enter worlds containing "copies" of ourselves without causing paradox and violating the consistency principle of the "megaverse"—hence only wild (or feral) worlds are open to Travel.

2. Other worlds exist, in a sense, only as probabilities; in order to "become fully real" they must be observed. In effect, the parallel universes are observer-created, as soon as a traveler "arrives" in one of them. Sohrawardi wanted a paleolithic world of endless forest, plentiful game and gathering, virgin, empty but slightly haunted—therefore, that's what he got! Either explanation raises problems in the light of what actually happened; perhaps there is a third, as yet unsuspected.

13. (Anonymous).
Ong's Hat: A Color Brochure of the Institute of Chaos Studies
(photocopy of the original color brochure) $25

This bizarre document, disguised as a brochure for a New Age health retreat, reveals some interesting information about the activities of Sohrawardi's group or a closely-associated group, a fairly accurate description of the Egg is provided, as well as a believable account of the first (or one of the first) Breakthroughs. However, everthing else in the pamphlet is sheer disinformation. The New Jersey Pine Barrens were never a center of alternate-worlds research, and all the names in the text are false. A non-existant address is included. Nevertheless, highly valuable for background.

14. "Sven Saxon".
The Stone Age Survivalist
(Loompanics, UnLtd., Port Townsend, WA 1985), Pb, $20

"Imagine yourself suddenly plunked down buck-nacked in the middle of a large dark forest with no resources except your mind," says the preface."What would you do?"

What indeed? and who could possibly care?—except a trans-dimensional Traveller! Loompanics specializes in books on dissapearances and survival involving a good deal of escapist fantasy—but as we know, this situation is all too real for the Visitor to Other Worlds.

Part I: Flint-knapping, an exellent illustrated handbook of paleolithic tool-production; II Zero-tech hunting and trapping; III, Gathering (incl. a materia medica); IV, Shelter; V, Primitive warfare; VI,Man & Dog: trans-species symbiosis; VII, Cold weather survival; VIII, Culture ("Sven" recommends memorizing a lot of songs, poems and stories—and ends by saying "Memorize this book—'cause you can't take it with you." Where is Mr.Saxon now, we wonder?).

15. Balcombe, Harold S.
Escape From Earth Prime!
(Foursquare Press, Denver, Colo., 1986), Pb, $15

This—unfortunately!—is the book that blew the lid off the Conspiracy for the first time. We say "unfortuantely" because ESCAPE!, to all appearances, is a piece of unmitigated paranoid pulp tripe. Written in breathless ungrammatical subFortean prose, unfootnoted and nakedly sensationalistic, the book sank without trace, ignored even by the kook-conspiracy fringe; we were able to buy out unsold stock from the vanity press which published it, just before they went out of business and stopped answering their mail.

Balcombe (whom we've been unable to trace and who may have "vanished"), is the author of one other book we've seen—but are not offering for sale—called "Drug Lords from the Hollow Earth" (1984) in which he claims that the CIA obtained LSD and cocaine from Dero-flying-saucer-nazis from beneath Antarctiac. So much for his credentials. How he got hold of even a bit of the authentic Other Worlds story is a miracle.

According to Balcombe, the first breakthrough was due not solely to K.Soharawardi—despite his importance as a theoretician—but also a "sinister webwork of cultists, anarchists, commies, fanatical hippies and renegade traitor scientists who made fortunes in the drug trade" (p.3). Balcombe promises to name names, and out of the welter of rant and slather, some hard facts about the pioneers actually emerge.

Funding (and some research) emanated in the 70's from a "chaos cabal" of early Silicon Valley hackers interested in complex dynamical systems, randomicity, and chance, and-gambling!—as well as a shadowy group of "drug lords" (Balcombe's favorite term of abuse), with connections to certain founders of the Discordian Illuminati. Money was channelled through a cult called the Moorish Orthodox Church, a loose knit confederation of jazz musicians, oldtime hipsters, white "sufis" and black moslems, bikers and street dealers (see" A Heresologist's Guide to Brooklyn", #24 in this list) who came into contact with Sohrawardi in Millbrook in the mid-60's.

Sohrawardi was a naive idealist and somewhat careless about his associations. He received clandestine support from people who were in turn connected to certain Intelligence circles with an interest in psychedelic and fringe mind-science. According to Balcombe this was not the CIA (MK-ULTRA) but an unofficial offshoot of several groups with Masonic connections! The Conspiracy was penetrated almost from the start, but was actually encouraged in the hope of gleaning useful information about parallel worlds, or at least about the "mental conditioning techniques" developed as part of the basic research.

By the mid-70's, Sohrawardi and his various cohorts and connections (now loosely referred to as "the Garden of Forked Paths" or GFP) had become aware of the Intelligence circles (now loosely grouped as "Probability Control Force" or PCF) and had in turn planted double-agents, and gone further underground. In 1978 or 79 an actual device for trans-dimensional Travel, the "Egg" (also called the Cocoon or the Cucurbit, which means both gourd and alchemical flask) was developed in deepest secrecy, probably at Sohrawardi's institute in Upstate New York, certainly not at a branch lab supposedly hidden away in the NJ Pine Barrens near the long-vanished village of Ong's Hat (see #13 in this list), since no such lab ever existed, nor does it exist now, despite what some fools think.

The PCF were unable to obtain an Egg for several years and did not succeed in Breakthrough until (Balcombe believes) 1982. The California groups, however, began Egg-production and broke through (into "Big-Sur2") in early 1980 (again, Balcombe's chronology). (Balcombe clearly knows nothing of the situation in Java.)

It remains unclear whether the East Coast and West Coast groups both entered the same alternate world, or two different but similar worlds. Communication between the two outposts has so far proved impossible because, as it happens, the Egg will not transport non-sentient matter. Travelers arrive Over There birth-naked in a Stone Age world—no airplanes, no radio, no clothes . . . no fire and no tools! Only the Egg, like a diamond Faberge easter gift designed by Dali, alone in the midst of "Nature naturing". Balcombe includes a dim out-of-focus photo of an Egg, and claims that the machine is part computer but also partly-living crystal, like virus or DNA, and also partly "naked quantumstuff".

Eggs are costly to produce, so the early pioneers had to return after each sortie and forego permanent settlement on E2 until a cheaper mode of transport could be discovered. However, emigration via the Egg proved possible when the "tantrik" or "double-yolk" effect was discovered: two people (any combination of age, gender, etc.) can Travel by Egg while making love, especially if one of the pair has already done the trip a few times and "knows the way" without elaborate visualization techniques and so forth. Balcombe has a field day with this juicy information and spends an entire chapter (VIII) detailing the "perversions" in use for this purpose. Talent for Travel ranges from brilliant to zero—probably no more than 15% of humanity can make it, although the less-talented and even children can be "translated" by the tantrik technique—and extensive training methods have somewhat improved the odds. California2 now contains about 1000 emigrants scattered along the coast, and the eastern settlements add up to 500 or 600. A few children have been born "over there"—some can Travel, some can't, although the talented percentage seems greater than among the general population of Earth-prime. And being "stuck" on E2 is no grave punishment in any case!, unless you object to the Garden of Eden and the "original leisure society" of the Paleolithic flintknappers.

Balcombe claims that the PCF was severely disappointed by the sentience "law" of Travel, since they had hoped to use the parallel worlds as a weapons-delivery system! Nevertheless they continued to experiment, hoping for a more "mechanistic" technique; meanwhile they devote their efforts to (a) suppressing all information leaks, (b) plotting against the independent GFP and infiltrating the E2 settlements, (c) attempting to open new worlds where technology might be possible. They are however handicapped by a shortage of talent: the kind of person who can Travel is not usually the kind of person who sympathizes with the "patriotic discipline

of the PCF" and rogue Masonic groups, but some of these end up defect-
ing and "doubling", and anyway most of them are much too weird for the
taste of the rigidly reactionary inner core of PCF leadership, who wonder
(as does Balcombe) whether these agents are "any better than the scum
they're spying on?"

More worlds have been discovered—E3 and E4 are mentioned in ES-
CAPE! (and we know that E5 was opened in 1988)—but all of these are
"empty" forest worlds apparently almost identical with E2.

In summary, Balcombe's style is execrable and attitude repulsive, but
his book remains the most accurate overview of the Conspiracy to date. If
you're only going to order one item from us, this is it.

16. (Anonymous).
Bionic Travel: An Orgonomic Theory of the Megaverse
(xerox of unpubl. typescript headed "Top Secret—Eyes Only"; 27pp), $15

If this paper emanates from PCF sources, as we believe, it indicates the
poor quality of original research carried out by the enemies of Sohrawardi
and the GFP, and may explain the PCF's relative lack of progress in the
field (especially considering their much larger budget!). The author attempts to revive W. Reich's Orgone Theory, with "bions" as "life-force
particles" and some sort of orgone accumulator (Reich's "box") as a possible substitute for the Egg. An unhealthy interest is shown in "harnessing
the force of Deadly Orgone" as a weapon for use on other worlds. References are also made to Aliester Crowley's "sex magick techniques" of the
Ordo Templi Orientis—even speculations on human sacrifice as a possible
source of "transdimensional energy". A morbid and crackpot document,
devoid of all scientific value (in our opinion) but affording a fascinating
insight into PCF mentality and method.

17. Corbin, Henry.
Creative Imagination in the Sufism of Ibn'Arabi
(trans. by R. Mannheim; Princeton, NJ, 1969), cloth, $50; Pb, $20

One of the few books mentioned by title in the Catalogue of the Inst.
of Chaos Studies & Imaginal Yoga (see #9 in this list). The "mundus
imaginalis", also called the World of Archetypes or the "Isthmus" (Ara-
bic, barzakh), lies in between the World of the Divine and the material
World of Creation. It actually consists of "many worlds", including two
"emerald cities" called Jabulsa and Jabulqa (very intriguing considering

the situation on Java2!). The great 14th-century Hispano-Moorish sufi Ibn'Arabi developed a metaphysics of the "Creative Imagination" by which the adept could achieve spiritual progress via direct contemplation of the archetypes, including the domains of djinn, spirits and angels. Ibn'Arabi also speaks of seven alternate Earths created by Allah, each with its own Mecca and Kaaba! Some parallel-universe theorists believe that Travel without any tech (even the Egg) may be possible, claiming that certain mystics have already accomplished it. If so, then Ibn'Arabi must have been one of them.

18. Gleick, James.
CHAOS: Making a New Science
(Viking Penguin, NY, 1987), cloth, 254pp, $30

The first and still the most complete introduction to chaos—required reading—BUT with certain caveats. First: Gleick has no philosophical or poetic depth; he actually begins the book with a quote from John Updike! No mention of chaos mythology or oriental sources. No mention of certain non-American chaos scientists such as Rene Thom and Ilya Prigogine! Instead, alongside the admittedly useful info, one gets a subtle indoctrination in "deterministic chaos", by which we mean the tendency to look on chaos as a weapon to fight chaos, to "save" Classical physics - and learn to predict the Stock Market! (As opposed to what we call the "quantum chaos" of Sohrawardi and his allies, which looks on chaos as a creative and negentropic source, the cornucopia of evolution and awareness.) Warning: we suspect Gleick of being a PCF agent who has embedded his text with subtle disinformation meant to distract the chaos-science community from any interest in "other worlds".

19. Pak Hardjanto.
Apparent Collapse of the Wave Function as an n-Dimensional Catastrophe
(trans. by "N.N.S." in Collected Papers of the *SE Asian Soc. for Advanced Research,* Vol.XXIX, 1980), 47pp, xerox of offprint, $15

An early paper by the little-known scientific director of the Javanese "Travel Cult" which succeeded in breakthrough, possibly in the year this essay was published or shortly thereafter. Hardjanto is known to have been in touch with Sohrawardi since the 60's; no doubt they shared all information, but each kept the other secret from their respective organizations. The pioneers of Java2 became known to the GFP and PCF only around 1984 or 85.

This article, the only scientific work we possess by Hardjanto, shows him to be a theoretician equal or even superior to Sohrawardi himself—and if Hardjanto is also the anonymous author of the following item, as we believe, then he appears a formidable "metaphysicist" as well!

"Apparent Collapse", while certainly not a blueprint for Egg construction, nevertheless constitutes one of the few bits of "hard" science published openly on our Subject. Unfortunately, its theorems and diagrams are doubtless comprehensible only to a handful of experts. The topological drawings literally boggle the mind, especially one entitled "Hypercube Undergoing 'Collapse' Into 5-Space Vortex"!

20. (Unsigned, probably by Pak Hardjanto).
A Vision of Hurqalya
(trans. by K.K. Sardono; Incunabula Press, 1988), Pb, 46pp, $20

The Indonesian original of this text appeared as a pamphlet in Yogjakarta (E.Java) in 1982. We ourselves at Incunabula commissioned the translation and have published this handsome edition, including all the illustrations from the original, at our own expense.

If one knew nothing about the Conspiracy or Many-Worlds Theory, A Vision would seem at first to be a mystical tract by an adherent of kebatinan, the heterodox sufi-influenced freeform esoteric/syncretistic complex of sects which has come to be influential in GFP circles, inasmuch as the idea of "spiritual master" (guru, murshed) has been replaced by "teacher" (pamong); some kebatinan sects utilize spontaneous non-hierarchical organizational structures.

However, in the light of our knowledge of the material existence of other worlds, Vision takes on a whole new dimension, as a literal description of what Hardjanto and his fellow pioneers found on Java2.

They discovered another uninhabited world, but with one huge difference. The author of Vision steps out of his "alchemical Egg" into a vast and ancient abandoned City! He calls it Hurqalya (after a traditional sufi name for the Other World or alam'e mithal). He senses his total aloneness, feels that the City's builders have long since moved on elsewhere, and yet that they still somehow somewhere exist.

The author compares Hurqalya to the ancient ruined city of Borobadur in E.Java, but notices immediately that there are no statues or images, all the decoration is abstract and severe, but "neither Islamic nor

Buddhist nor Hindu nor Christian nor any style I ever saw". The "palaces" of Hurqalya are grand, cyclopaean, almost monolithic, far from "heavy" in atmosphere, despite the black basalt from which they seem to have been carved. For the City is cut through by water ... it is in fact a water-city in the style of the Royal Enclave of Yogjakarta (now so sadly derelict), but incomparably bigger. Canals, aqueducts, rivers and channels crisscross and meander through the City; flowing originally from quiescent volcanic mountains looming green in the West, Water flows down through the City which is built on a steep slope gradually curving into a basin and down to the placid Eastern Sea, where a hundred channels flow dark and clear into the green salt ocean.

Despite the air of ruin—huge trees have grown through buildings, splitting them open—mosses, ferns and orchids coat the crumbling walls with viridescence, hosting parrots, lizards, butterflies—despite this desolation, most of the waterworks still flow: canal-locks broken open centuries ago allow cascades, leaks, spills and waterfalls in unexpected places, so that the City is wrapped in a tapestry of water-sounds and songbird voices. Most amazingly, the water flows at different levels simultaneously, so that aqueducts cross over canals which in turn flow above sunken streams which drip into wells, underground cisterns and mysterious sewers in a bewildering complex of levels, pipes, conduits and irrigated garden terraces which resemble (to judge by the author's sketches) a dreamscape of Escher or Piranesi. Viewed from above, the City would be mapped as an arabesque 3PD spiderweb (with waterbridges aboveground, streams at ground level and also underground) fanning out to fill the area of the basin, thence into the harbor with its huge cracked basalt-block docks.

The slope on which the City is built is irregularly terraced in ancient SE Asian style—as many staircases and streets thread their way up and down, laid out seemingly at random, following land-contours rather than grid-logic, adding to the architectural complexity of the layer of waterways with a maze of vine-encrusted overpasses, arched bridges, spiralling ramps, crooked alleyways, cracked hidden steps debouching on broad esplanades, avenues, parks gone to seed, pavilions, balconies, apartments, jungle-choked palazzos, echoing gloomy "temples" whose divinities, if any, seem to have left no forwarding address ... all empty, all utterly abandoned. And nowhere is there any human debris—no broken tools, bones or midden heaps, no evidence of actual habitation—as if the ancient builders of the City picked up and took everything with them when they departed—"perhaps to one of the other Seven Worlds of the alam'e mithal"—in other words, to a "higher dimension."

Thus ends the Vision of Hurqalya, raising more questions than it answers! There is no doubt that it describes exactly what was discovered in Java2 in 1980 or 81. But if the "observer-created" theory of other-worlds travel is true, "Hurqalya" represents the "imaginal imprint" of what Hardjanto (or whoever) expected to find. Yet again, if that theory is false ... who built Hurqalya? One current explanation (arising from time-distortion theorems which have so far remained unsolvable) suggests that the Builders "moved" in prehistoric times to Earth-prime and became the distant ancestors of the Javanese ("Java Man"). Another guess: the Builders have indeed moved on to a "distant" alternate universe, and eventually we may find them.

A small settlement now exists in Hurqalya. Once the American groups heard of the City's existence, members of both the GFP and PFC were able to visualize it and Travel to it from America (the Javanese can do the same from Java-prime to America2). Since 1985 all three groups have expanded most of their exploratory effort on "opening up" new worlds in the Java series. Apparently Indonesian sorcerers and trance adepts are very good at this, and we believe they have reached Java7—without, however, finding replications of the City or any trace of the Builders - only more empty forest.

21. Von Bitter Rucker, Dr R.
"The Cat Was Alive, But Looked Scared As Hell": Some Unexpected Properties of Cellular Automata in the Light of the Everett/Wheeler Hypothesis
(Complex Dynamical Systems Newsletter No. 8, 1989), offprint, $10

Who is this man and what does he know? No other serious mathematician has so far made any connection between cellular automata and the Many Worlds. Tongue-in-cheek (?), the author suggests that Schrodinger's poor cat might be both alive and dead, even after the box is opened, IF parallel universes are "stacked" in some arcane manner which he claims to be able to demonstrate with a piece of software he has hacked and is selling for an outrageous sum; we have also seen and ad for this program in a magazine called **MONDO 2000**, published in Berkeley and devoted to "reality hacking". We'd love to know what certain members of the Conspiracy would make of this bizarre concept!

22. Kennedy, Alison.
Psychotropic Drugs in 'Shared-World' & Lucid Dreaming Experiments
(Psychedelic Monographs & Essays, Vol.XIV, no.2,1981, offprint, $5

This writer appears to have inside information. The notion of a drug-induced hallucination so powerful it can be shared by many (in a proper "blind" experiment) and can actually come into existence, into material reality; the idea that drug-enhanced lucid dreaming can be used to discover objective information from "other ontological levels of being"; and finally the "prediction" that "a combination of these methods utilizing computer-aided biofeedback monitoring devices" will actually make it possible to "visit 'other' worlds in 'inner' space" (which suggests that the author adheres to the "observer-created" theory of parallel universes)—all this leads us to believe that the author is probably a member of one of the California Travel Cults—as well as an expert bruja!

23. (Anonymous).
A Collection of Cult Pamphlets, Flyers, Ephemera & Curiosa from the Library of a Traveller
(Looseleaf portfolio of photocopied originals) sold by lot, $25

The unknown compiler of this Collection (whom for convenience we'll call "X") left it behind when he "vanished", whence it came into our possession. We know something of the compiler's career from an untitled document written by him and found with the Collection, which we call "The Poetic Journal of a Traveller" (#24 in this list), as well as a pamphlet believed to be by the same author, Folklore of the Other Worlds (#25). (The Ong's Hat Color Brochure was also discovered in the same cache, and is sold by us as #13.)

The Collection contains the following items:

1) A History & Catechism of the Moorish Orthodox Church, which traces the origins of the sect to early (1913) American Black Islam, the "Wandering Bishops", the Beats of the 50s and the psychedelic churches movement of the 60s—deliberately vague about the 70s and 80s however.

2) The World Congress of Free Religions, a brochure-manifesto arguing for a "fourth way", a non-authoritarian spiritual movement in opposition to mainstream, fundamentalist and New Age religion.The WCFR is said to include various sects of Discordians, SubGeniuses, Coptic Orthodox People of the Herb, gay ("faery") neo-pagans, Magical Judaism, the Egyptian Church of New Zealand, Kaos Kabal of London, Libertarian Congregationalists, etc., and the Moorish Orthodox Church. Several of these sects are implicated in the Conspiracy, but no overt mention of the Travel Cults is made here.

3) Spiritual Materialism, by "the New Catholic Church of the Pantarchy, Hochkapel von SS Max und Marx", a truly weird flyer dedicated to

"Saints" Max Stirner and Karl Marx, representing a group claiming foundation by the 19th century Individualist Stephen Pearl Andrews, but more likely begun in the 1980s as a Travel Cult. Uses Nietzsche to contend that material reality itself constitutes a (or the) spiritual value and the principle of Infinity "which is expressed in the existence of many worlds." It argues for a utopia based on "individualism, telepathic socialism, free love, high tech, Stone Age wilderness and quantum weirdness"! No address is given, needless to say.

4) The Sacred Jihad of Our Lady of Chaos, this otherwise untraceable group calls for "resistance to all attempts to control probability." It quotes Foucault and Baudrillard on the subject of "disappearance", then suggests that "to vanish without having to kill yourself may be the ultimate revolutionary act ... The monolith of Consensus Reality is riddled with quantum-chaos cracks ... Viral attack on all fronts! Victory to Chaos in every world!"

5) The Temple of Antinous, a Travel Cult of pedophile boy-lovers and neo-pagans devoted to Eros and Ganymede. (Warning: this leaflet contains some just-barely-legal graphic material.) "Wistfully we wonder if the boygod can manifest only in some other world than this dreary puritanical polluted boobocracy—then, gleefully, we suddenly recall: there ARE other worlds!"

6) A Collage, presumably made by X himself, consisting of a "mandala" constructed from cut-outs of Strange Attractors and various Catastrophic topologies interwoven with photos of young girls and boys clipped from Italian fashion magazines. Eroticizing the mathematical imagery no doubt helps one to remember and visualize it while operating the Egg.

24. (Anonymous).
Poetic Journal of a Traveller; or, A Heresologist's Guide to Brooklyn
(Incunabula Press, pamphlet, $15. Believed to be by "X", the compiler of the Collection, & transcribed by us from manuscript.)

Apparently X began this MS with the intention of detailing his experiences with a Travel Cult and eventual "translation" to the various alternate-world settlements, but unfortunately abandoned the project early on, possibly due to PCF interference.

It begins with a summary account of X's spiritual quest, largely among the stranger sects of his native Brooklyn: Santeria in Coney Island, Cabala in Williamsburg, Sufis on Atlantica Avenue, etc. He is disappointed or turned away (and even mugged on one occasion). He becomes friendly with a Cuban woman of mixed Spanish, black, amerindian and Chinese ancestry who runs a botanica (magical supplies and herbs). When he asks her about "other worlds", she is evasive but promises to introduce him to someone who knows more about such matters.

She orders her grandpdaughter, a 14-year-old named Teofila, to escort X through the "rough neighborhoods" to the old man's shop. The girl is wearing a t-shirt that says "Hyperborean Skateboarding Association", and indeed travels by skateboard, "gliding on ahead of me like Hermes the Psychopomp." X is clearly attracted to Teofila and becomes embarrassedly tongue-tied and awkward.

The old man, called "the Shaykh", who claims to be Sudanese but speaks "pure Alabaman", runs a junk shop and wears a battered old Shriners fez. His attitude toward X is severe at first, but X is enchanted by his rather disjointed rambling and ranting—which reveal a surprisingly wide if erratic reading in Persian poetry, the Bible, Meister Eckhardt, William Blake, Yoruba mythology and quantum mechanics. Leaving the girl in the shop, the old man takes X into his back office, "crowded with wildly eclectic junk, naive paintings, cheap orientalismo, HooDoo candles, jars of flower petals, and an ornate potbellied stove, stoked up to cherryred, suffusing waves of drowsy warmth."

The Shaykh intimidates X into sharing a big pipe of hashish mixed with amber and mescaline, then launches into a stream-of-consciousness attack on "Babylon, the Imperium, the Con, the Big Lie that there's nowhere to go and nothing to buy except their fifth-rate imitations of life, their bullshit pie-in-the-sky religions, cold cults, cold cuts of self-mutilation I call 'em, and woe to Jerusalem!"

X, now "stoned to the gills", falls under the Shaykh's spell and bursts into tears. At once the old man unbends, serves X a cup of tea "sweetblack as Jamaica run and scented with cardamon", and begins to drop broad hints about "a way out, not to some gnostic-never-land with the body gone like a fart in a sandstorm, no brother, for the Unseen World is not just of the spirit but also the flesh—Jabulsa and Jabulqa, Hyperborea, Hurqalya—they're as real as Brooklyn but a damn sight prettier!"

Late afternoon; X must return home before dark, and prepare to take leave of the Shaykh—who gives him a few pamphlets and invites him to return. To X's surprise, Teofila is still waiting outside the shop, and offers to escort him to the subway. The girl is now in a friendlier mood and X less nervous. They strike up a conversation, X asking about Hyperborea and Teofila answering, "Yeah, I know where it is, I've been there."

The main narrative ends here, but we have added some other poetic fragments included with the original MS, despite the fact that they might offend some readers, in light of the importance of the "tantrik technique" of other-world Travel. (And let us remind you that a statement of age must be included with every order from Incunabula Inc.). These rather pornographic fragments suggest that X, too shy to attempt anything himself, was in fact seduced by Teofila, and that his subsequent "training" for Egg-navigation consisted of numerous "practice sessions for double-yolking" with a very enthusiastic young tutor.

We believe that X subsequently made an extended visit to America2 and Java2, that he returned to Earth-prime on some Intelligence or sabotage mission for the GFP, that he composed a paper on Folklore of the Other Worlds (see #25), that he and Teofila somehow came to the attention of PCF agents in New York, aborted their mission and returned to Java2, where they presumably now reside.

25. (Anonymous).
Folklore of the Other Worlds
(Incunabula Press, pamphlet,$15. By the same author as #24, transcribed by us from manuscript.)

Our anonymous Traveller from Brooklyn appears to have composed this little treatise after his first extended stay in E2. It deals with tales of Travellers and inhabitants of the other-world settlements, pioneers' experiences and the like. Of great interest is the claim that ESP and other paranormal abilities increase in the parallel universes, that the effect is magnified by passing through the series of discovered "levels", and that a small band of psychic researchers has therefore settled on Java7, the present frontier world. The "temple" of Hurqalya (or whatever these vast buildings may have been) are used for sessions of meditation, martial arts and psychic experimentation. X claims that telepathy is now accepted as fact "over there," with strong evidence for telekinesis and perhaps even Egg-less Travel.

Also intriguing are various accounts of "spirits" seen or sensed around the settlements, were animals supposedly glimpsed on higher levels, and legends which have arisen concerning the lost Builders of Hurqalya. Something of a cult has grown up around these hypothetical creatures who (it is said) are "moving toward us even as we move toward them, through the dimensions, through Time—perhaps backwards through Time"!

X points out that this legend strikes an eerie resonance with "complex conjugate wave theory" in quantum mechanics, which hypothesizes that the "present" (the megaverse "now") is the result of the meeting of two infinite quantum probabililty waves, one moving from past to future, the other moving from future to past—that space/time is an interference effect of these two waves—and that the many worlds are bubbles on this shoreline!

26. Eliade, Mircea.
Shamanism: Archaic Techniques of Ecstasy
(Univ. of Chicago Press), Pb, $30

This "bible" of the modern neo-shamanic movement also served as a metaphorical scripture for the pioneers of interdimensional consciousness physics and alternate-world explorers.Not only does it contain innumerable practical hints for the Traveller, as well as a spiritual ambience conducive to the proper state of mind for Travel, it is also believed that Eliade's mythic material on the prototypal Stone Age shamans who could physically and actually visit other worlds, offers strong evidence for the possibility of Egg-less Travel—which however so far remains in the realm of "folklore", speculation and rumor.

27. Lorde, John.
Maze of Treason
(Red Knight Books, Wildwood, NJ, 1988), Pb, 204 pp, $10

You may remember that after the Patty Hearst kidnapping it was discovered that a cheap pornographic thriller, published before the event, seemed to foretell every detail of the story. Jungian synchronicity? Or did the Symbionese Liberation Army read that book and decide to act it out? It remains a mystery.

Maze of Treason is also a pornographic thriller, complete with tawdry 4-color cover, sloppy printing on acidulous pulp, and horrendous style. It's marketed as Science Fiction, however. And there is no mystery about the author's inside knowledge. "John Lorde" not only knows about the Conspiracy, he's obviously *been there*. This book is probably a roman a clef, as it appears to contain distorted portraits of Sohrawardi and Harjanto (depicted as Fu-Manchu-type villains) as well as several actual agents of both the GFP and PCF—and even a character apparently based on the real-life "X", author of several titles in our list (#s 24 & 25).

The hero, Jack Masters, is an agent of an unnamed spyforce of American patriots who jokingly call themselves the Quantum Police. Their mission is to regain control of the alternate worlds for "the forces of reason and order" and "make trouble for agents of chaos in every known universe." The Q-Cops' secret underground HDQ contains a number of Eggs granting access to hidden bases on the other worlds, including "the Other America" and "the Other Indonesia".

Jack Masters is investigating the activities of a Chaote named Ripley Taylor, a "child-molester and black magician who runs a Travel Cult out of a comicbook store in a "racially-mixed neighborhood" of New York. The Cops hope to catch Taylor with his "juvenile delinquent girlfriend", blackmail him and turn him into a double agent.

The hero now becomes involved with Amanita, a beautiful woman performance artist from the Lower East Side who seems to know a lot about Taylor and the Travel Cult, but also seems quite attracted to the virile Jack Masters. At first he suspects her of duplicity, but soon decides he needs to "convert" her by making her "fall for me, and fall hard." Jack's problem is that his own "talent" will not suffice for solo Travelling, and in fact he has never managed to "get across"—since the Cops do not practice Tantrik techniques! He suspects her of being an "Other-Worlder" and hopes she can convey him thence via the "infamous 'double-yolk' method."

Meanwhile Taylor has laughed off the blackmail attempt, burned down the comic shop and escaped "into the fourth dimension—or maybe the fifth." Masters heats up his affair with the artist Amanita, and finally convinces her to "translate" him—after three chapters of unininterrupted porno depicting the pair in many little-known ritual practises, so to speak. (The author rises above his own mediocrity here, and attains something like "purple pulp", an inspired gush of horny prose, especially in the oral-genital area.) Masters now rises to the occasion for yet a fourth chapter in which a "government-issue Egg" becomes the setting for a "yab-yum ceremony of searing obscenity."

Immediately upon arrival in "Si Fan" (the author's name for Hurqalya), Amanita betrays our hero and turns him over naked to one of the tribes of "chaos-shamans who inhabit these Lemurian ruins". At this point Maze begins to add to our knowledge of the real-life situation by depicting more-or-less accurately the state of affairs and mode of life in present-day Hurqalya, at least as seen through the eyes of a paranoid right-wing spy.

The thousand or so inhabitants have made few changes in Hurqalya, preferring a life of "primitive sloth" and minimal meddling with Nature. Sex, hallucinogenic mushrooms and song-improvisation contests comprise the night-life, with days devoted to the serious business of "sorcery, skinnydipping, flintknapping and maybe a couple of hours of desultory fishing or berrypicking." There is no social order. "People with bones in their noses sitting around arguing about Black Hole Theory or recipes for marsupial stew, lazy smoke from a few clan campfires rising through the hazy bluegold afternoon, children masturbating in trees, bees snouting into orchids, signal drum in the distance, Amanita singing an old song by the Inkspots I remember from my childhood..."

Masters—or rather the author—claims to be disgusted by all this "anarchist punk hippy immorality—all this jungle love!"—but his ambivalence is revealed in his continued desire for Amanita, and the ease with which he falls into his own curmudgeonly version of *dolce far niente* in "Si Fan".

We won't give away the rest of the plot, not because it's so great, but because it's largely irrelevant (Taylor flees to distant dimensions, Masters gets Girl and returns to Earth-prime in triumph, etc.,etc.)—the book's true value lies in these pictures of daily life in Hurqalya. Sadly, Maze of Treason is still our only source for such material.

The Conspiracy to deny the world all knowledge of the Many Worlds is maintained by both the forces active in the parallel universes—the **GFP** and **PCF** both have their reasons for secrecy, evasion, lies, disinformation, distortion and even violence. Maze of Treason is not our only source for claiming that people have lost their lives as a result of getting too deeply involved in all this. But we at INCUNABULA believe that truth will out, because it must. To stand in the way of it is more dangerous than letting it loose. Freedom of information is our only protection—we will tell all, despite all scorn or threat, and trust that our "going public" will protect us from the outrage of certain private interests—if not from the laughter of the ignorant!

Remember: parallel worlds exist. They have already been reached. A vast cover-up denies YOU all knowledge. Only INCUNABULA can enlighten you, because only INCUNABULA dares.

Thank You, Emory Cranston, Prop.[1]

PREFACE

1. Shortly after Lang's death, a young Romanian religious scholar named Mircea Eliade suggested, in a 1937 article, that some supernatural tales are artistically embellished reports of real human experiences prompted by psychical abilities. Though Eliade's foray into psycho-folklorism was relatively short lived, over the next several decades a few other individuals have examined Lang's arguments. See Ward 1977, Lintrop 1996, and McClenon 2002 for examples. For an English translation of Eliade's 1937 article, "Folklore as an Instrument of Knowledge," see Rennie 2006.

2. See Hufford 1982; Rojcewicz 1987.

3. Paul Smith has long advocated for folklorists—especially those who study legends—to apply a "multi-media model of communication . . . which takes into account both *physiological* and *technological* elements." See Smith 1989; see also Smith 1975.

4. Ellwood 1973. See also Taylor 1999.

5. Ellis 2003, 167.

CHAPTER 1

1. This anecdote is often told within the UFO community, arguably to validate the subject of their interest as having precedent in antiquity. The original source of this incident seems to come from a non-cited reference in Frank Edwards's book, *Stranger Than Science* (New York: Ace Publications, 1958), so this tale might exemplify a fabricated or engineered legend. There have been many miraculous claims made of Alexander by ancient historians for political reasons, but I have been unable to find any primary source illustrating the Jaxartes incident.

2. This event is recounted in the anonymously written twelfth-century manuscript, *Annales Laurissenses Maioris*, in *Monumenta Germaniae Historica, Scriptores rerum Germanicarum* 6, 44.

3. Kean 2007.

4. Zhenxin and Wanpo 1979.

5. Sanderson 1960.

6. Podmore 2003 [1902], 254.

7. This collection was less popular than their publications on fairy tales, perhaps one reason being because the Grimms decontextualized legends and treated them as literature rather than as sociological phenomena.

8. Hand 1965.

9. See the Introduction in Bennett and Smith, 1996.

10. Interestingly, men report nearly all accounts of "vanishing hitchhikers," and the hitchhikers are almost always women.

11. For instance, urban legends are commonly transmitted in rural areas; many contemporary legends have their origins in the ancient world; and rumor legends present a conundrum—what *is* the difference between rumor and legend? Some legend scholars, such as Gillian Bennett, suggest that legends are capable of "straddling the divide between fact and fiction, partaking of the nature of both" (see p. 35 in Gillian Bennett and Paul Smith, eds., *Contemporary Legend: A Reader* [New York: Garland Publishing, 1996]), while others, like Jan Brunvand, propose that legends must be considered *false*, at least as literal accounts (see p. xii in *The Vanishing Hitchhiker: American Urban Legends and Their Meanings* [New York: W. W. Norton & Co., 1981]).

12. Georges 1971.

13. Lindahl 1986.

14. Ibid., 9.

15. I'm indebted to Jane McGonigal for developing the concept of the performance of belief as relating to immersive narratives. Source: http://www.avant-game.com/MCGONIGAL%20A%20Real%20Little%20Game%20DiGRA%202003. pdf (accessed March 2, 2006). See chapter 4 for more on McGonigal's concept.

16. Peuckert 1965, 80; see also Dégh 2001, 38.

17. Baer 1982, 275–76.

18. Ibid.

19. Victor 1990.

20. Ellis 2003, 199.

21. Mullen 1972.

22. 2003, 62.

23. Sleep paralysis consists of hypnogogic paralysis and is sometimes accompanied by hypnagogic hallucinations. The term *hypnagogic* refers to the border state of consciousness between sleep and wakefulness. Experiencing the effects of sleep paralysis can result in acute terror. For more, see Hufford 1982.

24. Fialkova and Yelenevskaya 2001.

25. Dégh 2001, 115.

26. See Davis 2004, Kochhar-Lindgren 2005.

27. Harris 2008, 5.

28. Lloyd 1995, 60.

29. Goldstein, Grider, and Thomas 2007, 174–75. Goldstein reports on the trend within real estate to advertise properties as being haunted by friendly spirits. These marketing strategies observe traditional views of the supernatural and decisions to advertise a place as haunted depend upon the nature of the spirit allegedly cohabitating the property. If the supernatural legend associated with the real estate depicts the ghost to have physically died by violence or disaster (as op-

posed to a natural, peaceful demise), then the legend may substantially decrease
the property's marketability and realtors may not choose to disclose these narratives unless forced to by law. In some states, realtors must inform potential buyers
of the regional folklore (supernatural legends) associated with the properties in
question.

30. Ibid., 200–202.

31. Ibid. 197.

32. Gabbert 2001.

33. Mylonas 1962.

34. Dundes 1997, referring to Claude Lévi-Strauss 1955.

CHAPTER 2

1. Jonathan Jurgenson, November 4, 2005, Lyndon, Kentucky. Interview recorded by Michael Kinsella. While Jonathan refers to a group called MESA, this is
actually an acronym standing for "multi-energy sensor array" and is a computer
system some paranormal researchers use to measure energies associated with pol-
tergeist activity. See Harte, Black, and Hollinshead, 1999.

2. Curiously, all ghostly images I've seen that have been taken at Waverly appear to be directly facing the camera, a fact pointed out to me by Jonathan during
one of our interviews.

3. The only ghost-sickness I was familiar with at the time was a series of
culture-related syndromes associated with certain Native American groups, such
as the Navajo, the Jicarilla, and the Lipan. Traditionally, ghost-sickness strikes
those Native Americans who have had contact with ghosts, who are preoccupied
with the dead, or who are the victims of witchcraft. Symptoms include weakness,
dizziness, confusion, and delusion. For commentary on Native American ghost-
sickness, see Holt 1983, Kluckhohn and Leighton 1946, and Opler 1959. For an
in-depth discussion on the European construction of culture-bound syndromes that
focuses on ghost-sickness, see Waldram 2004. While I can only speculate why one
particular spot apparently brings on sudden, temporary illness for some people, it
is an especially interesting theme within the Waverly Hills legend complex.

4. Folklorists coined the term "legend-tripping" sometime around the late
1960s to early 1970s.

5. In his study of Hispanic Texan legends about gravity hills, Mark Glazer
reports, "The narrative elements, the story context and the socio-cultural background of the narrators together result in a legend which is more than a narrative
and a belief which is less than a conviction." See Glazer 1989, 176.

6. See Ellis 2003, 2004.

7. Van Gennep 1909.

8. Turner 1967.

9. Thigpen 1971.

10. Ellis 2003, 167.

11. For examples, see Thigpen 1971, Hall 1973, Meley 1991, Bird 1994, Dégh
2001, Ellis 2004.

12. Lindahl 2005, 175.

13. Scott 1802. Bill Ellis makes reference to the original thirteenth-century work in his book, *Lucifer Ascending* (2004), 117–18.

14. Brady 1995, 147.

15. Ibid., 148.

16. Price 1996.

17. Koven 2008, 153.

18. Ibid. 154.

19. Ibid.

20. http://forums.scifi.com/index.php?showtopic = 2291677&hl = waverly&s t = 80 (accessed March 2, 2009).

21. Ibid.

22. http://forums.scifi.com/index.php?showtopic = 2291677&hl = waverly&s t = 100 (accessed March 2, 2009).

23. "Elijah Burke's spooky experience." Source: http://www.wwe.com/inside/overtheropes/news/elijahghosthuntersrecap (accessed July 6, 2009).

24. http://forums.syfy.com/index.php?showtopic = 2291677&hl = waverly&s t = 760 (accessed July 12, 2009).

25. http://forums.syfy.com/index.php?showtopic = 2291677&hl = waverly&s t = 740 (accessed July 12, 2009).

26. http://forums.scifi.com/index.php?showtopic = 2292549&hl = panic + but ton (accessed March 2, 2009).

27. http://forums.scifi.com/index.php?showtopic = 2292362 (accessed March 2, 2009).

28. Source: http://www.travelchannel.com/TV_Shows/Ghost_Adventures/ci.Ghost_A dventures_LIVE.show?vgnextfmt = show (accessed July 6, 2009).

29. Koven 2008, 152.

30. Lombard and Ditton 1997.

31. Ibid.

32. Lauria 1997.

CHAPTER 3

1. Frazer 1993 [1890], 12. Unlike Frazer, Malinowski believed magic was psychologically effective, but was convinced its practice would diminish with the more scientific knowledge people acquired.

2. Gmelch 1989, 295.

3. Bullard 2000.

4. Luhrmann 1989, 336.

5. Adler 1986, 8.

6. Ibid., 157.

7. Ibid., 6.

8. Crowley 1998 [1912], 147.

9. Luhrmann 1989.

10. Ibid., 317.

11. Ibid., 353.

12. Covino 1994, 12, referring to O'Keefe 1982.

13. O'Keefe 1982, xv.
14. Ellis 2003, 166.
15. Davis 2004, 216.
16. See Moore 1977; Oppenheim 1985; Owen 1989.
17. See John Harvey's 2004 article on Spiritualism and visual technology.
18. Firenze 2004, 73.
19. Harvey 2004.
20. Taylor 2004, 124
21. Warren 2003, 165.
22. Durant 2003, 14.
23. http://occultsoftware.com/thesourcesoftware/ (accessed December 12, 2007).
24. Ibid.
25. Keel 2006, 4.
26. Tucker 2007, 87–90.
27. Digital Dowsing, a company specializing in applied technologies for paranormal research, designed the Ovilus. http://www.digitaldowsing.com/products/ (accessed October 3, 2009).
28. "CyberSamhain Invitation." http://1997.webhistory.org/www.lists/www-vrml.1994/0642.html (accessed January 7, 2008).
29. Barkun 2003, 19.
30. McLuhan 1962.
31. The actual term "noosphere" was created by geochemist Vladimir Vernadsky to name a theoretical, yet-to-occur period of human development when human cognition would reshape Earth's biosphere.
32. Teilhard 1959, 251.
33. Ibid. 259.
34. Julian Huxley's "Introduction" to Teilhard de Chardin's *The Phenomenon of Man* (New York: Harper & Row, 1959), 17–18.

CHAPTER 4

1. For a brief introductory comparison, see Versluis 2007.
2. Mathers (translator) 1975 [1900].
3. See Vallee 1979, Keel 1996, Levenda 2005.
4. Raymond Fowler and Dr. R. Leo Sprinkle are two ufologists who, after investigating alien abductions for more than two decades each, eventually concluded that they themselves had been abducted. One of the more famous occult rumors that continues to circulate involves the magician Charles Stansfield Jones, otherwise known as Frater Achad. Jones was considered by Crowley to be his heir, or "magical child," and a future Magus. However, according to an unverified account given by Kenneth Grant, Jones's magical workings eventually led to mental instability; sometime around 1930, Jones was performing a magical operation in Vancouver when he suddenly ran outside and through the city naked, which led to his placement in a mental health institution (see Grant 1993).
5. Gunn 2005, 124.
6. Davis 2005.

7. Bendix 1997.

8. www.avantegame.com (accessed January 4, 2006).

9. This paper was a community-created resource put forth by the International Game Developers Association. Source: http://www.igda.org/arg/resources/IGDA-AlternateRealityGames-Whitepaper-2006.pdf (accessed January 4, 2006).

10. This term comes from Lewis Carroll's *Alice's Adventures in Wonderland,* in which Alice follows a mysterious white rabbit into a rabbit hole and discovers "Wonderland," an absurd, seemingly impossible world filled with bizarre characters. The phrase "rabbit hole" has also entered into colloquial speech as a reference to any portal or event leading to a strange location or situation (both supernatural legends and occult texts may be considered rabbit holes).

11. Szulborski 2005, 31.

12. McGonigal 2003.

13. Ibid., referring to Goffman 1974.

14. Source: http://www.avantgame.com/MCGONIGAL%20A%20Real%20Little%20Game%20DiGRA%202003.pdf (accessed March 2, 2006).

15. Orginal citation by McGonigal: T. "We are one, we are all." (July 25, 2001) http://groups.yahoo.com/group/cloudmakers/message/42523 (accessed January 21, 2003).

16. Original citation by McGonigal: Bonasia, Maria. "Editorials: MetaMystery." (May 30, 2001) http://cloudmakers.org/editorials/mbonasia530.shtml (accessed January 21, 2003).

17. Original citation by McGonigal: Moonlore. "Re: Cloudmakers link on Salla page." (May 3, 2001) http://groups.yahoo.com/group/cloudmakers/message/11912 (accessed January 21, 2003). SETI@Home—SETI stands for Search For Extraterrestrial Intelligence—is a software program that uses a distributed grid computer process enabling home computers to download and analyze data gathered from the SETI project.

18. McGonigal 2003.

19. Commercial and grassroots media producers continue to develop ARGs, sometimes to address real-world problems. *Tomorrow Calling* and *World Without Oil* are two examples of what has come to be called "serious ARGs," which are explicitly designed to creatively guide the collective intelligence of their performers/audiences toward affecting real solutions for environmental crises.

20. Kirshenblatt-Gimblett 1996, referring to Couey 1991.

21. Merrick 2004, quoting Jenkins 2002, 158.

22. Merrick 2004.

23. For more on memes, see Dawkins 1989, 192.

24. The artist and magician Austin Osman Spare initially popularized the act of sigilization for contemporary magicians. Sigils are any written symbol, work of art, or other creation that magicians make to impress their wills upon reality. One current trend in magical practice is the creation of hypersigils, more elaborate works of art that may incorporate transmedia storytelling explicitly for magical purposes. Some graphic novels and comic books, such as Grant Morrison's *The Invisibles,* are considered hypersigils.

25. Frauenfelder 1997.

26. Stang 1997, 1.

CHAPTER 5

1. Both these documents are included as appendices.

2. A version of this document seems to have appeared as a short story entitled "Ong's Hat" in the zine *Edge Detector* in 1988. The credited author, Peter Lamborn Wilson, purportedly received the document through mail art channels and, in the tradition of mail art, altered the materials and passed them on. A version of *Ong's Hat: Gateway* also appeared in the webzine *Grist On-Line* in February 1994; the credited author is Joseph Matheny. http://www.thing.net/~grist/golpub/golmag/gol5.txt (accessed March 5, 2008).

3. Rushkoff 1996, 190.

4. Eco 1994.

5. Source: http://web.archive.org/web/20030712174104/pub36.ezboard.com/fdarkplanet76000frm10.showMessage?topicID = 94.topic (accessed February 19, 2007).

6. Source: http://www.cassiopaea.org/cass/991204.htm (accessed January 5, 2007).

7. The following posts were accessed from http://deoxy.org/irc/59.htm on March 26, 2006. The website www.deoxy.org is a kind of online hub for future-oriented ideas about culture.

8. Source: http://www.geocities.com/harlaquinn_2000/cathedral.html (accessed January 22, 2007).

9. The phrase "parallel universes Q" simply refers to the multiple realities that folk interpretations of quantum physics envision.

10. Campion-Vincent 2005, 108.

11. Ellis 2004, 114.

12. Bulletin Board Systems are electronic message boards that usually serve specific interest groups. A precursor to the Internet, early BBS allowed users to connect to a computer system through phone lines.

13. Source: http://www.incunabula.org/inc4.html (accessed April 11, 2007).

14. Ibid., 36.

15. See Milford Connolly's interview with Matheny on "The Garden of Truth" podcast. http://gardenoftruth.blogspot.com/ (accessed March 13, 2009).

16. Culture-jamming (also known as reality-hacking and culture-hacking) can be defined as any disruptive tactic used to expose the ways mass culture "brain-washes" people. Groups commonly aligned with culture-jamming include the Dadaists and Surrealists (both are mentioned in later chapters).

17. Source: http://joseph.matheny.com/PDFS/mavericks.pdf (accessed March 17, 2006).

18. For an insightful study of the paranormal that focuses on its trickster qualities, see Hansen 2001.

19. "The Ong's Hat Mystery Revealed: An Interview with Joseph Matheny." No.2 Source: http://web.archive.org/web/20060713095419/www.newworld disorder.ca/issuethree/editorials/centripetalculture.html (accessed January 23, 2009).

20. See Sheldrake's Paper, "Morphic Resonance and Morphic Fields: An

Introduction." Source: http://www.sheldrake.org/Articles&Papers/papers/mor
phic/morphic_intro.html (accessed July 30, 2007).

21. Allegedly, Wilson forwarded this material to *Edge Detector* after hav-
ing received it himself through mail art channels. Both *Ong's Hat: Gateway* and
Incunabula: A Catalogue are considered to be anonymously written (Matheny and
Moon's 2002 book, *Ong's Hat: The Beginning*, cites versions of both *Incunabula: A
Catalogue* and *Ong's Hat: Gateway* as "authors unknown," and presents these docu-
ments as reference material.

22. Bey 1991. In the preface to his 2003 edition of *T.A.Z.*, Bey comments that
temporary (or permanent) autonomous zones *must* exist in physical space.

23. Bey 1994. Source: http://www.hermetic.com/bey/mailord.html (accessed
August 19, 2008).

24. Source: http://www.t0.or.at/hakimbey/radio.htm#Immediatism (accessed
October 8, 2008). Also see Bey 2001.

25. Source: http://www.incunabula.org/inc3.html (accessed April 3, 2007).

26. Neuro-Linguistic Programming (NLP) was developed in the 1970s by John
Grinder and Richard Bandler, and offers a series of models for how communication impacts and is impacted by subjective experience.

CHAPTER 6

1. Source: http://web.archive.org/web/20030712171108/pub36.ezboard.com/
fdarkplanet76000frm10.showMessage?topicID = 75.topic (accessed November 12,
2008).

2. McMahon 1987, 94–96.

3. Roth 2005, 72, referring to Berkhofer 1978 and Weatherford 1988, 117–31.

4. See Barkun 2003, 13.

5. The following posts were accessed from http://deoxy.org/irc/59.htm on
March 26, 2006. The website www.deoxy.org is an online hub for futurists.

6. This edition includes a host of new materials, such as Philip K. Dick's *Man In
the High Castle*, Jacques Vallee's *Messengers of Deception*, and the film, *The Matrix*.
It also contains other media, such as the shareware program "Cellular Automata."
Besides offering commentaries on the various catalogued items, this online and
updated catalogue includes links to where these various media may be down-
loaded or purchased (through the online store amazon.com). "The Incunabula
Catalogue: The Frequency Edition 2001–2012" can be found at http://www.sirba
con.org/dwc.html (accessed July 2, 2008).

7. Source: http://web.archive.org/web/20030910163546/pub36.ezboard.
com/fdarkplanet76000frm10.showMessage?topicID = 85.topic (accessed May 22,
2006). "Si Fan" was the secret society that the fictional character of Fu Manchu
(created by Sax Rohmer) belonged to. "YALU," "GANO," and "SILA" are found
in the book *bolo'bolo*, written by the anonymous Zurich-based author known as
"P.M.," and are parts of a terminology describing the operations of an alternative
society—a permanent autonomous zone. Yalu = one day's rations, Gano = hous-
ing, and Sila = a kind of social contract or utopian unit. *bolo'bolo* uses the phrase
"Planetary Work Machine" to refer our current social organization—this same
phrase is found at the beginning of *Ong's Hat: Gateway*.

8. Source: http://web.archive.org/web/20030712172314/pub36.ezboard.com/ fdark planet76000frm10.showMessage?topicID = 84.topic (accessed May 3, 2008).

9. Bishop's comments regarding "interviews" likely refers to both Matheny's 1992 online journal entry recounting a talk with Nick Herbert and a circulating audio clip of a phone interview Matheny conducted in 2000 with "Rupert" and "Abel," two people who claimed to have grown up in the Ong's Hat ashram (this recording was later transcribed in Matheny's book, *Ong's Hat: The Beginning*).

10. Source: http://www.geocities.com/harlaquinn_2000/ficgames.txt (accessed March 2, 2006).

11. Ellis 2003, 83–84.

12. Source: http://www.geocities.com/harlaquinn_2000/fictionsuits.html (accessed March 2, 2006).

13. Source: http://deoxy.org/wiki/fiction_suit (accessed March 2, 2006).

14. Source: http://www.disinfo.com/archive/pages/dossier/id987/pg4/index .html (accessed June 30, 2007).

CHAPTER 7

1. Ward 1977, 216.

2. Ellis 2003, 157–58.

3. Breton 1972, 123–24.

4. Hufford 1982.

5. See Owen 2004 for examples.

6. Source: http://web.archive.org/web/20030712165315/pub36.ezboard.com/ fdarkplanet76000frm10.showMessage?topicID = 110.topic (accessed March 28, 2009).

7. Owen 2004, 165.

8. Diverse supernatural traditions may represent ongoing, cumulative efforts to codify state-specific knowledge gathered during altered states of consciousness (ASCs) and to modulate access to these states. Because ASCs can offer therapeutic benefits and have the potential to positively transform the human psyche, we should notice culturally transmitted schemas that enhance people's natural ability to access these states. Because knowledge gathered in ASCs isn't fully knowable or translatable once ordinary or even another non-ordinary state of consciousness is entered, we should notice culturally transmitted schemas that preserve such knowledge. And since some people have a propensity for ASCs that can produce adverse effects, we should also notice culturally transmitted schemas that counter or control this susceptibility. We find all of these within a wide range of supernatural traditions, such as legend-telling, as well as within a number of traditions not specifically classifiable as supernatural.

9. Source: http://web.archive.org/web/20030712174825/pub36.ezboard.com/ fdarkplanet76000frm10.showMessage?topicID = 98.topic (accessed January 20, 2009).

10. Castaneda wrote of the "flyers," psycho-spiritual creatures who preyed on the imperfect thoughts of man and who implanted in mankind the flyers' own mind. Gurdjieff described a similar implanted organ of perception called "kund-

abuffer," which operates to limit man's spiritual evolution. Both the flyer-mind and the kundabuffer are said to increase the destructive qualities of egotism and diminish the capacity for spirituality. These ideas, in turn, are similar to ancient Gnostic concepts of the Archons, as well as countercultural ideas about the limitations of cultural belief systems. See Castaneda 1999, Gurdjieff 2000.

11. See Bennett 1999.

12. Source: http://web.archive.org/web/20030515044849/pub36.ezboard .com/fdarkplanet76000frm10.showMessage?topicID = 51.topic (accessed March 14, 2009).

13. Source: http://deoxy.org/irc/59.htm (accessed November 3, 2009).

14. Source: http://web.archive.org/web/20030713180330/pub36.ez board.com/fdarkplanet76000frm10.showMessageRange?topicID = 130 .topic&start = 21&stop = 32 (accessed March 3, 2009).

15. See Sannella 1992; see also Greenwell 1995.

16. Source: http://web.archive.org/web/20020415133521/pub36 .ezboard.com/fdarkplanet76000frm10.showMessageRange?topicID = 98 .topic&start = 21&stop = 29 (accessed November 30, 2009).

17. Source: http://web.archive.org/web/20021006235915/geocities.com/har laquinn_2000/chapel.html (accessed November 30, 2009).

18. Pauwels and Bergier chronicled other such efforts (including the Rosicrucian Manifestos) in their work, *The Morning of Magicians,* itself an example of "fantastic realism"—a point of view in which the fantastic is sought after in the real, leading to a "deeper participation in life" (xxvi–xxvii).

19. Source: http://web.archive.org/web/20021007010927/geocities.com/har laquin n_2000/mystery1.html (accessed December 12, 2009).

CHAPTER 8

1. The phrase "Akasa 'egg'" is an esoteric reference: "Akasa" (or "Akasha," as in the Akashic records) is a Sanskrit term meaning "sky." In an occult context, Akasa refers to the subtle spirit-matter that pervades all space as a sort of reservoir of conscious information; the Akasa egg then refers to the whole of existence—think of the noosphere. The "alchemical 'curcurbite'" and "Egg Philosophic" mentioned are terms used to describe the lower, oval-shaped part of a glass still containing the liquid to be transformed; these are also esoteric metaphors for the individual who will be transformed through magical initiation.

2. The acronyms LHP and RHP stand for "left hand path" and "right hand path." These are modern magical terms that emphasize different methods for acquiring magical or even mystical knowledge. Restraint, renunciation of the physical world, and devotion to a greater good characterize those practices commonly identified as RHPs, while antinomianism, embracement of the material world, and elevation of the ego typify LHPs.

3. Source: http://www.geocities.com/harlaquinn_2000/wrapup.html (accessed: March 2, 2007).

4. Source: http://www.geocities.com/harlaquinn_2000/gauntlet.html (accessed March 16, 2006).

5. Source: http://web.archive.org/web/20030713131420/pub36.ez board.com/fdarkplanet76000frm10.showMessageRange?topicID = 41. topic&start = 21&stop = 40 (accessed December 2, 2009).

6. Source: http://deoxy.org/forum (accessed March 15, 2006).

7. Matheny 2002, 172.

8. Moon 2004, 186, 187.

9. Ibid., 81.

10. Source: http://web.archive.org/web/20021007010927/geocities.com/har laquinn_2000/mystery1.html (accessed December 3, 2009).

CHAPTER 9

1. Source: http://amazingforums.com/forum/TRAVELLER/102.html (accessed January 23, 2008).

2. Moon 2004, 330–31.

3. "Macroteleport" refers to a now-defunct website that presented sculptures of teleportation devices for sale—this site gathered the considerable attention of alternative reality communities for a time, until its commercial aspects came into focus.

4. Source: http://amazingforums.com/forum/TRAVELLER/102.html (accessed January 23, 2008).

5. Source: http://www.darkplanetonline.com/whatreally.html (accessed March 3, 2006).

6. Ibid.

7. Ibid.

8. Whitehead 2000.

9. Communities developed around or otherwise concerned with UFO lore are especially sensitive to the presence of hoaxes, ARGs, and viral marketing campaigns. For instance, MUFON (the Mutual U.F.O. Network, an international organization devoted to the study and dissemination of the UFO phenomenon) spent considerable time investigating a series of photographs and videos containing "drones," an aesthetically unique type of machinery or craft of unknown origins that appeared repeatedly throughout 2007. These drones were connected to an anonymous figure known only as "Isaac," who maintains a website detailing his involvement with a company ("CARET") that reverse engineers alien technology (a popular motif in current UFO lore). After exploring the case at length, MUFON found a possible motive to be a viral marketing campaign. Other UFO enthusiasts have also suggested that the "Isaac/CARET" phenomenon is part of an alternate reality game. See http://www.mufon.com/documents/Drones-CARET.ppt (accessed July 22, 2009); see also http://isaaccaret.fortunecity.com/ (accessed July 22, 2009).

10. Keel 1983. This letter was later revealed by Palmer to have been written by Fred Lee Crisman, a figure who, interestingly, appears in several paranormal and conspiratorial accounts throughout the middle of the twentieth century. This letter's contents are strikingly similar to contemporary accounts of firefights with aliens that allegedly occurred underground at Ducle, New Mexico, in the late 1970s.

APPENDIX 2

1. Source: http://deoxy.org/inc2.htm (accessed December 4, 2005).

APPENDIX 3

1. Source: http://deoxy.org/inc1.htm (accessed December 4, 2005).

Adler, Margot. 1986. *Drawing Down the Moon*. Boston: Beacon Books.

Baer, Florence E. 1982. "Give me . . . your huddled masses": Anti-Vietnamese Refugee Lore and the "Image of Limited Good." *Western Folklore* 41:4, 275–91.

Barkun, Michael. 2003. *A Culture of Conspiracy: Apocalyptic Visions in Contemporary America*. Berkeley and Los Angeles: University of California Press.

Bendix, Regina. 1997. *In Search of Authenticity: The Formation of Folklore Studies*. Madison: University of Wisconsin Press.

Bennett, Gillian. 1999. *Alas, Poor Ghost! Traditions of Belief in Story and Discourse*. Logan: Utah State University Press.

———. 1996. "Legend: Performance and Truth." *Contemporary Legend: A Reader*, ed. Gillian Bennett and Paul Smith. New York: Garland Publishing.

Bennett, Gillian, and Paul Smith. 1996. "Introduction." *Contemporary Legend: A Reader*, ed. Gillian Bennett and Paul Smith. New York: Garland Publishing.

Ben-Yehuda, Nachman. 1985. *Deviance and Moral Boundaries: Witchcraft, the Occult, Science Fiction, Deviant Sciences and Scientists*. Chicago: University of Chicago Press.

Berkhofer, Robert F., Jr. 1978. *The White Man's Indian: Images of the American Indian from Columbus to the Present*. New York: Vantage.

Bey, Hakim. 2001. *Immediatism*. Oakland: AK Press.

———. 1991. *The Temporary Autonomous Zone*. http://www.hermetic.com/bey/taz_cont.html. Accessed March 2, 2006.

Bird, S. Elizabeth. 2002. "It Makes Sense To Us: Cultural Identity in Local Legends of Place." *Journal of Contemporary Ethnography* 31:519–47.

———. 1994. "Playing With Fear: Interpreting the Adolescent Legend Trip." *Western Folklore* 53:191–209.

Borges, Jorge Luis. 1966. *Labyrinths: Selected Stories and Other Writings*, ed. Donald A. Yates and James E. Irby. New York: New Directions Publishing.

Brady, Erika. 1995. "Bad Scares and Joyful Hauntings: 'Priesting' the Supernatural Predicament." Barbara Walker, ed. *Out of the Ordinary: Folklore and the Supernatural*. Logan: Utah University Press. 145–58.

Breton, André. 1972. "Second Manifesto of Surrealism." *Manifestoes of Surrealism*, trans. Richard Seaver and Helen Lane. Ann Arbor: University of Michigan Press.

Brookes-Smith, C., and D. W. Hunt. 1970. "Some Experiments in Psychokinesis." *Journal of the Society for Psychical Research* 47:69–89.

Brown, David Jay, and Rebecca Novack. 1993. "MediaKaos Interview." http://joseph.matheny.com/PDFS/mavericks.pdf. Accessed March 17, 2006.

Brunvand, Jan. 1981. *The Vanishing Hitchhiker: American Urban Legends and Their Meanings.* New York: W. W. Norton.

Bullard, Thomas. 2000. "Lost in the Myths." *UFOs and Abductions: Challenging the Borders of Knowledge,* ed. David Jacobs. Lawrence: University Press of Kansas.

Campion-Vincent, Véronique. 2005. "A Dominant Pattern in Conspiracy Theories Today." *Rumor Mills: The Social Impact of Rumor and Legend,* ed. Chip Heath. Piscataway, NJ: Aldine Transaction.

Castaneda, Carlos. 1999. *The Active Side of Infinity.* New York: Harper Perennial.

Corbin, Henry. 1995. *Swedenborg and Esoteric Islam,* trans. Leonard Fox. New York: Swedenborg Foundation Publishers.

Couey, Anna. 1991. "Cyber Art: The Art of Communication Systems." *Matrix News* 1:4.

Covino, William. 1994. *Magic, Rhetoric, and Literacy: An Eccentric History of the Composing Imagination.* Buffalo: SUNY Press.

Crowley, Aleister. 1998 [1912]. *Magick: Liber Aba : Book 4*; 2 Rev Sub edition. Newburyport: Weiser Books.

———. 1992. *Magick in Theory and Practice.* Minneapolis: Consortium Book Sales & Distribution.

Davis, Erik. 2005. "Calling Cthulhu: H. P. Lovecraft's Magick Realism." http://www.techgnosis.com/chunks.php?sec = articles&cat = phantasy&file = chunkfrom-2005-12-13-1057-0.txt. Accessed November 2, 2006.

———. 2004. *TechGnosis: Myth, Magic and Mysticism in the Age of Information.* London: Serpent's Tail.

Dawkins, Richard. 1989. *The Selfish Gene.* Oxford: Oxford University Press.

Dégh, Linda. 2001. *Legend and Belief.* Bloomington: Indiana University Press.

Dégh, Linda, and Andrew Vázsonyi. 1983. "Does the Word 'Dog' Bite? Ostensive Action: A Means of Legend Telling." *Journal of Folklore Research* 20:5–34.

———. 1974. "The Memorate and the Proto-Memorate." *Journal of American Folklore* 87:225–39.

Dundes, Alan. 1997. "Binary opposition in myth: The Propp/Levi-Strauss debate in retrospect." *Western Folklore* 56:1

Durant, Mark Alice. 2003. "The Blur of the Otherworldly." *Art Journal* 62 (3): 6–17.

Eco, Umberto. 1994. *The Limits of Interpretation.* Bloomington: Indiana University Press.

———. 1990. *Foucault's Pendulum.* New York: Ballantine Books.

Edwards, Frank. 1958. *Stranger Than Science.* New York: Ace Publications.

Ellis, Bill. 2004. *Lucifer Ascending: The Occult in Folklore and Popular Culture.* Lexington: University Press of Kentucky.

———. 2003. *Aliens, Ghosts, and Cults: Legends We Live.* Jackson: University Press of Mississippi.

Ellwood, Robert S., Jr. 1973. *Religious and Spiritual Groups in Modern America.* Englewood Cliffs, NJ: Prentice Hall, Inc.

Ferris, Alison. 2003. "Disembodied Spirits: Spirit Photography and Rachel Whiteread's Ghost." *Art Journal* 62 (3): 45–53.

Fialkova, Larisa, and Maria Yelenevskaya. 2001. "Ghosts in the Cyber World: An Analysis of Folklore Sites on the Internet." *Fabula* 42:64–89.

Firenze, Paul. 2004. "Spirit Photography." *Skeptic* 11 (2): 70–78.

Frauenfelder, Mark. 1997. "Cheap Memes: Zines, Metazines and the Virtual Press." http://www.zinebook.com/resource/memes.html. Accessed February 3, 2007.

Frazer, James. 1993 [1890]. *The Golden Bough.* Hertfordshire: Wordsworth Editions Lt.

Friedman, R. Seth. 1997. *The Factsheet Five Zine Reader.* New York: Three Rivers Press.

Gabbert, Lisa. 2000. "Religious Belief and Everyday Knowledge: A Functional Analysis of the Legend Dialectic." *Contemporary Legend New Series Volume 3*: 108–26.

Gennep, Arnold Van. 1909. *The Rites of Passage.* Translated by Monika B. Vizedom and Gabrielle L. Caffee. London: Routledge and Kegan Paul.

Georges, Robert. 1971. "The General Concept of Legend: Some Assumptions to Be Reexamined and Reassessed." *American Folk Legend: A Symposium,* ed. Wayland Hand. Berkeley and Los Angeles: University of California Press.

Gettings, Fred. 1978. *Ghosts in Photographs: The Extraordinary Story of Spirit Photography.* New York: Harmony Books.

Glazer, Mark. 1989. "Gravity Hill: Belief and Belief Legend." *The Questing Beast: Perspectives on Contemporary Legend Volume IV,* ed. Gillian Bennett and Paul Smith. Sheffield: Sheffield Academic Press.

Gmelch, George. 1989 (1985), "Baseball Magic." *Magic, Witchcraft, and Religion: An Anthropological Study of the Supernatural,* ed. Arthur Lehmann and James E. Myers, 2nd ed. Mountainview: Mayfield Publishing Co.

Goffman, Erving. 1974. *Frame Analysis: An Essay on the Organization of Experience.* London: Harper and Row.

Goldstein, Diane, Sylvia Grider, and Jeannie Banks Thomas. 2007. *Haunting Experiences: Ghosts in Contemporary Folklore.* Logan: Utah State University Press.

Grant, Kenneth. 1993. *The Magical Revival.* London: Skoob Books.

Greenwell, Bonnie. 1995. *Energies of Transformation: A Guide to the Kundalini Process.* Saratoga: Shakti River Press.

Gunn, Joshua. 2005. *Modern Occult Rhetoric: Mass Media and the Drama of Secrecy in the Twentieth Century.* Tuscaloosa: University of Alabama Press.

Gunning, Tom. 1995. "Phantom Images and Modern Manifestation: Spirit Photography, Magic Theater, Trick Film, and Photography's Uncanny." *Fugitive Images: From Photography to Video,* ed. Patrice Petro. Bloomington: Indiana University Press. 42–71.

Gurdjieff, G. I. 2000. *Beelzebub's Tales to His Grandson: All and Everything.* New York: Penguin.

Hall, Gary. 1973. "The Big Tunnel." *Indiana Folklore Quarterly* 6:139–73.

Hand, Wayland D. 1965. "Status of European and American Legend Study." *Current Anthropology* 4:439–46.

Hansen, George P. 2001. *The Trickster and the Paranormal.* Xlibris.

Harris, Jason Marc. 2008. *Folklore and the Fantastic in Nineteenth-Century British Fiction.* Burlington: Ashgate Publishing Co.

Harte, T. M., D. L. Black, and M. T. Hollinshead. 1999. "MESA: A new configuration for measuring electromagnetic field fluctuations." *Behavior Research Methods, Instruments & Computers* 31:680–83.

Harvey, John. 2004. "The Photographic Medium: Representation, Reconstitution, Consciousness, and Collaboration in Early-Twentieth-Century Spiritualism." *Technoetic Arts: A Journal of Speculative Research* 2:109–23.

Holt, H. Barry. 1983. "A Cultural Resource Management Dilemma: Anasai Ruins and the Navajos." *American Antiquity* 48:594–99.

Hufford, David J. 1982. *The Terror That Comes in the Night: An Experience-Centered Study Of Supernatural Assault Traditions*. Philadelphia: University of Pennsylvania Press.

Hufford, Mary. 1992. *Chaseworld: Foxhunting and Storytelling in New Jersey's Pine Barrens*. Philadelphia: University of Pennsylvania Press.

International Game Developers Association. 2006. *2006 Alternate Reality Games White Paper*. http://igda.org/arg. Accessed January 2, 2007.

Jenkins, Henry. 2002. "Interactive Audiences?: The 'Collective Intelligence' of Media Fans." *The New Media Book,* ed. Dan Harries. London: British Film Institute.

Kean, Leslie. 2007. "Symington confirms he saw UFO 10 years ago." *Daily Courier,* March 18.

Keel, John. 1996. *Operation Trojan Horse*. Lilburn: IllumiNet Press.

———. 1983. "The Man Who Invented Flying Saucers." *Fortean Times* 41:52–57.

Kirshenblatt-Gimblett, Barbara. 1996. "Electronic Vernacular." *Connected: Engagements with Media,* ed. George E Marcus. Chicago: University of Chicago Press.

Klinkman, Sven-Erik. 2002. "Theorizing Popular Imagination." *Popular Imagination: Essays on Fantasy and Cultural Practice*. Turku: NNF Publications.

Kluckhohn, Clyde, and Dorothea Leighton. 1946. *The Navaho*. Cambridge, MA: Harvard University Press.

Kochhar-Lindgren, Gray. 2005. *Technologics: Ghosts, the Incalculable, and the Suspension of Animation*. Albany: State University of New York Press.

Koven, Mikel J. 2007. *Film, Folklore, and Urban Legends*. Lanham: Scarecrow Press.

Kurzweil, Ray. 2005. *The Singularity Is Near: When Humans Transcend Biology*. New York: Viking.

Landow, George P. 1989. "Hypertext in Literary Education, Criticism and Scholarship." *Computers and the Humanities* 23:173–98.

Lauria, Rita. 1997. "Virtual Reality: 'An Empirical-Metaphysical Testbed.'" *Journal of Computer-mediated Communication* 3:2. http://jcmc.indiana.edu/vol3/issue2/lauria.html. Accessed July 8, 2006.

Levenda, Peter. 2005. *Sinister Forces: A Grimoire of American Political Witchcraft*. Walterville: Trine Day.

Lévi-Strauss, Claude. 1955. "The Structural Study of Myth." *Journal of American Folklore* 68:428–44.

Lindahl, Carl. 2005. "Ostensive Healing: Pilgrimage to the San Antonio Ghost Tracks." *Journal of American Folklore* 118:164–85.

———. 1986. "Psychic Ambiguity at the Legend Core." *Journal of Folklore Research* 23:1.

Lintrop, Aado. 1996. "Hereditary Transmission in Siberian Shamanism and the
    Concept of the Reality of Legends." *Folklore: Electronic Journal of Folklore Vol.
    1.* Tartu: Institute of the Estonian Language & Estonian Folklore Archives.
    http://www.folklore.ee/folklore/nr1/heredit.htm. Accessed February 4, 2008.
Lloyd, Timothy C. 1995. "Folklore, Foodways, and the Supernatural." *Out of the
    Ordinary: Folklore and the Supernatural,* ed. Barbara Walker. Utah: Utah State
    University Press.
Lombard, Matthew, and Theresa Ditton. 1997. "At the Heart of It All: The Concept
    of Presence." *Journal of Computer-mediated Communication* 3:2. http://www
    .ascusc.org/jcmc/vol3/issue2/lombard.html. Accessed July 8, 2006.
Luhrmann, Tanya M. 1989. *Persuasions of the Witch's Craft: Ritual Magic in
    Contemporary England.* Cambridge, MA: Harvard University Press.
Matheny, Joseph. 2002. *Ong's Hat: The Beginning.* New York: SkyBooks.
———. 1999. *The Incunabula Papers: Ong's Hat and Other Gateways to New
    Dimensions.* eXe Active Media Group.
———. 1992. "Advances in Skin Science: Quantrum Tantra. An Interview with
    Nick Herbert." http://www.incunabula.org/PDFS/herbert.zip. Accessed March
    2, 2006.
Mathers, S. L. MacGregor. 1975 [1900]. *The Book of the Sacred Magic of Abramelin
    the Mage.* Ontario: Dover Publications.
McClenon, James. 2002. *Wondrous Healing: Shamanism, Human Evolution, and the
    Origin of Religion.* Dekalb: Northern Illinois University Press.
McGonigal, Jane. 2005. "All Game Play is Performance: The State of the Art
    Game." www.avantgame.com. Accessed April 2, 2006.
———. 2003. "A Real Little Game: The Performance of Belief in Pervasive
    Play." Digital Games Research Association (DiGRA) "Level Up" Conference
    Proceedings. www.avantgame.com. Accessed April 2, 2006.
McLuhan, Marshall. 1962. *The Gutenberg Galaxy: The Making of Typographic Man.*
    Toronto: University of Toronto Press.
McMahon, William. 1987. *Pine Barrens Legends, Lore and Lies.* Moorestown: Middle
    Atlantic Press.
Meley, Patricia M. 1991. "Adolescent Legend Trips as Teenage Cultural Response:
    A Study of the Lore in Context." *Children's Folklore Review* 14:5–25.
Merrick, Helen. 2004. "'We Was Cross-dressing 'Afore You Were Born!' Or,
    How SF Fans Invented Virtual Community." *Refractory: A Journal of Media
    Entertainment* (6). http://www.refractory.unimelb.edu.au/journalissues/vol6/
    HMerrick.html. Accessed: January 12, 2007.
Moon, Peter. 2004. *Synchronicity and the Seventh Seal.* New York: Sky Books.
Moore, R. Laurence. 1977. *In Search of White Crows: Spiritualism, Parapsychology,
    and American Culture.* New York: Oxford University Press.
Mullen, Patrick. 1972. "Modern Legend and Rumor Theory." *Journal of the Folklore
    Institute* 9:95–109.
Mylonas, George E. 1962. *Eleusis and the Eleusinian Mysteries.* Princeton: Princeton
    University Press.
New World Disorder Magazine. "The Ong's Hat Mystery Revealed: An Interview
    with Joseph Matheny." No.2 http://www.newworlddisorder.ca/issuetwo/
    interviews/matheny.html. Accessed March 1, 2006.

Nicolaisen, W. F. H. 1984. "Legend As Narrative Response." In *Perspectives On Contemporary Legend: Proceedings Of The Conference On Contemporary Legend*, ed. Paul Smith. Sheffield: Sheffield Academic Press.

O'Keefe, Daniel Lawrence. 1982. *Stolen Lightning: The Social Theory of Magic*. New York: Continuum.

Opler, Morris E. 1959. "Component, Assemblage, and Theme in Cultural Integration and Differentiation." *American Anthropologist*, New Series 61:6.

Oppenheim, Janet. 1985. *The Other World: Spiritualism and Psychical Research in England, 1850–1914*. New York: Cambridge University Press.

Owen, Alex. 2004. *The Place of Enchantment: British Occultism and the Culture of the Modern*. Chicago: University Press of Chicago.

———. 1989. *The Darkened Room: Women, Power, and Spiritualism in Late Victorian England*. Chicago: University Press of Chicago.

Patel, Nitin. 2008. "The Beast." http://www.scribd.com/doc/6470266/The-Beast-ARG-Presentation-10208. Accessed July 15, 2010.

Pauwels, Louis, and Jacques Bergier. 2008 [1960]. *The Morning of the Magicians: Secret Societies, Conspiracies, and Vanished Civilizations*. Rochester: Destiny Books.

Peuckert, Will-Erich. 1965. *Sagen: Geburt und Antwort der mythischen Welt*. (Legends: Birth and answer of the mythical world.) Berlin: Erich Schmidt.

P.M. 1984. *bolo'bolo*. Brooklyn: Autonomedia.

Podmore, Frank. 2003 [1902]. *Mediums of the 19th Century, Part 1*. Whitefish: Kessinger Publishing.

Price, E. Alan. 1996. "The Uri Geller Effect." The South African Institute for Parapsychology, Johannesburg. http://www.uri-geller.com/books/geller-papers/g24a.htm. Accessed June 3, 2008.

Rennie, Bryan S. 2006. *Mircea Eliade: A Critical Reader*. London: Equinox Publishing.

Revolution Magazine. 2000. "Convergence: Where the Body Meets the Mind." http://joseph.matheny.com/PDFS/ED-Rev.pdf. Accessed December 30, 2006.

Rojcewicz, Peter M. 1987. "The 'Men in Black' Experience and Tradition: Analogues with the Traditional Devil Hypothesis." *Journal of American Folklore* 100:148–60.

Roth, Christopher F. 2005. "Ufology as Anthropology." *E.T. Culture: Anthropology in Outerspaces*, ed. Debora Battaglia. Durham: Duke University Press.

Rushkoff, Douglas. 1996. *Media Virus! Hidden Agendas in Popular Culture*. New York: Ballantine Books.

Sanderson, Ivan T. 1960. "A New Look at America's Mystery Giant." *True Magazine*, March.

Sannella, Lee. 1992. *The Kundalini Experience*. Lower Lake: Integral Publishing.

Scott, Walter. 1802. *Minstrelsy of the Scottish Border, Vol. II (of 3) Consisting Of Historical And Romantic Ballads, Collected In The Southern Counties Of Scotland; With A Few Of Modern Date, Founded Upon Local Tradition*. The Project Gutenberg Ebook. http://www.gutenberg.org/files/12882/12882-h/12882-h.htm. Accessed June 20, 2007.

Shea, Robert, and Robert Anton Wilson. 1983. *The Illuminatus! Trilogy*. New York: Dell.

Shumaker, John F. 1990. *Wings of Illusions: The Origin, Nature and Future of Paranormal Belief*. New York: Prometheus Books.

Smith, Paul. 1989. "Contemporary Legend: A Legendary Genre?" *The Questing Beast: Perspectives on Contemporary Legend Volume IV*, ed. Gillian Bennett and Paul Smith. Sheffield: Sheffield Academic Press.

———. 1975. "Tradition—A Perspective: Part II—Transmission." *Lore and Language* 2:8–13.

Southall, Richard. 2003. *How to Be a Ghost Hunter*. Woodbury, MN: Llewllyn Publications.

Stang, Rev. Ivan. 1988. *High Weirdness By Mail: A Directory of The Fringe: Mad Prophets, Crackpots, Kooks & True Visionaries*. New York: Fireside, Simon and Schuster.

Szulborski, Dave. 2005. *This Is Not A Game: A Guide to Alternate Reality Gaming*. New-Fiction Publishing.

Tangherlini, Timothy R. 2007. "Rhetoric, Truth and Performance: Politics and the Interpretation of Legend." *Indian Folklife* 25. http://www.indianfolklore.org/pdf/newsletter/currentissue/jan_2007/ifl_25-8.pdf. Accessed February 2, 2007.

———. 1994. *Interpreting Legend: Danish Storytellers and Their Repertoires*. New York: Garland Publishing.

Taves, Ann. 2009. *Religious Experience Reconsidered: A Building-Block Approach to the Study of Religion and Other Special Things*. Princeton: Princeton University Press.

Taylor, Eugene. 1999. *Shadow Culture: Psychology and Spirituality in America*. Washington, D.C.: Counterpoint.

Taylor, Troy. 2004. *The Ghost Hunters Guidebook*. Alton: Whitechapel Press.

Teilhard, de Chardin, Pierre. 1959. *The Phenomenon of Man*. New York: Harper & Row.

Thigpen, Kenneth. 1971. "Adolescent Legends in Brown County: A Survey." *Indiana Folklore* 4:141–215.

Tolkien, J. R. R. 1966. *The Tolkien Reader*. New York: Ballantine.

Tucker, Elizabeth. 2007. *Haunted Halls: Ghostlore of American College Campuses*. Jackson: University Press of Mississippi.

———. 2006. "Legend Quests." *Voices: The Journal of New York Folklore* 32. http://www.nyfolklore.org/pubs/voic32-1-2/legend.html. Accessed November 2, 2008.

Turner, Victor. 1967. *The Forest of Symbols: Aspects of Ndembu Ritual*. Ithaca: Cornell University Press.

Vallee, Jacques. 1979. *Messengers of Deception: UFO Contacts and Cults*. Berkeley: And/Or Press.

———. 1991. *Revelations: Alien Contact and Human Deception*. New York: Ballantine Books.

Versluis, Arthur. 2007. *Magic and Mysticism: An Introduction to Western Esotericism*. Lanham: Rowman and Littlefield Publishers.

Victor, Jeffrey. 1990. "Satanic Cult Rumors as Contemporary Legend." *Western Folklore* 49:51–81.

Waldram, James B. 2004. *Revenge of the Windigo: The Construction of the Mind and Mental Health of North American Aboriginal Peoples*. Toronto: University of Toronto Press.

Ward, Donald. 1977. "The Little Man Who Wasn't There: Encounters With the Supranormal." *Fabula* 18:212–25.

Warren, Joshua P. 2003. *How to Hunt Ghosts.* New York: Fireside.

Weatherford, Jack. 1988. *Indian Givers: How the Indians of the Americas Transformed the World.* New York: Fawcett Columbine.

Whitehead, Charles. 2000. "The Anthropology of Consciousness: Keeping Body and Soul Together? Society for Anthropological Consciousness, Tucson, 5–9." *Anthropology Today* 16:20–22.

Zhenxin, Yuan, and Huang Wanpo. 1979. "'Wild man'—fact or fiction?" *China Reconstructs* (July): 56–59.

Mr. Nowhere (screen name), 106
MUFON (Mutual UFO Network), 196n9
Mumler, William, 48

N N (screen name), 102–3
Necronomicon, 59
Negativeland, 79
Nergalus (screen name), 100
New World Disorder Magazine, 79, 84
Nichols, Preston, 143
noosphere, 54–55, 95

O'Bryan, Ronald Clark, 13–14
O'Bryan, Timothy, 13
occult software, 51, 52–53
occultism, 56–58, 74, 77
O'Keefe, Daniel Lawrence, 46
Ong's Hat: Gateway, 64, 66–67, 68,
    73, 80, 93, 95. *See also* Incunabula
    Papers
Ong's Hat, New Jersey, 86
online communities, 15–16
ostension, 12–15, 36, 40. *See also*
    Incunabula Papers: ostension and;
    legends: ostension and; legend-
    tripping: ostension and
Ouija board, 29, 34–35, 122
Ovilus, 52
Owen, Alex, 115

Pahana (screen name), 115–16, 117,
    125–26, 129–30, 134–36
Palmer, Raymond A., 145, 146, 196n10
Paranormal Activity, 145
Parsifal (screen name), 140–41
Parsons, Jack, 110
Pauwels, Louis, *Le Matin de Magiciens*,
    124
performing belief, 7, 18, 62, 120; ARGs
    and, 63; Bey and, 82; conspiracy
    theories and, 75; legends and,
    45–46; ritual and, 99; Waverly
    Hills Sanitarium and, 105. *See also*
    Incunabula Papers: performing belief
    and; legend-tripping: performing
    belief and
Pesche, Mark, 52–53

Peuckert, Will-Erich, 4, 7
Pine Barrens (New Jersey), 85, 86
Podmore, Frank, 4
Poetic Journal of a Traveller, 69–70
presencing, 40–41, 44. *See also*
    Incunabula Papers: presencing and;
    legend-tripping: presencing and
Price, Allan, 35
priesting, 35
Probability Control Force (PCF), 67
prophecy, 4

Qu Yuan, 3

rabbit holes, 61
Regardie, Israel, 57
Rev. Justin (screen name), 140
Roe, William, 3, 12
Rosicrucian Manifestos, 59–60
Roth, Christopher, 86
Rythmaning (screen name), 119–20

sacred sites, 4
Sasquatch, 3
satanic conspiracies, 4, 9–10
Schreiber, Klaus, 52
Scott, Walter, 32
700 Club, The, 36, 40
Shaver, Richard, 146
Shea, Robert, *Illuminatus! Trilogy*, 72,
    75
Sidney, Ohio, 9
sigils, 64, 107, 109, 114
Situationist International, 79
Sky Books Publishing, 143
sleep paralysis, 14, 187n23
Spare, Austin Osman, 107, 109, 191n24
Sparky (screen name), 141
Spielberg, Steven, *A.I.*, 61, 138
spirit photography, 21, 23–24, 48–51
Spiritualism, 47–49. *See also* spirit
    photography
Sprinkle, R. Leo, 190n4
Stockton Record, 8
Stonehenge, 33
Stseamonelmo (screen name), 103–5,
    122

CPSIA information can be obtained at www.ICGtesting.com
Printed in the USA
LVOW08*2020171213

365619LV00003B/7/P